VIRTUAL ROOTS 2.0

First published 2003

Printed and bound in the United States of America

Scholarly Resources Inc.

104 Greenhill Avenue

Wilmington, DE 19805-1897

www.scholarly.com

Library of Congress Cataloging-in-Publication Data

Kemp, Thomas Jay.
    Virtual roots 2.0 : a guide to genealogy and local history on the
World Wide Web / Thomas Jay Kemp.— Rev. and updated.
        p. cm.
    ISBN 0-8420-2922-2 (alk. paper) — ISBN 0-8420-2923-0 (pbk. : alk.
paper)
     1. Genealogy—Computer network resources. 2. Web sites—Directories.
     3. Internet—Handbooks, manuals, etc. 4. Genealogy—Databases.
     5. World Wide Web. I. Title.
CS14.K46 2003
025.06'9291—dc21   2002154366

∞ The paper used in this publication meets the minimum requirements of the American National Standard for permanence of paper for printed library materials, Z39.48, 1984.

VIRTUAL ROOTS 2.0

A Guide to
Genealogy and Local History
on the World Wide Web

REVISED AND UPDATED

THOMAS JAY KEMP

A Scholarly Resources Inc. Imprint
Wilmington, Delaware

*Dedicated to my wife Vi
and children Andrew and Sarah*

A Family without a Genealogy
Is Like a Country without a History
—Traditional Chinese Saying

ABOUT THE AUTHOR

THOMAS JAY KEMP, a well-known librarian and archivist for more than twenty-five years, is the assistant director of the Godfrey Memorial Library in Middletown, Connecticut. He is the chair of the American Library Association's Genealogy and Local History Discussion Group and has served on the Board of Directors of the Federation of Genealogical Societies. He also has been chair of the Council of National Library and Information Associations and president of the American Society of Indexers.

Kemp is a life member of the Association for the Bibliography of History, the New York Genealogical and Biographical Society, the New England Archivists, and the New Hampshire Library Association. The author of more than two dozen books and databases, he has also written numerous articles that regularly appear in state and national library, archival, and genealogical journals.

A partial bibliography of his works includes:

BOOKS

1930 Census: A Reference and Research Guide. North Salt Lake, UT: ProQuest, HeritageQuest, 2002. 250p.

The American Census Handbook. Wilmington, DE: Scholarly Resources, 2001. 517p.

International Vital Records Handbook. 4th. ed. Baltimore, MD: Genealogical Publishing, 2001. 603p.

The Genealogist's Virtual Library: Full-text Books on the World Wide Web. Wilmington, DE: Scholarly Resources, 2000. 257p.

Genealogy Annual: A Guide to Published Sources, 1995– . Wilmington, DE: Scholarly Resources, 1996– .

Connecticut's Historians and Genealogists, 1890–1990. Stamford, CT: Little Factory Press, 1991. 32p.

Connecticut Researcher's Handbook. Detroit, MI: Gale Research Company, 1981. 755p.

ARTICLES

"Genealogy and the Virtual Library." *Oregon Library Association Quarterly* (Winter 2001).

"Minnesota eBooks: Local History on the World Wide Web." *Minnesota History* (Spring 2001).

"Conversation with Tom Kemp, Author of *Genealogist's Virtual Library.*" *Today's Librarian* (July 2000).

"Local History: Histories of Nearby States Can Bolster Local History Collections." *Today's Librarian* (July 2000).

"Access to Connecticut History, Full-text Books Are on the Web, Now!" *Connecticut Libraries* (September 1999).

"I Read It on the Web: African American Full-text Books on the Web." *Archival Outlook* (September–October 1999).

"Genealogists Read It on the Web." *Illinois Library Association Reporter* (October 1999).

"Internet Resources Genealogy: Finding Roots on the Web." *College and Research Libraries News* (June 1999).

"Promise of the Web: Full-text New York Books on the Web." *NYGandB Newsletter* (Summer 1999); continued in (Fall 1999).

"Collection Development: Genealogy." *Library Journal* (April 1999).

"Family History Resources in Print, Video and on the Web." *CBC (Children's Book Council) Features* (Fall 1998).

"Roots on the Web." *School Library Journal* (January 1998).

"I Read It on the Web." *Archival Outlook* (September–October 1997).

"Slavery: Resources on the Internet." *Library Journal* (September 1997).

"Online Genealogy Resources." *Library Journal* (July 1997).

"Best Websites for Helping Genealogists." *NAGARA Clearinghouse* (June 1997).

CONTENTS

INTRODUCTION

Virtual Roots 2.0 is a road map, guide, and detailed directory to hundreds of the best genealogy and local history sites on the Internet, and serves as the most comprehensive all-in-one genealogical reference work available today. It provides web sites from around the world and explains what will be found at each site. Included with each entry are the e-mail and postal addresses, as well as telephone and fax numbers, when available, for the reference staff. Instead of surfing the net exploring endless lists of sites, *Virtual Roots 2.0* allows users to plan their research offline, thereby saving time and money when going online.

With more than one million web sites or home pages currently on the Internet—and more being added every day—researchers will find sites ranging from a one-page promotional flyer to those filled with book-length guides and scanned images of original documents. Genealogists, historians, librarians, and archivists internationally have joined with computer engineers and mounted original documents, indexes, and guides to the World Wide Web. The Internet has made the world much smaller, communication more instantaneous, and the searching of data from the world's archives a practical reality.

Virtual Roots 2.0 divides the best and most useful of the Internet sites into three sections: **General Subjects, United States Sources,** and **International Sources.** This valuable reference tool does not simply provide web sites but outlines in detail the guides and resources that researchers will want to use that are listed on each site.

The full contact information included with each entry enables researchers to be in touch immediately with archives, libraries, or historical societies from around the world while still viewing the repository's web site from their home computer. By bringing together all the key data in one handy guide, it is possible to examine documents from across the country and send the archives reference staff questions, and receive answers instantly.

The **General Subjects** section includes those sites and repositories that focus on a specific category of records such as church or military records. Entries for **United States Sources** contain the official state home page, state archives, state library, state genealogical society, and state historical society sites, along with the other important web sites for that state. The **International Sources** section lists sites for national libraries, archives, and record offices as well as for genealogical and historical societies from around the world.

Out of the many sites documented in *Virtual Roots 2.0,* there are some that have changed the way in which genealogy is researched. Throughout this guide nearly 100 of the web sites highlighted have been designated as either **Extraordinary** or **Outstanding Sites.** Individuals and institutions are encouraged to follow the examples of these web sites in planning and designing their own sites.

Among the **Extraordinary Sites** found in this guide, thirteen have set the highest standard for providing solid, reliable information to researchers (see list, with links, on page xvii). These **Most Extraordinary Sites** include the Family History Library of The Church of Jesus Christ of Latter-day Saints (the single most important genealogical web site online today); one of the largest libraries in the country (the Library of Congress); one of the smallest public libraries (the Lane Memorial Library); the Caleb Johnson's Mayflower Web Page (the effort of a single individual); and the U.S. government's National Archives and Records Administration site.

What is not presented in this guide is a discussion of the growing number of commercial web sites with genealogical content. ProQuest http://www.proquest.com and Ancestry.com are the two leading commercial providers, both of which sell and license portions of their content to other vendors such as Genealogy.com. The major difference between them is that ProQuest is comprehensive in what it provides and digitizes the critical sources that genealogists rely upon for research. ProQuest's material is prepared with the thorough documentation expected in a library market, with printouts of its digital documents including the complete bibliographical citation of the source used.

ProQuest also offers resources such as ProQuest Historical Newspapers, which contains digital copies of the complete runs of newspapers, among them the *New York Times*, the *Wall Street Journal*, and the *Washington Post*. Well produced and indexed, this service allows researchers to retrieve articles and advertisements from the first issue of a newspaper. Once located the article can be printed or saved as an electronic file. In addition, ProQuest's HeritageQuestOnline includes the complete U.S. Census, 1790–1930; daily updates of newspaper obituaries from 150 newspapers across the country; complete digital copies of the Revolutionary War Pension and Bounty Land Warrant Files; and digital copies of more than 25,000 genealogies and local histories. Every word is searchable. This massive collection dwarfs the offerings of other commercial firms.

Ancestry.com has been the clear dominant provider of genealogy data to the consumer market, and has been the first to complete the online offering of the U.S. Census and to provide images for the entire 1790 through 1930 censuses. Its online indexes are easy to use, quick, and reliable. While not nearly as large as the data provided by ProQuest, Ancestry.com has critical resources that genealogists depend on; for example, it is the provider of choice for the Social Security Deathfile Index—http://www.ancestry.com/ search/rectype/vital/ssdi/main.htm?rc=locale%7E&us=0, which is probably the most used database on its web site.

Ancestry.com also provides two landmark indexes: the Periodical Source Index (PERSI) http://www.ancestry.com/search/rectype/periodicals/persi/main.htm, prepared by the Allen County Library (Indiana); and the American Genealogical and Biographical Index (AGBI) http://www.ancestry.com/search/rectype/inddbs/3599a.htm, prepared by the Godfrey Memorial Library (Connecticut).

LIST OF THE MOST EXTRAORDINARY SITES

Genealogical Society of Utah—Family History Library of The Church of
Jesus Christ of Latter-day Saints (pp. 7, 192)
www.FamilySearch.org
This is the single most important genealogical web site online today.

AfriGeneas: African Ancestored Genealogy (p. 3)
http://www.afrigeneas.com/

Caleb Johnson's Mayflower Web Page (p. 28)
http://members.aol.com/calebj/mayflower.html

JewishGen: The Home of Jewish Genealogy (p. 11)
http://www.jewishgen.org/

Lane Memorial Library (p. 134)
http://www.hampton.lib.nh.us/

Library of Congress (p. 63)
http://www.loc.gov/

Library of Virginia (p. 195)
http://www.lva.lib.va.us/

National Archives and Records Administration (p. 66)
http://www.archives.gov

New Orleans Public Library (p. 100)
http://www.nutrias.org/

USGenWeb Project (p. 22)
http://www.usgenweb.com/index.html

University of Kansas—Kansas Collection (p. 93)
http://www.kancoll.org/

University of Michigan—Dearborn (p. 115)
http://www.umd.umich.edu/

University of North Carolina at Chapel Hill (p. 153)
http://www.unc.edu/

GENERAL SUBJECTS

AFRICAN AMERICANS

African American Cemeteries Online

E X T R A O R D I N A R Y   S I T E
One of the Most Extraordinary Web Sites Online

AfriGeneas: African Ancestored Genealogy
http://www.afrigeneas.com/

P.O. Box 4250
Anniston, AL 36204

Phone   (256) 820-8794
Fax   (256) 820-8339
E-mail   listowner@afrigeneas.com

Baltimore, Maryland, Blacks in City Directories, 1810–1866
http://afrigeneas.com/library/baltimore/

Baltimore County, Maryland, Runaway Slave Ads. 1842–1863
http://www.afrigeneas.com/library/runaway_ads/balt-intro.html

Cherokee Freedmen in Indian Territory
http://www.afrigeneas.com/library/cherokee/

Ex-Slave Pension Movement
http://www.afrigeneas.com/library/hillarticle.html#note11

Fairfax County, Virginia, Slave and Colored Births, 1853
http://www.afrigeneas.com/library/va-fairfax-births.html

Genealogy, Online Tutorial
http://www.afrigeneas.com/guide/

Georgia Slave Bills of Sale
http://www.afrigeneas.com/library/ga-slavebills/

Granville County, North Carolina, Slave Records Contained in the County Records 1746–1864
http://www.afrigeneas.com/library/ncdeeds/

Jamaica. African Americans in the Public Acts, 1760–1810
http://afrigeneas.com/library/jamaica/acts.html

Jamaica. Manumissions, 1820–1825
http://afrigeneas.com/library/jamaica/manumissions/

Little Rock, Arkansas, Class Rosters and Yearbooks. 1876–1882
http://www.afrigeneas.com/library/schoolrosters/

New Orleans. Inward Slave Manifests, 1818–1860
   http://www.afrigeneas.com/slavedata/manifests.html

Obituaries, Death Notices, and Funeral Programs
   http://www.afrigeneas.com/obituaries/

Richmond, Virginia, City Directory, 1852
   http://www.afrigeneas.com/library/richmond-fc-1852.html

Slave Data Collection
   http://www.afrigeneas.com/slavedata/

Texas. Slave Narratives
   http://www.afrigeneas.com/library/SlaveNarrTX.html

Utica, New York, City Directory. People of Color. 1854
   http://www.afrigeneas.com/library/utica-poc-1854.html

Wilkinson County, Mississippi, Marriages, 1865–1870
   http://www.afrigeneas.com/library/ms-wilkinson/aamarriages.html

Williamson County, Texas, Slave Bills of Sale, 1850–1858
   http://www.afrigeneas.com/library/tx-williamson/slavebills.html

ARCHIVES

National Association of Government Archives and Records Administrators (NAGARA)
   http://www.nagara.org/

48 Howard Street	*Phone*	*(518) 463-8644*
Albany, NY 12207	*Fax*	*(518) 463-8656*
	E-mail	*nagara@caphill.com*

Crossroads: Developments in Electronic Records Management and Information Technology. (Serial). No. 1 (1996)– .
   http://www.nagara.org/crossroads/ch.html

NAGARA Clearinghouse. (Serial). Quarterly. Vol. 13, No. 1 (Winter 1997)– .
   http://www.nagara.org/clearinghouse/clearinghousehome.html

National Archives and Records Administration

See: District of Columbia

New England Archivists
   http://www.lib.umb.edu/newengarch/

c/o Massachusetts Archives	*Phone*	*(207) 786-6354*
Office of the Secretary of State	*Fax*	*(207) 786-6035*
220 Morrissey Blvd.		
Boston, MA 02125		

NEA Newsletter
http://nils.lib.tufts.edu/newengarch/newsletter/index.html

NEA Newsletter. (Serial). Quarterly. Index. (1972–1993).
http://nils.lib.tufts.edu/newengarch/newsletter/newsindex.html

Society of American Archivists
http://www.archivists.org/

527 S. Wells St., 5th Floor   *Phone   (312) 922-0140*
Chicago, IL 60607-3922   *E-mail   info@archivists.org*

Associated Archival Organizations
http://www.archivists.org/assoc-orgs/index.asp

Code of Ethics
http://www.archivists.org/governance/handbook/app_ethics.asp

SAA Council Handbook
http://www.archivists.org/governance/handbook/index.asp

CEMETERIES

Association for Gravestone Studies
http://www.gravestonestudies.org/

278 Main Street, Suite 207   *Phone   (413) 772-0836*
Greenfield, MA 01301   *E-mail   info@gravestonestudies.org*

Hartshorn. Stephen and Charles Hartshorn of Providence
http://www.gravestonestudies.org/Carvers--Hartshorn%20Shop.htm

John Anthony Angel and Seth Luther, Early Providence Gravestone Carvers
http://www.gravestonestudies.org/Carvers--Angel%20Luther%20Shop.htm

Library, Book Loan Collection
http://www.gravestonestudies.org/lending_library.htm

Markers. (Serial). Annual. Table of Contents. Vol. 1 (1980)– .
http://www.gravestonestudies.org/markers.htm

Preservation
http://www.gravestonestudies.org/preservation.htm

Stevens Family of Carvers
http://www.gravestonestudies.org/Carvers--Stevens%20Shop.htm

CENSUS RECORDS

USGenWeb Archives Census Project
http://www.rootsweb.com/~usgenweb/census/

Online Census Images, by State
http://www.rootsweb.com/~usgenweb/cen_img.htm

State List, Completed Online Census Indexing Projects
http://www.rootsweb.com/~cenfiles/

CHURCH RECORDS

ADVENTIST

Adventist Heritage Center
http://www.andrews.edu/library/ahc/index.html

Andrews University	*Phone*	*(616) 471-3274*
James White Library	*Fax*	*(616) 471-6166*
P.O. Box 1400	*E-mail*	*ahc@andrews.edu*
Berrien Springs, MI 49104-1400		

Association of Seventh-day Adventist Librarians
http://www.asdal.org/

Seventh-day Adventist Periodical Index. (Serial). Online.
http://www.andrews.edu/library/ahc/sdapi.cgi

Seventh-day Adventist Obituary Index
http://www.andrews.edu/library/ahc/sdapi.cgi

Seventh-day Adventist Church
http://www.adventist.org/

12501 Old Columbia Pike	*Phone*	*(301) 680-6000*
Silver Spring, MD 20904-6600	*Fax*	*(301) 680-6090*
	E-mail	*info@adventist.org*

Adventist Review. (Serial). Weekly. (January 7, 1999)– .; Index. (July 1996)– .
http://www.adventistreview.org/thisweek/archives.html

Seventh-day Adventist Yearbook. (Serial). Annual.
http://www.adventist.org/ast/yearbook.shtml

ASSEMBLIES OF GOD

Assemblies of God Archives
http://www.ag.org/

1445 Boonville Avenue	*Phone*	*(417) 862-2781*
Springfield, MO 65802-1894	*E-mail*	*info@ag.org*

History, "85 Years Ago."
http://ag.org/enrichmentjournal/199904/004_prologue.cfm

BAPTIST

SBCNet

http://www.sbc.net/

901 Commerce Street   *Phone (615) 244-2355 Southern Baptist*
Nashville, TN 37203-3699   *Convention Phone*

BPNews. (Serial). Online. Daily.

http://sbcbaptistpress.org/

THE CHURCH OF JESUS CHRIST OF
LATTER-DAY SAINTS

SINGLE MOST IMPORTANT GENEALOGICAL
WEB SITE ONLINE

Genealogical Society of Utah
Family History Library of The Church of Jesus Christ of Latter-day Saints
www.FamilySearch.org

35 North West Temple Street   *Phone   (800) 453-3860 Ext. 22331*
Salt Lake City, UT 84150-3400   *E-mail   fhl@ldschurch.org*

Directory of Family History Centers (Branch Libraries)

http://www.familysearch.org/Eng/Library/FHC/frameset_fhc.asp

Genealogy Research Guides

http://www.familysearch.org/Eng/Search/RG/frameset_rg.asp

Letter Writing Guides

http://www.familysearch.org/Eng/Library/Education/frameset_education.asp?PAGE=education_publications.asp

Word Lists (Multilingual Genealogical Vocabulary Lists)

http://www.familysearch.org/Eng/Library/Education/frameset_education.asp?PAGE=education_publications.asp

Online Library Catalog

http://www.familysearch.org/Eng/Library/FHLC/frameset_fhlc.asp

National Society of the Sons of Utah Pioneers

http://www.sonsofutahpioneers.org/

3301 East 2920 South   *Phone   (888) 827-2746*
Salt Lake City, UT 84109-4260   *Fax   (801) 484-2067*
                              E-Mail   info@sonsofutahpioneers.org

Library
http://www.sonsofutahpioneers.org/p5300.htm

Trail Markers
http://www.sonsofutahpioneers.org/p4300.htm

OUTSTANDING SITE

Tracing Mormon Pioneers
http://www.xmission.com/~nelsonb/pioneer.htm

Australian LDS Emigration for 1853–1868
http://www.xmission.com/~nelsonb/australia.htm

Missionary Record Index, 1830–1971
http://www.xmission.com/~nelsonb/mission.htm

Pioneer Companies, 1847–1868
http://www.xmission.com/~nelsonb/company.htm

Scandinavian Pioneer Index
http://www.xmission.com/~nelsonb/sindex.htm

Tracing Mormon Pioneers
http://www.xmission.com/~nelsonb/quick_menu.htm

CONGREGATIONAL

OUTSTANDING SITE

Congregational Library and Archives
http://www.14beacon.org/

14 Beacon Street   *Phone   (617) 523-0470*
Boston, MA 02108   *Fax   (617) 523-0491*
                           E-mail hworthley@14beacon.org

American Congregational Association Records
http://www.14beacon.org/aca.htm

Guide, Associations, Conventions, etc.
http://www.14beacon.org/assocrec.htm

Guide, Local Church Records
http://www.14beacon.org/guidech.htm

Guide, Manuscript Collections
http://www.14beacon.org/papers.htm

Guide, Missionary, Charitable etc.
http://www.14beacon.org/organrec.htm

Guide, Periodical Holdings
http://www.14beacon.org/period.htm

Women, Collections Relating to
http://www.14beacon.org/women.htm

EPISCOPAL

Episcopal Divinity School
Weston Jesuit School of Theology
http://www.edswjst.org/home.htm

99 Brattle Street	*Phone*	*(617) 349-3602*
Cambridge, MA 02138-3402	*Fax*	*(617) 349-3603*
	E-mail	*skuehler@edswjst.org*

Episcopal Church History, Basic Sources
http://www.edswjst.org/episcopal.htm

Historical Society of the Episcopal Church
http://www.hsec-usa.org/

P.O. Box 2098	*Phone*	*(512) 282-3234*
Manchaca, TX 78652-2098		*(800) 553-7745*
	Fax	*(512) 280-3902*
	E-mail	*mlofgreen@austin.rr.com*

Anglican and Episcopal History. (Serial). Quarterly. Ten-Year Index, 1978–1988.
http://www.hsec-usa.org/journal/10yrindex.htm

EVANGELICAL COVENANT

Covenant Archives and Historical Library
http://campus.northpark.edu/library/archives/cahl.htm

3225 West Foster Avenue	*Phone*	*(312) 244-6224*
Chicago, IL 60625-4895	*Fax*	*(312) 267-2362*
	E-mail	*eengseth@northpark.edu*

Karl A. Olsson Papers
http://campus.northpark.edu/library/archives/series_612132a.htm

JEWISH

American Jewish Archives

http://www.huc.edu/aja/

3101 Clifton Avenue   *Phone*   *(513) 221-1875*
Cincinnati, OH 45220-2488   *Fax*   *(513) 221-7812*
                               E-mail   *AJA@cn.huc.edu*

American Jewish Archives. (Serial). Semi-annual. Vol. 50– .
http://www.huc.edu/aja/journal.htm

Archives
http://www.huc.edu/aja/collect.htm

Cincinnati Jewry Manuscripts
http://www.huc.edu/aja/cinti.htm

Creating the Synagogue Archives
http://www.huc.edu/aja/create1.htm

Family and Personal Papers
http://www.huc.edu/aja/family.htm

Future of the Past. (Serial). Online. Irregular.
http://www.huc.edu/aja/news.htm

Genealogy
http://www.huc.edu/aja/collect.htm#gen

"Jewish Women in the Central Appalachian Coal Fields, 1890–1960, From Breadwinners to Community Builders" by Deborah Weiner
http://www.huc.edu/aja/00-1.htm

Synagogue Records
http://www.huc.edu/aja/syn.htm

American Jewish Historical Society

http://www.ajhs.org/

15 West 16th Street   *Phone*   *(212) 294-6160*
New York, NY 10011   *Fax*   *(212) 294-6161*
                          E-mail   *lslome@ajhs.cjh.org*

American Jewish History. (Serial). Quarterly. Vol. 84 (1996)– .
http://muse.jhu.edu/journals/american_jewish_history/index.html

Archival Collections
http://www.ajhs.org/research/index.cfm

Electronic Discussion Group
http://www.ajhs.org/about/Electronic.cfm

Genealogical Resources
http://www.ajhs.org/research/Gene_RelevantC.cfm

Heritage. (Serial). (Spring/Summer 2000)– .
http://www.ajhs.org/about/newsletter/

OUTSTANDING SITE

Avotaynu
http://www.avotaynu.com/

P.O. Box 99   *Phone   (201) 387-7200*
Bergenfield, NJ 07621   *Fax   (201) 387-2855*
                                                      E-mail   info@avotaynu.com

Avotaynu Consolidated Jewish Surname Index
http://www.avotaynu.com/csi/csi-home.html

Avotaynu. (Serial). Quarterly. Index. (1985–1998).
http://www.avotaynu.com/indexsum.htm

Getting Started Tracing Your Jewish Roots
http://www.avotaynu.com/jewish_genealogy.htm

Shtetl Photographs, Pictures of Jewish Life in Europe
http://www.avotaynu.com/postcards/

EXTRAORDINARY SITE
One of the Most Extraordinary Web Sites Online

JewishGen: The Home of Jewish Genealogy
http://www.jewishgen.org/

Association of Jewish   *Phone   (415) 424-1622*
Genealogical Societies   *E-mail   RWeissJGS@aol.com*
P.O. Box 50245   *support@jewishgen.org*
Palo Alto, CA 94303

International Association of Jewish Genealogical Societies
http://www.jewishgen.org/iajgs/

JewishGen Online Worldwide Burial Registry (JOWBR)
http://www.jewishgen.org/databases/cemetery/

Yizkor Book Project
http://www.jewishgen.org/Yizkor/

Jewish Theological Seminary of America

http://www.jtsa.edu/

Library
3080 Broadway
New York, NY 10027

Phone   (212) 678-8075
E-mail   library@jtsa.edu

Between the Lines. (Serial). Semi-annual. Vol. 8, No. 1 (Spring 1995)– .
http://www.jtsa.edu/library/news/

Library
http://www.jtsa.edu/library/

Online Catalog
http://catalog.jtsa.edu/

Special Collections
http://www.jtsa.edu/library/collections/special.shtml

Leo Baeck Institute

http://www.users.interport.net/~lbi1/

15 West 16th Street
New York, NY 10011

Phone   (212) 744-6400
Fax   (212) 988-1305
E-mail   lbaeck@lbi.cjh.org

Library Online Catalog
http://users.rcn.com/lbi1/mclinkpage.htm

Research Library
http://users.rcn.com/lbi1/library.html

University of Arizona

Special Collections Department,
Library

P.O. Box 210055
Tucson, AZ 85721-0055

Phone   (520) 621-4345
Fax   (520) 621-9733
E-mail   stuartg@u.arizona.edu

Archival Guides
http://www.library.arizona.edu/images/swja/findingaids/findingaids.htm

Arizona Jewish Pioneers
http://www.library.arizona.edu/images/swja/arizona.htm

Bibliography
http://www.library.arizona.edu/images/swja/suggreads.htm

Jewish Pioneers of the Southwest
http://www.library.arizona.edu/images/swja/pioneers.htm

Leona G. and David Bloom Southwest Jewish Archives
http://www.library.arizona.edu/images/swja/swjalist.html

Manuscript Collections
http://dizzy.library.arizona.edu/branches/spc/homepage/alphlist/alphlist.htm

New Mexico Jewish Pioneers
http://www.library.arizona.edu/images/swja/newmexico.htm

Southwest Jewish History. (Serial). Vol. 1 (Fall 1992–Winter 1995).
http://www.library.arizona.edu/images/swja/newsletter.html

Synagogues of the Southwest
http://www.library.arizona.edu/images/swja/synagogues.htm

West Texas Jewish Pioneers
http://www.library.arizona.edu/images/swja/westtexas.htm

University of Texas at Austin
http://www.utexas.edu/

Benson Latin American Collection
http://www.lib.utexas.edu/benson/index.html

Sid Richardson Hall 1.108	*Phone*	*(512) 495-4520*
University of Texas at Austin	*Fax*	*(512) 495-4568*
Austin, TX 78713-8916	*E-mail*	*blac@lib.utexas.edu*

Jews in Latin America
http://www.lib.utexas.edu/benson/bibnot/bn-61-1.html

Yad Vashem
The Holocaust Martyrs' and Heroes' Remembrance Authority
http://www.yad-vashem.org.il/

P.O. Box 3477	*Phone*	*(011) + 972-2-6751-611*
Jerusalem 91034, Israel	*Fax*	*(011) + 972-2-4335-11*
	E-mail	*library@yadvashem.org.il*
		names.search@yadvashem.org.il

Hall of Names
http://www.yadvashem.org/remembrance/index_remembrance.html

Yad Vashem Online Magazine. (Serial). Online. Vol. 1– .
http://www.yadvashem.org/about_yad/index_about_yad.html

Yivo Institute
http://www.yivoinstitute.org/

The Center for Jewish History	*Phone*	*(212) 246-6080*
15 West 16th Street	*Fax*	*212) 292-1892*
New York, NY 10011-6301	*E-Mail*	*yivomail@yivo.cjh.org*

Archives
http://www.yivoinstitute.org/archlib/archlib_fr.htm

Genealogy Resources
http://www.yivoinstitute.org/archlib/archlib_fr.htm

Holocaust Resources
http://www.yivoinstitute.org/archlib/archlib_fr.htm

Library
http://www.yivoinstitute.org/archlib/archlib_fr.htm

Preserving Rare Books and Documents
http://www.yivoinstitute.org/archlib/archlib_fr.htm

LUTHERAN

Evangelical Lutheran Church in America
http://www.elca.org/os/archives/intro.html

Archives	*Phone*	*(847) 690-9410*
321 Bonnie Lane	*Fax*	*(847) 690-9502*
Elk Grove Village, IL 60007	*E-mail*	*archives@elca.org*

Archives
http://www.elca.org/os/archives/intro.html

Genealogy Help
http://www.elca.org/os/archives/geneal.html

Guide for ELCA Congregation Archives
http://www.elca.org/os/records.html

History of the ELCA
http://www.elca.org/co/roots.html

Maintaining the Parish Register
http://www.elca.org/os/parishre.html

Microfilm Loan Collection
http://www.elca.org/os/archives/filmloan.html

Oral History Collections
http://www.elca.org/os/archives/oralhist.html

Published Guides
http://www.elca.org/os/archives/publist.html

Lutheran Historical Conference
http://luthhist.org/

5732 White Pine Drive	*Phone*	*(314) 487-9884*
Saint Louis, MO 63129-2936	*Fax*	*(314) 894-1945*

Bibliography
http://luthhist.org/bibliography/lbibin.html

Essays and Reports. (Serial). Bi-annual. Table of Contents. Vol. 2 (1996)– .
http://luthhist.org/essays/ervol.html

Author Index. Vol. 2 (1966)– .
http://luthhist.org/essays/erauth.html

Lutheran Historical Society Newsletter. (Serial). Quarterly. Vol. 34, No. 1 (February 1996)– .
http://luthhist.org/news/index.htm

Lutheran Historical Society
http://www.abs.net/~lhs/

61 Seminary Ridge   Phone   (301) 713-7000
Gettysburg, PA 17325   E-mail   lhs@abs.net

Lutheran Historical Society, Constitution
http://www.abs.net/~lhs/constitution.html

Lutheran Historical Society of the Mid-Atlantic Newsletter. (Serial). Semi-annual. Vol. 7, No. 2 (Winter 1996)– .
http://www.abs.net/~lhs/previousNL.html

MENNONITE

Center for Mennonite Brethren Studies
http://www.fresno.edu/affiliation/cmbs/

1717 S. Chestnut Avenue
Fresno, CA 93702

Archival Collections
http://www.fresno.edu/affiliation/cmbs/archives.htm

California Mennonite Historical Society
http://www.fresno.edu/affiliation/cmhs/index.htm

4824 East Butler Street
Fresno, CA 93727-5097

California Mennonite Historical Society Bulletin. (Serial). Irregular. Nos. 32–37 (June 1995–December 1999).
http://www.fresno.edu/affiliation/cmhs/bulletin.htm

Genealogy Resources
http://www.fresno.edu/affiliation/cmbs/geneal.htm

GRANDMA (Genealogical Registry and Database of Mennonite Ancestry)
http://www.fresno.edu/affiliation/cmhs/gpc/home.htm

Historical Commission of the General Conference of Mennonite Brethren Churches
http://www.fresno.edu/affiliation/hc/index.htm

Mennonite Brethren Archives
http://www.fresno.edu/affiliation/cmbs/archives/mbsystem.htm

Molotschna 1835 Census Index
http://www.mmhs.org/russia/1835cens.htm

Lancaster Mennonite Historical Society
http://www.lmhs.org/index.html

2215 Millstream Road   *Phone   (717) 393-9745*
Lancaster, PA 17602-1499   *Fax   (717) 393-8751*
                               E-mail lmhs@lmhs.org

Genealogical Resources
http://www.lmhs.org/index.html

Mennonite Research Journal. (Serial). Quarterly. Table of Contents. (April
1960–October 1977).
http://www.lmhs.org/index.html

Pennsylvania Mennonite Heritage. (Serial). Quarterly. Table of Contents. (1978)– .
http://www.lmhs.org/index.html

METHODIST

General Commission on Archives and History Center of the United Methodist Church
http://www.gcah.org/index.htm

P.O. Box 127   *Phone   (973) 408-3189*
36 Madison Avenue   *Fax   (973) 408-3909*
Madison, NJ 07940   *E-mail research@gcah.org*

Archives and Manuscripts Collections
http://www.gcah.org/umac_inv.htm

Directory for Local and Regional United Methodist Archives
http://www.gcah.org/Conference/umcdirectory.htm

Handling and Care of Photographs
http://www.gcah.org/care.html

Historical Societies
http://www.gcah.org/Directory/HistSoc.htm

Library Online Catalog
http://www.gcah.org/inventory.htm

Manual for Annual Conference Commissions on Archives and History, 2001–2004.
(Serial).
http://www.gcah.org/AC_Manual/acmanual.htm

Menking, Stanley J. and Paul Riemann. *200 Years of United Methodism. An
Illustrated History.* Electronic Edition. 1984.
http://www.drew.edu/books/200Years/200UM/homepage.htm

Mission Biographical Reference Files
http://www.gcah.org/ead/framgcah2101.htm

Researching Your Methodist Ancestor
http://www.gcah.org/Searching.htm

PENTECOSTAL

Institute for the Study of American Evangelicals
http://www.wheaton.edu/isae/

Wheaton College   *E-mail   isae@wheaton.edu*
Wheaton, IL 60187-5593

Bibliograhies
http://www.wheaton.edu/isae/ESB_bibliography.html

Evangelical Studies Bulletin. (Serial). Varies, Currently Quarterly. Table of Contents.
Vol. 1, No. 2 (May 1984)– .
http://www.wheaton.edu/isae/ESB_past.html

PRESBYTERIAN

Presbyterian Church, USA
http://www.pcusa.org/

100 Witherspoon Street   *Phone   (502) 569-5000*
Louisville, KY 40202   *Fax   (502) 569-5018*
                                       E-mail presbytel@pcusa.org

Presbyterian Historical Society
http://www.history.pcusa.org/contents.html

425 Lombard Street   *Phone   (215) 627-1852*
Philadelphia, PA 19147-1516   *Fax   (215) 627-0509*
                                       E-mail refdesk@history.pcusa.org
                                       Dept.of.History.Phil@pcusa.org

Celebrate! Your Church's Anniversary
http://www.history.pcusa.org/cong/anniv1.html

Genealogical Research
http://www.history.pcusa.org/famhist/general.html

Journal of Presbyterian History. (Serial). Quarterly. Table of Contents. Vol. 77
(Spring 1999)– .
http://www.history.pcusa.org/pubs/journal/index.html

Minister and Missionary Biographical Files
http://www.history.pcusa.org/famhist/bio_ref.html

Ministerial Directories
http://www.history.pcusa.org/famhist/cler_bib.html

ROMAN CATHOLIC

Archdiocese of Atlanta
http://www.archatl.com

Archives of the Archdiocese of Atlanta
http://www.archatl.com/offices/archives/

The Catholic Center	*Phone*	*(404) 885-7203*
680 West Peachtree Street, NW	*Fax*	*(404) 885-7230*
Atlanta, GA 30308-1984	*E-mail*	*abritton@archatl.com*

Georgia Bulletin: Official Newspaper of the Archdiocese of Atlanta. (Serial). Weekly. (January 4, 1963)– .
http://www.archatl.com/gabulletin/gb-year.html

Necrology of Deceased Priests
http://www.archatl.com/offices/archives/necrology.html

Parish Profiles
http://www.archatl.com/parishes/index_bydate.html

Catholic Archives of Texas
http://www.onr.com/user/cat/

Diocese of Austin Chancery Building	*Phone*	*(512) 476-4888*
1600 North Congress Avenue	*Fax*	*(512) 476-3715*
Austin, TX 78701	*E-mail*	*cat@onr.com*

Mailing Address:
P.O. Box 13327, Capitol Station
Austin, TX 78711

Corporate Records
http://www.onr.com/user/cat/cathol95.html#corporate_records

Manuscripts
http://www.onr.com/user/cat/cathol95.html

Personal Papers
http://www.onr.com/user/cat/cathol95.html#personal_papers

Sacramental Records
http://www.onr.com/user/cat/sacraments.htm

Seton Hall University
http://www.shu.edu/

Walsh Library
http://library.shu.edu/

Special Collections Center
http://library.shu.edu/SpecColl.htm

Walsh Library, First Floor	*Phone*	*(973) 761-9476*
400 South Orange Avenue	*E-mail*	*DeloziAl@shu.edu*
South Orange, NJ 07079-2696		

New Jersey Catholic Historical Records Commission

> *History Department*   *Phone*   *(973) 275-2773*
> *South Orange, NJ 07079-2696*   *E-mail   MahoneJo@shu.edu*

Archdiocese of Newark
> http://library.shu.edu/SpecColl-anc.htm

New Jersey Catholic Records Newsletter. (Serial). 3/year. Vol. 15, No. 3
(Spring 1996)– .
> http://library.shu.edu/catholicrec/njhrc.htm

Texas Catholic Historical Society
> http://www.onr.com/user/cat/TCHS.htm

> *c/o Texas Catholic Conference*   *E-mail   jd10@swt.edu*
> *1625 Rutherford Lane, Bldg. D*
> *Austin, TX 78754-5105*

Catholic Southwest, A Journal of History and Culture. (Serial). Annual. Vols. 1–4
(1990–1993). Table of Contents. Vol. 2 (1991); Vol. 5 (1994)– .
> http://www.history.swt.edu/Catholic_Southwest.htm

U.S. Catholic Historical Society
> http://www.catholic.org/uschs/index.html

> *The Catholic Center*   *Phone*   *(800) 225-7999*
> *1011 First Avenue*   *E-mail   catholichistory@aol.com*
> *New York, NY 10022*

Archives Guide
> http://cf.catholic.org/uschs/searchphase1.cfm

GENEALOGICAL SOCIETIES

American Society of Genealogists
> http://www.fasg.org/

> *P.O. Box 1515*
> *Derry, NH 03038-1515*

ASG Scholar Award
> http://www.fasg.org/asg_scholar_award.html

Donald Lines Jacobus Award and Recipients
> http://www.fasg.org/jacobus_award.html

Fellows, Active
> http://www.fasg.org/ActiveFellows.html

Fellows, Roster of All Elected, 1940–
> http://www.fasg.org/AllFellows.html

Association of Professional Genealogists

http://www.apgen.org/

P.O. Box 40393   E-mail   admin@apgen.org
Denver, CO 80204-0393

APG-L, Listserv

http://www.apgen.org/publications/index.html#APG-L

APG Quarterly. (Serial). Index. (1979–1999).

http://www.apgen.org/publications/quarterly/archives/index.html

Chapter Directory

http://www.apgen.org/localchapters/index.html

Membership Directory

http://www.apgen.org/directory/index.php

Board for Certification of Genealogists

http://www.bcgcertification.org/

P.O. Box 14291   E-mail   office@bcgcertification.org
Washington, DC 20044

Certification FAQ

http://www.bcgcertification.org/certification/faq.html

Roster

http://www.bcgcertification.org/associates/index.php

OUTSTANDING SITE

Eastman's Online Genealogy Newsletter
http://www.rootsforum.com/newsletter/

OUTSTANDING SITE

Federation of East European Family History Societies
http://feefhs.org/

P. O. Box 51089
Salt Lake City, UT 84151-0898

Ethnic, Religious, and National Index

http://feefhs.org/ethnic.html

Map Room

http://feefhs.org/maps/indexmap.html

OUTSTANDING SITE

Federation of Genealogical Societies
http://www.fgs.org/

P.O. Box 200940
Austin, TX 78720-0940

Phone (888) FGS-1500
Fax (888) 380-0500
E-mail fgs-office@fgs.org

Calendar of Genealogical Events
http://www.fgs.org/fgs-calendar.asp

Conferences
http://www.fgs.org/fgs-conference.htm

Federation of Genealogical Societies History and Awards
http://www.fgs.org/fgs-awards.htm

Society Hall, Directory of Member Societies
http://www.familyhistory.com/societyhall/main.asp

Stern-NARA Gift Fund
http://www.fgs.org/fgs-naragift.htm

Genealogical Speakers Guild
http://www.genspeakguild.org/

P.O. 2818 Pennsylvania Ave., NW
Suite 159
Washington, DC 20007

E-mail rhondam@thegenealogist.com

Membership Directory
http://www.genspeakguild.org/

Guild of One-Name Studies
http://www.one-name.org/

EXTRAORDINARY SITE

National Genealogical Society
http://www.ngsgenealogy.org/

4527 17th Street, North
Arlington, VA 22207-2399

Phone (703) 525-0050 Office
(703) 841-9065 Library
Fax (703) 525-0052
E-mail ngs@ngsgenealogy.org

GEDCOM Testbook Project
http://www.gentech.org/ngsgentech/projects/TestBook2001/

GENTECH Genealogical Data Model
http://www.gentech.org/ngsgentech/projects/Gdm/Gdm.asp

Library Catalog
http://www.ngsgenealogy.org/libprecat.htm

National Genealogical Society Awards
http://www.ngsgenealogy.org/comngsawards.htm

National Genealogical Society GENTECH
http://www.gentech.org/ngsgentech/main/Home.asp

EXTRAORDINARY SITE
One of the Most Extraordinary Web Sites Online

USGenWeb Project
http://www.usgenweb.com/index.html

Links, by State
http://www.usgenweb.com/thestates.html

HERALDRY

OUTSTANDING SITE

François Velde's Heraldry Site
http://www.heraldica.org/

Bibliography
http://www.heraldica.org/biblio/index.html

Ecclesiastical Heraldry
http://www.heraldica.org/topics/ecclesia.htm

Heraldry, by Country
http://www.heraldica.org/topics/national/index.html

Knighthood and Orders of Chivalry
http://www.heraldica.org/topics/orders/

Nobility
http://www.heraldica.org/topics/nobility/

Origins of Heraldry
> http://www.heraldica.org/topics/origins.htm

Royalty
> http://www.heraldica.org/topics/royalty/

HISTORICAL SOCIETIES

American Association of State and Local History
> http://www.aaslh.org/

530 Church Street	*Phone* *(615) 320-3203*
Nashville, TN 37219-2325	*Fax* *(615) 327-9013*
	E-mail *history@aaslh.org*

AASLH Operating Plan
> http://www.aaslh.org/operatingplan.htm

Ethics Statement
> http://www.aaslh.org/ethics.htm

American Historical Association
> http://www.theaha.org/

400 A Street, SE	*Phone* *(202) 544-2422*
Washington, DC 20003-3889	*Fax* *(202) 544-8307*
	E-mail *aha@theaha.org*

Affiliated Societies
> http://www.theaha.org/affiliates/

American Historical Review. (Serial). Quarterly. Vol. 104, No. 3 (June 1999)– .
> http://www.historycooperative.org/ahrindex.html

Calendar
> http://www.theaha.org/calendar/

Common-Place. (Serial). Quarterly. Vol. 1 (September 2000)– .
> http://www.historycooperative.org/cpindex.html

Dissertations in Progress, Online
> http://www.theaha.org/pubs/dissertations/

Gutenberg-E Prizes
> http://www.theaha.org/prizes/gutenberg/

History Teacher. (Serial). Quarterly.
> http://www.historycooperative.org/htindex.html

Journal of American History. (Serial). Quarterly. Vol. 86, No. 1 (June 1999)– .
> http://www.historycooperative.org/jahindex.html

Law and History Review. (Serial). Quarterly. Vol. 17, No. 1 (Spring 1999)– .
> http://www.historycooperative.org/lhrindex.html

Online Directory of History Departments and Organizations in the United States and Canada. (Serial). Limited Edition.
  http://www.theaha.org/pubs/directory/index.cfm

Online Papers
  http://www.theaha.org/pubs/olpubs.htm

Perspectives Online. (Serial). Current Issue.
  http://www.theaha.org/perspectives/

Teaching
  http://www.theaha.org/teaching/

Western Historical Quarterly. (Serial). Quarterly. Vol. 32 (January 2001)– .
  http://www.historycooperative.org/whqindex.html

William and Mary Quarterly. (Serial). Quarterly. Vol. 58 (January 2001)– .
  http://www.historycooperative.org/wmindex.html

Conference on Historical Journals
  http://www.h-net.msu.edu/~chj/index.html

Book Reviews, Some Basics for Authors and Reviewers
  http://www.h-net.msu.edu/~chj/reviews.html

Guidelines for Editorial Procedures and Ethics
  http://www.h-net.msu.edu/~chj/guidelines.html

Member Directory
  http://www.h-net.msu.edu/~chj/members.html

What Journal Editors Wish Authors Knew
  http://www.h-net.msu.edu/~chj/whateds.html

EXTRAORDINARY SITE

H-Net
http://h-net2.msu.edu/

310 Auditorium Building   *Phone*   *(517) 355-9300*
Michigan State University   *Fax*   *(517) 355-8363*
East Lansing, MI 48824

Directory of the 50+ Discussion Lists
  http://www2.h-net.msu.edu/lists/

H-California
  http://www2.h-net.msu.edu/~cal/

H-Florida
> http://www2.h-net.msu.edu/~florida/

H-HISTBIBL (Historians, Bibliographers, Librarians, Archivists)
> http://www2.h-net.msu.edu/~histbibl/

H-Indiana
> http://www2.h-net.msu.edu/~indiana/

H-Itam (Italian American History)
> http://www2.h-net.msu.edu/~itam/

H-Local
> http://www2.h-net.msu.edu/~local/

H-Maryland
> http://www2.h-net.msu.edu/~maryland/

H-Michigan
> http://www2.h-net.msu.edu/~michigan/

H-New Mexico
> http://www2.h-net.msu.edu/~newmex/

H-Ohio
> http://www2.h-net.msu.edu/~ohio/

H-Public (History)
> http://www2.h-net.msu.edu/~public/

H-Tennessee
> http://www2.h-net.msu.edu/~tenn/

H-Texas
> http://www2.h-net.msu.edu/~texas/

National Council on Public History
> http://www.ncph.org/

327 Cavanaugh Hall   *Phone*   *(317) 274-2716*
IUPUI   *Fax*   *(317) 274-2347*
425 University Blvd.   *E-mail* *ncph@iupui.edu*
Indianapolis, IN 46202-5140

Code of Ethics
> http://www.ncph.org/code_of_ethics.htm

Museum Exhibit Standards
> http://www.ncph.org/exhibit%20standards.html

Public Historian. (Serial). Vol. 23, No. 1 (Winter 2001)–.
> http://www.ucpress.edu/journals/tph/

Public History News. (Serial). Vol. 21, No. 4 (Summer 2001)– .
> http://www.ncph.org/PHN%20Online.htm

Public History News. (Serial). Table of Contents. Vol. 1, No. 1– .
   http://www.ncph.org/Public%20History%20News%20article%20index.htm

Organization of American Historians
   http://www.oah.org/

112 Bryan Street	*Phone (812) 855-7311*
Bloomington, IN 47408-4199	*Fax (812) 855-0696*
	E-mail oah@oah.org

Awards
   http://www.oah.org/activities/awards/index.html

OAH Magazine. (Serial). Index. (1985–2001).
   http://www.oah.org/pubs/magazine/mohidx.html

LIBRARIES

American Library Association
   http://www.ala.org/

50 East Huron Street	*Phone (800) 545-2433*
Chicago, IL 60606	*E-mail ala@ala.org*

Genealogical Publishing Company Award Committee
   http://www.ala.org/rusa/hs/awa.html

Genealogy and Local History Discussion Group
   http://www.ala.org/rusa/hs/disc1.html

Genealogy Committee
   http://www.ala.org/rusa/hs/gen.html

Guidelines for a Unit or Course of Instruction in Genealogical Research at Schools of Library and Information Science
   http://www.ala.org/rusa/stnd_gencourse.html

Guidelines for Developing Beginning Genealogical Collections and Services
   http://www.ala.org/rusa/stnd_beg_gene_col.html

Guidelines for Editors of Historical and Genealogical Bulletins and Family Newsletters
   http://www.ala.org/rusa/stnd_editors.html

Guidelines for Establishing Local History Collections
   http://www.ala.org/rusa/stnd_localhis.html

Guidelines for Preservation, Conservation, and Restoration of Local History and Local Genealogical Materials
   http://www.ala.org/rusa/stnd_gen_local.html

History Librarians Discussion Group
   http://www.ala.org/rusa/hs/disc2.html

History Section
http://www.ala.org/rusa/hs/

Local History Committee
http://www.ala.org/rusa/hs/loc.html

RUSA, Reference and User Services Association
http://www.ala.org/rusa/

EXTRAORDINARY SITE

Libweb
http://sunsite.berkeley.edu/Libweb/

Africa and the Middle East, List of Libraries
http://sunsite.berkeley.edu/Libweb/africa.html

Asian Libraries
http://sunsite.berkeley.edu/Libweb/Asia_main.html

Australia and New Zealand, Libraries
http://sunsite.berkeley.edu/Libweb/aus.html

Canada
http://sunsite.berkeley.edu/Libweb/Canada_main.html

Consortia
http://sunsite.berkeley.edu/Libweb/usa-consortia.html

Europe
http://sunsite.berkeley.edu/Libweb/Europe_main.html

Library Online Catalogs, Gateways
http://staffweb.library.vanderbilt.edu/Breeding/libwebcats.html

Mexico, the Caribbean, Central America, and South America
http://sunsite.berkeley.edu/Libweb/mex.html

School Libraries (K–12)
http://www.sldirectory.com/

United States, Academic Libraries
http://sunsite.berkeley.edu/Libweb/Academic_main.html

United States, National Libraries and Library Organizations
http://sunsite.berkeley.edu/Libweb/usa-org.html

United States, Public Libraries
http://sunsite.berkeley.edu/Libweb/Public_main.html

United States, State Libraries
   http://sunsite.berkeley.edu/Libweb/usa-state.html

MAPS

U.S. Geological Survey
   http://www.usgs.gov/

   508 National Center   *Phone*   *(703) 648-4544*
   Reston, VA 20192   *(800) 872-6277*
                                    E-mail   www-nmd@usgs.gov

Foreign Gazetteers
   http://www-nmd.usgs.gov/www/gnis/foreigninstr.html

Geographic Names Information System
   http://www-nmd.usgs.gov/www/gnis/

Mapping Information Service
   http://www-nmd.usgs.gov/www/html/nmp_prog.html

Regional Mapping Centers
   http://www-nmd.usgs.gov/www/html/1nmdsite.html

Topographic Mapping
   http://www-nmd.usgs.gov/misc/evolution.html

MAYFLOWER

EXTRAORDINARY SITE
One of the Most Extraordinary Web Sites Online

Caleb Johnson's Mayflower Web Page
http://members.aol.com/calebj/mayflower.html

E-mail   MayfloWeb@aol.com

Bibliography
   http://members.aol.com/calebj/bibliography.html

Common Mayflower Genealogical Hoaxes
   http://members.aol.com/calebj/hoaxes.html

Contemporary Accounts about the Pilgrims
   http://members.aol.com/mayflo1620/writings.html

Crew of the Mayflower
   http://members.aol.com/calebj/crew.html

Early Plymouth Letters
   http://members.aol.com/mayflo1620/letters.html

Hypocricie Unmasked, 1646
   http://members.aol.com/calebj/hypocricie.html

Mayflower, Ship
   http://members.aol.com/calebj/ship.html

Mayflower Compact
   http://members.aol.com/calebj/compact.html

Mayflower Passenger List
   http://members.aol.com/calebj/passenger.html

U.S. Presidents, Vice-Presidents, First Ladies with Mayflower Ancestors
   http://members.aol.com/calebj/presidents.html

Wills of Mayflower Passengers
   http://members.aol.com/mayflo1620/wills.html

Women on the Mayflower
   http://members.aol.com/calebj/women.html

General Society of Mayflower Descendants
   http://www.themayflowersociety.com/

P.O. Box 3297   *Phone   (508) 746-3188*
Plymouth, MA 02361-3297

State Chapters, Directory
   http://www.themayflowersociety.com/contact.htm

California Chapter
   http://www.mayflowersociety.com/

Canadian Society of Mayflower Descendants
   http://users.rootsweb.com/~canms/canada.html

Connecticut Society
   http://www.ctmayflower.org/

Florida Society
   http://www.geocities.com/flmayflower/

Hawaii Society
   http://www.geocities.com/Heartland/Ridge/4602/index.html

Miane Society
   http://www.blazenetme.net/~rthivier/memayflower.html

Maryland Society
   http://members.aol.com/MdMayflower2001/

Massachusetts Society
   http://www.massmayflowersociety.org/

Missouri Society
http://www.rootsweb.com/~mosmd/missouri/

New Hampshire Society
http://www.blazenetme.net/~rthivier/nhmayflower.html

North Carolina Society
http://home.nc.rr.com/ncmayflower/

Pennsylvania Society
http://www.sail1620.org/

Rhode Island Society
http://www.mayflower-ri.org/

Texas Society
http://www.geocities.com/texasmayflower/index.html

Utah Society
http://www.northernutah.com/mayflower/

Vermont Society
http://members.aol.com/samatyas/

Wisconsin Society
http://www.mayflowerwi.org/

MILITARY RECORDS

Air Force Historical Research Agency
http://www.au.af.mil/au/afhra/

600 Chennault Circle   *Phone   (334) 953-2395*
Maxwell AFB, AL 36112-6424   *E-mail   AFHRANEWS@maxwell.af.mil*

Air Force Heraldry
http://www.au.af.mil/au/afhra/heraldry.htm

Archives, Personal Papers
http://www.au.af.mil/au/afhra/wwwroot/personal_papers/personal_papers.html

Army Air Force Statistical Digest
http://www.au.af.mil/au/afhra/wwwroot/aafsd/aafsd_index_table.html

Historical Studies Series
http://www.au.af.mil/au/afhra/hisstud.htm

Korean War
http://www.au.af.mil/au/afhra/wwwroot/korean_war/korean_war.html

Unit, Division Histories
http://www.au.af.mil/au/afhra/wwwroot/rso/rso_index.html

Air Force History Support Office, AFHSO/HOS

http://www.airforcehistory.hq.af.mil/

Reference and Analysis Division   *Phone   (202) 404-2264*
200 McChord Street, Box 94
Bolling AFB, DC 20332-1111

Online Publications

http://www.airforcehistory.hq.af.mil/publications.htm

USAAF, WWII, Combat Chronology, 1941–1945

http://www.airforcehistory.hq.af.mil/PopTopics/chron/title.htm

---

O U T S T A N D I N G   S I T E

Center of Military History

http://www.army.mil/cmh-pg/

Historical Resources Branch   *Phone   (202) 761-5416*
U.S. Army Center of Military History
1099 14th Street NW
Washington, DC 20005-3402

Army Museum Directory

http://www.army.mil/cmh-pg/Museums/Memo/AM-Memo.htm

Army Museum Memo. Serial.

http://www.army.mil/cmh-pg/Museums/Memo/AM-Memo.htm

Army Museum System

http://www.army.mil/cmh-pg/Museums/museums.htm

Gulf War Bibliography

http://www.army.mil/cmh-pg/reference/gulfbib.htm

Medal of Honor Recipients

http://www.army.mil/cmh-pg/moh1.htm

Online Book Collection

http://www.army.mil/cmh-pg/online/Bookshelves/books-era.htm

Military History Institute

http://carlisle-www.army.mil/usamhi/

Carlisle Barracks   *Phone   (717) 245-3601*
Carlisle, PA 17013   *E-mail   MHI-HR@carlisle-emh2.army.mil*
                              Archives MHI-AR@carlisle-emh2.army.mil
                              Photos MHI-SC@carlisle-emh2.army.mil

Civil War Biographical Bibliography

http://carlisle-www.army.mil/usamhi/ACWBiogs.html

Civil War Unit Bibliographies
http://carlisle-www.army.mil/usamhi/ACWUnits.html

Collection Index (RefBibs)
http://carlisle-www.army.mil/usamhi/RefBibs.html

Finding Aids
http://carlisle-www.army.mil/usamhi/1findingaidssubheaders.html

Korean War Individual Interview Project Information Form
http://carlisle-www.army.mil/usamhi/KoreanWarQuestionnaire.html

Manuscripts Index
http://carlisle-www.army.mil/usamhi/ArchivesDB.html

Photograph Collection Index
http://carlisle-www.army.mil/usamhi/PhotoDB.html

WWII Individual Interview Project Information Form
http://carlisle-www.army.mil/usamhi/WWIIquestionnaire.html

OUTSTANDING SITE

Naval Historical Center
http://www.history.navy.mil/

Washington Navy Yard	*Phone*	*(202) 433-4132*
901 M Street SE	*Fax*	*(202) 433-9553*
Washington, DC 20374-5060	*E-mail*	*dlriley@hop-uky.campus.mci.net*
Marine Corps Historical Center	*Phone*	*(202) 433-3483*
Washington Navy Yard, Building 58	*E-mail*	*homepage.usmc@notessmtp.*
Washington, DC 20374-0580		*hqi.usmc.mil*

Bibliographies
http://www.history.navy.mil/nhc6.htm#anchor52857

Manuscripts, Guide
http://www.history.navy.mil/biblio/biblio3/biblio3.htm

Naval Vessel Register
http://www.nvr.navy.mil/nvrships/NAME.HTM

Reestablishment of the Navy, 1787–1801
http://www.history.navy.mil/biblio/biblio4/biblio4.htm

Spanish-American War, Bibliography
http://www.history.navy.mil/biblio/biblio7/biblio7.htm

USAF Museum

http://www.wpafb.af.mil/museum/index.htm

1100 Spaatz Street   Phone   *(937) 255-3286*
Wright-Patterson AFB, OH 45433-7102

Aircraft Index

http://www.wpafb.af.mil/museum/ind/ind.htm

WWII Bombardiers

http://www.wpafb.af.mil/museum/history/wwii/bomb.htm

OUTSTANDING SITE

U.S. Coast Guard
http://www.uscg.mil/

African Americans in the Coast Guard

http://www.uscg.mil/hq/g-cp/history/MINORITY%20BIB.html

Bibliographies

http://www.uscg.mil/hq/g-cp/history/generalbib.html

Biographical Sources

http://www.uscg.mil/hq/g-cp/history/CoastGuardPeople.html

Chronology of Coast Guard History

http://www.uscg.mil/hq/g-cp/history/Chronology_index.html

Coast Guard at War

http://www.uscg.mil/hq/g-cp/history/h_militaryindex.html

Lighthouses, Lightships, etc.

http://www.uscg.mil/hq/g-cp/history/h_lhindex.html

Locating Personnel Records

http://www.uscg.mil/hq/g-cp/history/Genealogy.html

Women in the Coast Guard

http://www.uscg.mil/hq/g-cp/history/WOMEN%20BIB.html

NEWSPAPERS

Newspaper Association of America

http://www.naa.org/

1921 Gallows Road, Suite 600   Phone   *(703) 902-1600*
Vienna, VA 22182-3900   Fax   *(703) 917-0636*

Links, Newspapers by State
   http://www.newspaperlinks.com/home.cfm

U.S. Newspaper Program
   http://lcweb.loc.gov/preserv/usnppr.html

   Library of Congress
   101 Independence Ave., SE   *E-mail   rhar@loc.gov*
   Washington, DC 20540

Links to State Newspaper Projects
   http://www.neh.gov/projects/usnp.html

Preserving Newspapers
   http://lcweb.loc.gov/preserv/care/newspap.html

USNSP Preservation Microfilming Guidelines
   http://lcweb.loc.gov/preserv/usnpguidelines.html

PHOTOGRAPHS

Daguerreian Society
   http://www.daguerre.org/

   3045 West Liberty Avenue, Suite 9   *Phone   (412) 343-5525*
   Pittsburgh, PA 15216-2460   *Fax   (412) 563-5972*
                                           E-mail   dagSocPgh@aol.com

Daguerreian Annual. (Serial). Table of Contents. (1990)– .
   http://www.daguerre.org/society/annual/toc.html

Daguerreian Process: A Description
   http://www.daguerre.org/resource/process/remin.html

Daguerreotype Bibliography
   http://www.daguerre.org/resource/biblio/biblio.html

Daguerreotypist. (Serial). Ceased. (February 5, 1997–September 20, 1999).
   http://www.daguerre.org/resource/dagtypist/dagtypist.html

eTexts, Online Books and Articles
   http://www.daguerre.org/resource/texts.html

SURNAMES

U.S. Surname Distribution Map
   http://www.hamrick.com/names/

TELEPHONE DIRECTORIES

OUTSTANDING SITE

International Telephone Directories
http://www.infobel.com/World/

Kapitol   *E-mail   info@infobel.com*
Chaussée de Saint Job
506 Sint Jobsesteenweg
1180 Bruxelles–Brussel
Belgium

Belgium Telephone Books
http://www.infobel.com/Belgium/

France Telephone Books
http://www.infobel.com/France/

Denmark Telephone Books
http://www.infobel.com/Denmark/

Italy Telephone Books
http://www.infobel.com/italy/

Netherlands Telephone Books
http://www.infobel.com/netherlands/

Spain Telephone Books
http://www.infobel.com/Spain/

United Kingdom
http://www.infobel.com/uk/

United States
http://www.infobel.com/usa/

OUTSTANDING SITE

Switchboard.com™
http://www.switchboard.com/

WOMEN'S HISTORY

OUTSTANDING SITE

Women's History
http://frank.mtsu.edu/~kmiddlet/history/women.html

Todd Library
Middle Tennessee State University
Murfreesboro, TN 37132

Phone   (615) 904-8524
E-mail   kmiddlet@frank.mtsu.edu

Biographical Sources
http://frank.mtsu.edu/~kmiddlet/history/women/wh-bio.html

Guide to Sources, by State
http://frank.mtsu.edu/~kmiddlet/history/women/wh-bio.html

UNITED STATES SOURCES

ALABAMA

Alabama State Home Page
http://www.alabama.gov/

Vital Records Office
http://ph.state.al.us/chs/VitalRecords/VRECORDS.HTMl

STATE ARCHIVES

Alabama Department of Archives and History (ADAH)
http://www.archives.state.al.us/

624 Washington Avenue	*Phone (334) 242-4235*
Montgomery, AL 36130-0024	*Fax (334) 240-3433*
	E-mail ndupree@archives.state.al.us

African American Records
http://www.archives.state.al.us/afro/afro.html

Alabama County Historical and Genealogical Societies
http://www.archives.state.al.us/referenc/hsglist.html

Alabama Historical Quarterly. (Serial). Quarterly. Table of Contents. (1930–1982).
http://www.lib.auburn.edu/special/docs/ahistqtr.html

Alabama History On-line
http://www.archives.state.al.us/aho.html

Archives, Preparation Guidelines for Volunteers, Alabama Microfilming Project
http://www.archives.state.al.us/ol_pubs/looserep.html

Association Records
http://www.archives.state.al.us/referenc/assoc.html

Bibliography of Alabama History Books
http://www.archives.state.al.us/biblio/biblio.html

Bibliography of Alabama Women's History Books
http://www.archives.state.al.us/referenc/cover.html

Biographical Sources
http://www.archives.state.al.us/famous/famous.html

Business Records
http://www.archives.state.al.us/referenc/business.html

Census Records
http://www.archives.state.al.us/referenc/census.html#federal

Church Records
http://www.archives.state.al.us/referenc/church.html

City Directories
  http://www.archives.state.al.us/referenc/micro.html

County Records
  http://www.archives.state.al.us/referenc/procount.html

Digital Imaging Guidelines for Alabama Records
  http://www.archives.state.al.us/ol_pubs/digital.html

Government Officials
  http://www.archives.state.al.us/govtoff.html

Government Records News. (Serial). Quarterly. No. 1 (July 1996)– .
  http://www.archives.state.al.us/ol_pubs/olpubs.html

Military Records
  http://www.archives.state.al.us/referenc/military.html

Newspapers on Microfilm
  http://www.archives.state.al.us/newsp/newsp.html

Online Research Request Form
  http://www.archives.state.al.us/referenc/newform2.html

Public Records, Responsibilities of Public Officials
  http://www.archives.state.al.us/ol_pubs/pub_off.html

Records Not at the ADAH
  http://www.archives.state.al.us/referenc/notat.html

Statistical Information
  http://www.archives.state.al.us/stats.html

Teachers, Using Primary Sources in the Classroom
  http://www.archives.state.al.us/teacher/psources.shtml

Vital Records on Microfilm
  http://www.archives.state.al.us/referenc/vital.html

OTHER STATE SITES

AlabamaInfo
  http://www.alabamainfo.com/

Alabama Cities Index
  http://www.alabamainfo.com/cities/

Alabama Media Index
  http://www.alabamainfo.com/media/

Auburn University
http://www.auburn.edu/

Special Collections Department   Phone   *(334) 844-1700*
Draughon Library
231 Mell Street
Auburn University, AL 36849

Alabama Authors
http://www.lib.auburn.edu/madd/docs/ala_authors/contents.html

Alabama Collection, Accessions List
http://www.lib.auburn.edu/special/docs/alaindex.html

Alabama Heritage. (Serial). Quarterly. Table of Contents. (Summer 1986)– .
http://www.lib.auburn.edu/special/docs/alaheritage.html

Alabama Historical Quarterly. (Serial). Quarterly. Table of Contents. Vol. 1, No. 1 (Spring 1930)– .
http://www.lib.auburn.edu/special/docs/ahistqtr.html

Alabama Review. (Serial). Quarterly. Table of Contents. Vol. 1, No. 1 (January 1948)– .
http://www.lib.auburn.edu/special/docs/alarevu.html

Gulf South Historical Review. (Serial). Semi-annual. Table of Contents. Vol. 1, No. 1 (Fall 1985)– .
http://www.lib.auburn.edu/special/docs/gchr.html

ALASKA

STATE HOME PAGE

Alaska State Government
http://www.state.ak.us

Alaska Court System
http://www.state.ak.us/courts/courtdir.htm

Bureau of Vital Statistics
http://www.hss.state.ak.us/dph/bvs/

STATE ARCHIVES

Alaska State Archives
http://www.archives.state.ak.us/

Department of Education   Phone   *(907) 465-2270*
Division of Libraries, Archives   Fax   *(907) 465-2465*
*   and Museums*
Archives and Records Manage-
*   ment Services*
Willoughby Avenue
Juneau, AK 99801-1720

Alaska State Library
http://www.library.state.ak.us/

P.O. Box 110571   *Phone*   *(907) 465-2925*
Juneau, AK 99811-0571   *Fax*   *(907) 465-2990*
                                     E-mail *asl@muskox.alaska.edu*
                                               gladik@muskox.alaska.edu

Alaska Genealogy
http://www.library.state.ak.us/pub/online/akgene.html

Alaska Gold, Teaching Tool
http://www.library.state.ak.us/goldrush/HOME.HTM

Alaska Historical Collections
http://www.library.state.ak.us/hist/hist.html#Intro

Alaska Library Directory
http://www.library.state.ak.us/dev/aslld99.html

Alaska Newspaper Project
http://www.library.state.ak.us/hist/newspaper.html

Alaska Newspapers, Chronologies
http://www.library.state.ak.us/hist/newspaper/chron.html

Alaska Newspapers on Microfilm, 1866–1998
http://www.library.state.ak.us/hist/newspaper/news.html

Alaska Statistics Index
http://library.state.ak.us/asp/statestatistics.html

How to Find Your Gold Rush Relative
http://www.library.state.ak.us/hist/parham.html

Online Library Catalog
http://www.ccl.lib.ak.us/webclienttest.html

ARIZONA

State of Arizona WWW Page
http://www.az.gov/webapp/portal/

Links to Arizona Local and County Government
http://www.az.gov/webapp/portal/subtopic.jsp?id=2186&name=Arizona+Government

Office of Vital Records
http://www.hs.state.az.us/vitalrcd/index.htm

STATE LIBRARY AND ARCHIVES

Arizona Department of Library, Archives, and Public Records

http://www.dlapr.lib.az.us/

State Capitol, Suite 442	*Phone*	*(602) 542-4159*
1700 West Washington	*Fax*	*(602) 542-4402*
Phoenix, AZ 85007	*E-mail*	*archive@lib.az.us*

Arizona History

http://www.lib.az.us/archives/azhistory.htm

Arizona Newspaper Project

http://www.lib.az.us/anp/index.html

Checklist of Arizona State Agency Publications

http://www.lib.az.us/is/state/index.html

County Records

http://www.lib.az.us/archives/local.htm

Genealogy

http://www.lib.az.us/archives/famhistory.htm

Map Collections

http://www.lib.az.us/is/maps.htm

Museum

http://www.lib.az.us/museum/index.html

Online Catalog

http://aslaprcat.lib.az.us/

Teacher Resource Guide (Arizona History)

http://www.lib.az.us/museum/teachmanual2000.pdf

OTHER STATE SITES

Arizona State University Library

http://www.asu.edu/lib/

Department of Archives and	*Phone*	*(602) 965-4932*
Manuscripts	*Fax*	*(602) 965-0776*
Charles Trumbull Hayden Library,		
4th Level		
Tempe, AZ 85287		

Archives and Manuscripts Department

http://www.asu.edu/lib/archives/

Arizona Collection

http://www.asu.edu/lib/archives/arizona.htm

Arizona Historical Foundation

http://www.users.qwest.net/~azhistoricalfdn/

Arizona Southwest Index
    http://www.asu.edu/lib/resources/db/azsw.htm

Chicano Research Collection
    http://www.asu.edu/lib/archives/chicano.htm

George H. N. Luhrs Family in Phoenix and Arizona, 1874–1984
    http://www.asu.edu/lib/archives/luhrs/title.htm

Hayden Arizona Pioneer Biographies Collection
    http://www.asu.edu/lib/archives/azbio/bios.htm

Labriola National American Indian Data Center
    http://www.asu.edu/lib/archives/labriola.htm

Manuscript Collections
    http://www.asu.edu/lib/archives/msscoll.htm

Southwestern Autobiography Index
    http://www.asu.edu/lib/archives/swbio.htm

Promise of Gold Mountain: Tucson's Chinese Heritage
    http://dizzy.library.arizona.edu/promise/

Bibliography
    http://dizzy.library.arizona.edu/promise/sources_041801.html

Biographies of Prominent Chinese-American Tucsonans
    http://dizzy.library.arizona.edu/promise/bios_041801.html

Farms and Small Businesses
    http://dizzy.library.arizona.edu/promise/farmb_041801.html

Hi Wo Family
    http://www.library.arizona.edu/soza/hiwo.htm

"Immigrants to a Developing Society: The Chinese in Northern Mexico, 1875–1932,"
by Evelyn Hu DeHart
    http://dizzy.library.arizona.edu/promise/hu_041801.html

"Sojourners and Settlers, the Chinese Experience in Arizona," by
Lawrence Michael Fong
    http://dizzy.library.arizona.edu/promise/lmfong_041801.html

Southern Pacific Railroad Workers
    http://dizzy.library.arizona.edu/promise/railroad_041801.html

Tucson's Chinatowns
    http://dizzy.library.arizona.edu/promise/chinat_041801.html

Video Clips
    http://dizzy.library.arizona.edu/promise/video_041801.html

Tempe Historical Museum

http://www.tempe.gov/museum/

809 E. Southern Avenue	*Phone*	*(480) 350-5100*
Tempe, Arizona 85282	*Fax*	*(480) 350-5150*
	TDD	*(480) 350-5050*

Barrios Oral History Project

http://www.tempe.gov/museum/barrios.htm

Biographical Database

http://www.tempe.gov/museum/abiodb.htm

Tempe Historic Property Survey

http://www.tempe.gov/museum/ahpsfile.htm

University of Arizona

Special Collections Department,	*Phone*	*(520) 621-4345*
Library	*Fax*	*(520) 621-9733*
P.O. Box 210055	*E-mail*	*stuartg@u.arizona.edu*
Tucson, AZ 85721-0055		

Archival Guides

http://www.library.arizona.edu/images/swja/findingaids/findingaids.htm

Arizona Jewish Pioneers

http://www.library.arizona.edu/images/swja/arizona.htm

Bibliography

http://www.library.arizona.edu/images/swja/suggreads.htm

Biography Collections

http://dizzy.library.arizona.edu/branches/spc/azbiogr/azbiog.htm

http://dizzy.library.arizona.edu/branches/spc/uabiogr/uabio.htm

Jewish Pioneers of the Southwest

http://www.library.arizona.edu/images/swja/pioneers.htm

Leona G. and David Bloom Southwest Jewish Archives

http://www.library.arizona.edu/images/swja/swjalist.html

Manuscript Collections

http://dizzy.library.arizona.edu/branches/spc/homepage/alphlist/alphlist.htm

New Mexico Jewish Pioneers

http://www.library.arizona.edu/images/swja/newmexico.htm

Southwest Jewish History. (Serial). Vol. 1 (Fall 1992–Winter 1995).

http://www.library.arizona.edu/images/swja/newsletter.html

Synagogues of the Southwest

http://www.library.arizona.edu/images/swja/synagogues.htm

West Texas Jewish Pioneers

http://www.library.arizona.edu/images/swja/westtexas.htm

ARKANSAS

STATE HOME PAGE

State of Arkansas Home Page
http://www.state.ar.us/

Arkansas Department of Health Services, Vital Records
http://www.healthyarkansas.com/certificates/certificates.html

STATE ARCHIVES

Arkansas History Commission and State Archives
http://www.state.ar.us:80/ahc/index.htm

One Capitol Mall   *Phone   (501) 682-6900*
Little Rock, AR 72201

Resources
http://www.ark-ives.com/resource_types/index.php

STATE LIBRARY

Arkansas State Library
http://www.asl.lib.ar.us/

One Capitol Mall   *Phone   (501) 682-1527*
Little Rock, AR 72201-1081

Arkansas Libraries Online
http://www.asl.lib.ar.us/web_catalogs.htm

News. (Serial). Monthly. (January–February 1999)– .
http://www.asl.lib.ar.us/news/news.htm

OTHER STATE SITES

Department of Arkansas Heritage
http://www.arkansasheritage.com/

1500 Tower Building   *Phone   (501) 324-9150*
Little Rock, AR 72201   *Fax   (501) 324-9154*
                               E-mail info@arkansasheritage.com

African, Asian, European Americans
http://www.arkansasheritage.com/about/

University of Arkansas Library Home Page

Special Collections Division
http://libinfo.uark.edu/specialcollections/

Fayetteville, AR 72701-1201   *Phone   (479) 575-5577*
                                Fax   (479) 575-6656

Biography and Genealogy
http://cavern.uark.edu/libinfo/speccoll/shortguides/genealogy.html

Church Records
http://cavern.uark.edu/libinfo/speccoll/index.html#churches

Civil War, Manuscript Resources
http://cavern.uark.edu/libinfo/speccoll/civilwar1.html

Japanese American Internment
http://libinfo.uark.edu/specialcollections/manuscripts/japaneseamericans.asp

Manuscripts, Guide to Selected Collections
http://cavern.uark.edu/libinfo/speccoll/civilwar1.html

Personal and Family Papers
http://www.uark.edu/libinfo/speccoll/indexnew.html#family

University of Arkansas History and Records
http://www.uark.edu/libinfo/speccoll/indexnew.html#uofa

Women's Studies, Manuscript Resources
http://www.uark.edu/libinfo/speccoll/indexnew.html#women

World War II Prisoner of War Records
http://cavern.uark.edu/depts/speccoll/findingaids/ww2priswar.html

CALIFORNIA

STATE HOME PAGE

California State Home Page
http://www.state.ca.us/state/portal/myca_homepage.jsp

Vital Records Office
http://www.dhs.ca.gov/hisp/chs/OVR/ordercert.htm

STATE ARCHIVES

California State Archives
http://www.ss.ca.gov/archives/archives.htm

1020 "O" Street	*Phone (916) 653-2246*
Sacramento, CA 95814	*Fax (916) 653-7363*
	E-mail ArchivesWeb@SS.CA.GOV

Collections
http://www.oac.cdlib.org/dynaweb/ead/csa

Education Outreach: Learn California
http://www.learncalifornia.org/

Family History Resources
http://www.ss.ca.gov/archives/level3_genie.htm

Local Government Records Program
http://www.ss.ca.gov/archives/level3_locgovrec.html

Oral Histories, California State Government Officials
http://www.ss.ca.gov/archives/level3_ohguide1.html

Photograph Collections
http://www.ss.ca.gov/archives/level3_phguide1.html

Spanish and Mexican Land Grants
http://www.ss.ca.gov/archives/level3_ussg3.html

State Historical Records Advisory Board
http://www.ss.ca.gov/archives/level3_shrab.html

STATE LIBRARY

California State Library
http://www.library.ca.gov/

P.O. Box 942837	*Phone*	*(916) 654-0174*
Sacramento, CA 94237-0001	*E-mail*	*csl-adm@library.ca.gov*

Library and Courts Building I	*Phone* *(415) 731-4477*
914 Capitol Mall, Room 220	
Sacramento, CA 95814	

Sutro Library	*Phone* *(916) 654-0176* *CA History Room*
480 Winston Drive	
San Francisco, CA 94132	

"California As We Saw It": Exploring the California Gold Rush
http://www.library.ca.gov/goldrush/

California Library Directory
http://www.library.ca.gov/html/main.cfm

Genealogy Research
http://www.library.ca.gov/html/genealogy.html

STATE GENEALOGICAL SOCIETY

California Genealogical Society
http://www.calgensoc.org/

1611 Telegraph Avenue, Suite 200   *Phone*   *(510) 663-1358*
Oakland, CA 94612-2152

Library
http://www.calgensoc.org/library/index.htm

Name Index, Find Your California Forebears
    http://www.calgensoc.org/library/forebears.htm

STATE HISTORICAL SOCIETY

California Historical Society
    http://www.californiahistoricalsociety.org/

678 Mission Street   *Phone   (415) 357-1848*
San Francisco, CA 94105-4014   *Fax   (415) 357-1850*
                                  E-mail   info@calhist.org

California City Directories
    http://www.calhist.org/Support_Info/Collections/Library-Misc/CalifCityDir.html

California Historical Agencies by County
    http://www.calhist.org/Support_Info/CHAs.htmld/

California History. (Serial). Quarterly. Table of Contents. Vol. 1, No. 3 (1922)–Vol. 9, No. 4 (1930).
    http://www.californiahistoricalsociety.org/publications/index_page.html

Guide to California County Histories
    http://www.calhist.org/Support_Info/Collections/Library-Misc/CACountyHistoriesGuide.htmld/

Manuscript Collection, Descriptive Guides
    http://www.calhist.org/Support_Info/Collections/Manuscripts/MSDescriptiveGuides.htmld/

Photography Collections
    http://www.californiahistoricalsociety.org/collections/photography_coll.html

San Francisco Manuscript Collections. Preliminary Listing
    http://www.calhist.org/Support_Info/Collections/Manuscripts/MSS-SF-Guide/MS-SFColl1-Intro.html

OTHER STATE SITES

California State University, Chico
    http://www.csuchico.edu/

Meriam Library, Room 305a   *Phone   (530) 898-6342*
California State University, Chico *E-mail   BJones2@csuchico.edu*
Chico, CA 95929-0295

Association for Northern California Records and Research
    http://www.csuchico.edu/ancrr/

P.O. Box 3024   *E-mail   ANCRR@csuchico.edu*
Chico, CA 95927-3024

Bibliography of the History of the University
    http://www.csuchico.edu/lspr/bib.htm

Library
    http://www.csuchico.edu/library/

Maps
http://maps.csuchico.edu/

Newspaper Index
http://aphid.csuchico.edu/lso/newspaper/search.asp

Photograph Collections
http://cricket.csuchico.edu/spcfotos/photos2.html

Special Collections Department
http://www.csuchico.edu/lbib/spc/iepages/home.html

University Archives
http://www.csuchico.edu/lspr/

California State University, Fresno
http://duchess.lib.csufresno.edu/

Special Collections Department	*Phone*	*(559) 278-2595*
Henry Madden Library	*Fax*	*(559) 278-6952*
5200 North Barton Avenue	*E-mail*	*specialc@listserv.csufresno.edu*
M/S ML 34		
Fresno, CA 93740-8014		

Japanese Americans in World War II Collection
http://www.oac.cdlib.org/dynaweb/ead/csuf/jainwwii

June English Collection (Local History and Genealogy)
http://duchess.lib.csufresno.edu/subjectresources/specialcollections/photographs/englishcollectionphotos.html

Kneeland Family Photograph Collection, Guide
http://www.oac.cdlib.org/dynaweb/ead/csuf/kneelaph

Local, Regional, and California History Collections
http://duchess.lib.csufresno.edu/SubjectResources/SpecialCollections/Local.html

Special Collections Department
http://duchess.lib.csufresno.edu/subjectresources/specialcollections/introduction.html

University Archives
http://duchess.lib.csufresno.edu/subjectresources/specialcollections/archives.html

California State University, Northridge
http://www.csun.edu/

Special Collections Department
http://www.csun.edu/~spcoll/hbspcoll.html

Oviatt Library, Room 4	*Phone*	*(818) 677-2832*
California State University,	*E-mail*	*tgardner@csun.edu*
Northridge		
Northridge, CA 91330-8326		

Center for Southern California Studies
http://www2.h-net.msu.edu/~cal/resources/index.html

College of Social and Behavioral Sciences
18111 Nordhoff Street   *Phone*   *(818) 677-6518*
Northridge, CA 91330-8371   *E-mail   cscs@csun.edu*

California Studies Collection
http://www.csun.edu/~spcoll/hpsclist.html#calif

Guide to Collections on Los Angeles
http://www.csun.edu/~spcoll/laguide.html

Japanese American Internment, 1942–1945
http://www.csun.edu/~spcoll/fdgds6.html#heart

California Views
http://www.caviews.com/

Pat Hathaway Collection of Historical Photos
469 Pacific Street   *Phone*   *(831) 373-3811*
Monterey, CA 93940-2702   *E-mail   hathaway@caviews.com*

Guide to California Historical Photographs
http://www.caviews.com/

Chinese Historical Society of America
http://www.chsa.org/

965 Clay Street   *Phone*   *(415) 391-1188*
San Francisco, CA 94108   *Fax*   *(415) 391-1150*
                                     E-mail   info@chsa.org

Bulletin. (Serial). Monthly. Table of Contents. No. 1 (February 1999)– .
http://www.chsa.org/resources/bulletin.htm

Chinese America: History and Perspectives. (Serial). Annual. Table of Contents.
Vol. 1 (1987)– .
http://www.chsa.org/resources/index.htm#Publications

Chinese Americans in the Civil War
http://www.chsa.org/resources/civilwar.htm

Chinese Historical Society of Southern California
http://www.chssc.org/

P.O. Box 862647   *E-mail   chssc@chssc.org*
Los Angeles, CA 90086-2647

Chinese Americans in World War II
http://www.chssc.org/ww2photos/index.html

Memorial Shrine, 1888
http://www.chssc.org/shrinededication.html

Timeline, Chinese Americans in California
http://www.chssc.org/timeline.html

H-California
http://h-net2.msu.edu/~cal/

Introduction
http://www2.h-net.msu.edu/~cal/about/about.html

Listserv Subscription Information
http://www2.h-net.msu.edu/~cal/about/about.html

OUTSTANDING SITE

Museum of the City of San Francisco
http://www.sfmuseum.org

2801 Leavenworth Street   *Phone   (415) 928-0289*
San Francisco, CA 94116   *Fax   (415) 731-4204*

Data and Links about San Francisco History
http://www.sfmuseum.org/hist1/subjects.html

San Francisco History by Subject
http://www.sfmuseum.org/hist1/index0.html

San Francisco History by Year
http://www.sfmuseum.org/hist1/index.html

San Francisco History Index
http://www.sfmuseum.org/hist1/subjects.html

San Diego Historical Society
http://edweb.sdsu.edu/SDHS/histsoc.html

Casa de Balboa, Lower Level   *Phone   (619) 232-6203*
1649 El Prado, Balboa Park
P.O. Box 81825
San Diego, CA 92138-1825

Collections
http://www.sandiegohistory.org/mainpages/locate6.htm

Photograph Collections
http://www.sandiegohistory.org/slideshow/mainphoto.htm

San Diego Biographies
http://www.sandiegohistory.org/bio/biographies.htm

San Diego History. (Serial). 3/year. No. 1 (January 1955)– .
http://www.sandiegohistory.org/journal/journal.htm

University of California, Berkeley
http://www.berkeley.edu/

The Bancroft Library   *Phone   (510) 642-6481*
Berkeley, CA 94720-6000

California Studies Association
http://geography.berkeley.edu/ProjectsResources/californiastudies.html

c/o Department of Geography   Phone   (510) 642-3903
Mailbox CSA, 507 McCone Hall   E-mail   walker@socrates.berkeley.edu
University of California,
Berkeley, CA 94720-4740

Bancroft Library
http://www.lib.berkeley.edu/BANC/

California Digital Library
http://www.cdlib.org/

California Heritage Collection Digital Image Access Project
http://sunsite.berkeley.edu/CalHeritage/

California Newspaper and Periodical Indexes
http://bancroft.berkeley.edu/reference/newsindexes.html#calnews

Collection Guides
http://www.lib.berkeley.edu/BANC/#collect

Finding Aids for Archival Collections
http://sunsite.berkeley.edu/FindingAids/

Friends of the Bancroft Library
http://bancroft.berkeley.edu/friends/

A Geographer Looks at the San Joaquin Valley
http://geography.berkeley.edu/ProjectsResources/Publications/Parsons_SauerLect.html

Manuscript Finding Aids
http://www.oac.cdlib.org/dynaweb/ead/ead/berkeley/bancroft/

Rare Book Collection
http://bancroft.berkeley.edu/collections/rarebooks.html

COLORADO

STATE HOME PAGE

Colorado State Home Page
http://www.state.co.us/

Vital Records

http://www.cdphe.state.co.us/hs/certs.asp

STATE ARCHIVES

Colorado State Archives

http://www.archives.state.co.us/index.html

1313 Sherman Street, Room 1B-20	*Phone*	*(303) 866-2358*
Denver, CO 80203		*(800) 305-3442*
	Fax	*(303) 866-2257*
	E-mail	*archives@state.co.us*

Arapahoe County Poor Hospital Records Index 1895–1899

http://www.archives.state.co.us/hospital/index.html

Bibliography

http://www.archives.state.co.us/bib/alpha.htm

Biography

http://www.archives.state.co.us/arcbiog.html

Children's Home Records

http://www.archives.state.co.us/cch/home.htm

City Directory. 1866 Denver Auraria City Directory

http://www.archives.state.co.us/dcd/dirhome.htm

Civilian Conservation Corps (CCC) Index

http://www.archives.state.co.us/ccc/index.html

Colorado State Penitentiary Inmate Index, 1871–1973

http://www.archives.state.co.us/pen/index.htm

Divorce Records, County Level

http://www.archives.state.co.us/divorce/

Divorce Records, State Supreme Court, and State Court of Appeals

http://www.archives.state.co.us/court.html

Genealogy and Family History

http://www.archives.state.co.us/geneal.html

History

http://www.archives.state.co.us/info.html

Kit Carson County Land Records Index, 1913–1919

http://www.archives.state.co.us/land/kit_carson_land_index.html

Maps, Historical

http://www.archives.state.co.us/histmaps.html

Marriage Records

http://www.archives.state.co.us/marr1.html

Marriage Records. Gilpin County Index, 1864–1944
   http://www.archives.state.co.us/marriage/gilpin_index.htm

Military Records
   http://www.archives.state.co.us/military.html

Military Records. Civil War, Casualties
   http://www.archives.state.co.us/ciwardea.html

Military Records. Civil War, Volunteers Index
   http://www.archives.state.co.us/trans/index.html

Military Records. Civil War, Volunteers, New Mexico Campaign
   http://www.archives.state.co.us/trans/civwar2.htm

Military Records. Spanish American War, Index
   http://www.archives.state.co.us/spamwar.html

Military Records. Veteran's Graves Index. 1862–1949
   http://www.archives.state.co.us/grave_dir/cograv.html

Military Records. World War I. Conejos County Enlistments Index
   http://www.archives.state.co.us/military/enlistments/conejos_county.html

Military Records. World War I. Denver, War Risk Insurance Index
   http://www.archives.state.co.us/military/war_risk_insurance/

Naturalization Records
   http://www.archives.state.co.us/natural.html

Old Age Pension Records Index
   http://www.archives.state.co.us/oap/index.html

Alfred Packer Collection
   http://www.archives.state.co.us/packer.html

Photograph Collections
   http://www.archives.state.co.us/photo/home.htm

Probate Records Index
   http://www.archives.state.co.us/wills/index.html

Probate Records, Inheritance Tax Records Index, by County
   http://www.archives.state.co.us/inh_tax/index.html

Rio Grande County Teacher Certificates, 1874–1893
   http://www.archives.state.co.us/rio.htm

School Records
   http://www.archives.state.co.us/school.html

Spanish, Mexican Land Grants
   http://www.archives.state.co.us/mlg/mlg.html

STATE LIBRARY

Colorado Virtual Library
http://www.aclin.org/

Colorado Department of Education   *Phone*   *(303) 866-6900*
201 East Colfax Avenue   *Fax*   *(303) 830-0793*
Denver, CO 80203

STATE GENEALOGICAL SOCIETY

Colorado Genealogical Society
http://www.rootsweb.com/~cocgs/

P.O. Box 9218   *Phone*   *(303) 571-1535*
Denver, CO 80209-0218

Colorado Genealogical Societies
http://www.rootsweb.com/~cocgs/genealogyorg.htm

OTHER STATE SITES

Colorado College
http://anakin-www-hp.cc.colorado.edu/Library/SpecialCollections/Special.html

Special Collections and Archives   *Phone*   *(719) 389-6668*
Tutt Library   *Fax*   *(719) 389-6859*
1021 North Cascade Avenue   *E-mail*   *jrandall@ColoradoCollege.edu*
Colorado Springs, CO 80903

Colorado Collection
http://www2.colorado.edu/Library/SpecialCollections/Colo.html

Colorado Prospector. (Serial). Index.
http://anakin-www-hp.cc.colorado.edu/Library/SpecialCollections/Colorado/Prospector.html

Diaries
http://anakin-www-hp.cc.colorado.edu/Library/SpecialCollections/Colorado/Diaries.html

History
http://www2.coloradocollege.edu/library/Reference/Resources/Colo.html

Manuscript Collection Index
http://anakin-www-hp.cc.colorado.edu/Library/SpecialCollections/Manuscripts.html

Photograph Collection Index
http://www2.coloradocollege.edu/library/SpecialCollections/Colorado/ColoradoPhotos.html

Denver Public Library
http://www.denver.lib.co.us/

10 West 14th Avenue Parkway   *Phone*   *(303) 640-6200*
Denver, CO 80204

Western History Photograph Collection
http://gowest.coalliance.org/

CONNECTICUT

STATE HOME PAGE

Connecticut State Home Page
http://www.state.ct.us

Vital Records Section
http://www.dph.state.ct.us/OPPE/hpvital.htm

STATE LIBRARY AND ARCHIVES

OUTSTANDING SITE

Connecticut State Library
http://www.cslib.org

231 Capitol Avenue
Hartford, CT 06106

Phone (860) 566-4301
Fax (860) 566-8940
E-mail rakeroyd@csunet.ctstateu.edu

History and Genealogy Section

Phone (860) 757-6580
Fax (860) 757-6521

African American Resources
http://www.cslib.org/blagen.htm

Bible Records Index
http://www.cslib.org/bible.htm

Canadian Genealogical Research
http://www.cslib.org/canada.htm

Church Records
http://www.cslib.org/church.htm

Civil War
http://www.cslib.org/civwar.htm

German Genealogical Research
http://www.cslib.org/germans.htm

History, Connecticut
http://www.cslib.org/history.htm

Irish Genealogy Resources
http://www.cslib.org/irish.htm

Italian Genealogy Resources
http://www.cslib.org/italians.htm

Land Records
http://www.cslib.org/landrec.htm

Military, Colonial Wars
http://www.cslib.org/colwars.htm

Military, Civil War
http://www.cslib.org/civwar.htm

Military, Mexican War
http://www.cslib.org/mexwar.htm

Military, Revolutionary War
http://www.cslib.org/revwar.htm

Military, War of 1812
http://www.cslib.org/war1812.htm

Military Records
http://www.cslib.org/miltrec.htm

Native American Resources
http://www.cslib.org/indians.htm

Naturalization Records
http://www.cslib.org/natural.htm

Newspapers, History of in Connecticut
http://www.cslib.org/cnp/biblio.htm

Passenger Lists
http://www.cslib.org/passlist.htm

Polish American Genealogical Resources
http://www.cslib.org/polish.htm

Probate Records
http://www.cslib.org/probintr.htm

Vital Records
http://www.cslib.org/vitals.htm

Vital Records, Divorce Records
http://www.cslib.org/divorce.htm

Women's History
http://www.cslib.org/women.htm

STATE HISTORICAL SOCIETY

Connecticut Historical Society

http://www.chs.org/

1 Elizabeth Street   *Phone   (860) 236-5621*
Hartford, CT 06105   *Fax   (860) 236-2664*

African American Resources

http://www.chs.org/afamcoll/default.htm

Civil War Manuscripts

http://www.chs.org/kcwmp/default.htm

Civil War Monuments of Connecticut

http://www.chs.org/ransom/default.htm

Library

http://www.chs.org/library/default.htm

Manuscripts

http://www.chs.org/library/msscoll.htm

Online Library Catalog

http://www.chs.org/library/request.htm

OTHER STATE SITES

Mystic Seaport

http://www.mystic.org/welcome.html

G. W. Blunt White Library   *Phone   (860) 572-5367*
P.O. Box 6000   *Fax   (860) 572-5394*
Mystic, CT 06355   *TDD   (860) 572-5319*

Collections

http://www.mystic.org/research/ru-libresearchresources.htm

Library

http://www.mysticseaport.org/research/ru-libspecial.htm

Manuscripts

http://www.mysticseaport.org/library/manuscripts/registers.html

OUTSTANDING SITE

Stamford Historical Society

http://www.stamfordhistory.org/

1508 High Ridge Road   *Phone   (203) 329-1183*
Stamford, CT 06903   *Fax   (203) 322-1607*

Bibliography by Ronald Marcus
http://www.cslib.org/stamford/biblio.htm

Collections
http://www.stamfordhistory.org/records.htm

Grand Lists, 1641–1821
http://www.cslib.org/stamford/Granlist.htm

Guide to Nature. (Serial). Index for Stamford Items. (1908–1919).
http://www.cslib.org/stamford/g2n.htm

History of Stamford
http://www.cslib.org/stamford/HISTORY.HTM

Marcus Research Library
http://www.stamfordhistory.org/libr_1.htm

Photograph Archives
http://www.stamfordhistory.org/photo_a.htm

Stamford, Scenes from Yesteryear
http://www.stamfordhistory.org/murals.htm

DELAWARE

STATE HOME PAGE

State of Delaware Home Page
http://www.state.de.us

Office of Vital Statistics
http://www.state.de.us/dhss/dph/vs.htm

STATE ARCHIVES

Delaware Public Archives
http://www.state.de.us/sos/dpa/

121 Duke of York Street   *Phone   (302) 744-5000*
Dover, DE 19901   *Fax   (302) 739-2578*
                              E-mail archives@state.de.us

Coroner's Inquests
http://www.state.de.us/sos/dpa/exhibits/Coroner/index.htm

Digital Map Collections
http://www.state.de.us/sos/dpa/exhibits/MapCollection/index.htm

Friends of the Archives
http://www.state.de.us/sos/dpa/admin/friends.htm

Guide to Holdings
http://www.state.de.us/sos/dpa/collections/index.htm

Historical Markers
    http://www.state.de.us/sos/dpa/markers-htm/index.htm

Jackson and Sharp Company Photograph Collection
    http://www.state.de.us/sos/dpa/exhibits/jsc/index.htm

Naturalization Records Database
    http://www.state.de.us/sos/dpa/collections/natrlzndb/index.htm

Photograph Collections
    http://www.state.de.us/sos/dpa/exhibits/hpe/index.htm

School Insurance Evaluation Reports
    http://www.state.de.us/sos/dpa/exhibits/SchoolVal/index.htm

17th-Century Records
    http://www.state.de.us/sos/dpa/exhibits/17thcentury/index.htm

State Highway Photograph Collection
    http://www.state.de.us/sos/dpa/exhibits/HighwayDept/index.htm

World War II Photograph Collection
    http://www.state.de.us/sos/dpa/exhibits/WWII/index.htm

STATE GENEALOGICAL SOCIETY

Delaware Genealogical Society
    http://delgensoc.org/
    505 Market Street Mall   *E-mail   tdoherty@magpage.com*
    Wilmington, DE 19801-3091

Delaware Genealogical Society Journal. (Serial). Quarterly. Table of Contents. Vol. 1, No. 1 (October 1980)– .
    http://delgensoc.org/dgsj.html

Delaware Genealogical Society Journal. (Serial). Quarterly. Index. Vol. 1, No. 1 (October 1980)– .
    http://delgensoc.org/dgsjindx.htm

Delaware Jurisdictions: Counties, Hundreds
    http://delgensoc.org/delhund.html

Delaware Jurisdictions: Towns and Places
    http://delgensoc.org/deltowns.html

STATE HISTORICAL SOCIETY

Historical Society of Delaware
    http://www.hsd.org/
    505 North Market Street   *Phone   (302) 655-7161*
    Wilmington, DE 19801   *Fax   (302) 655-7844*
                                     E-mail hsd@dca.net

Genealogy
http://www.hsd.org/gengd.htm

Published Genealogies
http://www.hsd.org/gengd.htm

Women's History, Bibliography
http://www.hsd.org/Womens_Bibliography.htm

OTHER STATE SITES

University of Delaware
http://www.udel.edu/

Special Collections Department
http://www.lib.udel.edu/ud/spec/

181 South College Avenue   *Phone   (302) 831-6952*
Newark, DE 19717-5267   *Fax   (302) 831-1046*
                                    E-mail   tdm@udel.edu

Delaware in Wartime
http://www.lib.udel.edu/ud/spec/exhibits/wartime.html

History (Post-1880) Resources
http://www.lib.udel.edu/ud/spec/guides/post1880.htm

Manuscript and Archives Collections
http://www.lib.udel.edu/ud/spec/findaids/index.htm

Maps
http://www.lib.udel.edu/ud/spec/mapsnote.htm

New Castle County, Delaware Resources
http://www.lib.udel.edu/ud/spec/guides/newcastl.htm

Newark, Delaware, Resources
http://www.lib.udel.edu/ud/spec/guides/newark.htm

DISTRICT OF COLUMBIA

DISTRICT HOME PAGE

District Home Page
http://dc.gov/

Vital Records Division
http://dchealth.dc.gov/services/vital_records/index.shtm

EXTRAORDINARY SITE
One of the Most Extraordinary Web Sites Online

Library of Congress
http://www.loc.gov/

Local History and Genealogy
Reading Room
Jefferson Building, Room LJ G20
Washington, DC 20540-4720

NUCMC Team
101 Independence Ave., SE
Washington, DC 20540-4375

Phone   (202) 707-5537
Fax   (202) 707-1957
E-mail   nucmc@mail.loc.gov

African American Family Histories
http://www.loc.gov/rr/genealogy/bib_guid/aframer/

African American Genealogical Research
http://www.loc.gov/rr/genealogy/bib_guid/afro.html

African American Ohio Experience
http://memory.loc.gov/ammem/award97/ohshtml/aaeohome.html

American Folklife Center
http://lcweb.loc.gov/folklife/afc.html

American Memory Project
http://lcweb2.loc.gov/ammem/ammemhome.html

California, As I Saw It: First Person Narratives
http://memory.loc.gov/ammem/cbhtml/cbhome.html

Center for the Book
http://lcweb.loc.gov/loc/cfbook/

City Directories
http://www.loc.gov/rr/microform/uscity/

Civil War Maps
http://memory.loc.gov/ammem/gmdhtml/cwmhtml/cwmhome.html

Civil War Photographs
http://memory.loc.gov/ammem/cwphtml/cwphome.html

Civil War Regimental Histories
http://www.loc.gov/rr/genealogy/uscivilwar/

County Studies, Area Handbooks
http://lcweb2.loc.gov/frd/cs/cshome.html

Daguerreotype Collection
http://memory.loc.gov/ammem/daghtml/daghome.html

Danish Immigration to America
http://www.loc.gov/rr/genealogy/bib_guid/danish.html

English Genealogy
http://www.loc.gov/rr/genealogy/bib_guid/england.html

Genealogical Periodical in the Local History and Genealogy Reading Room
http://www.loc.gov/rr/genealogy/bib_guid/genperio.html

Genealogical Research
http://www.loc.gov/rr/genealogy/bib_guid/guide0.html

Grand Army of the Republic and Kindred Societies
http://www.loc.gov/rr/main/gar/

Great Plains Photograph Collection
http://memory.loc.gov/ammem/award97/ndfahtml/ngphome.html

Guides to Genealogical Research
http://www.loc.gov/rr/genealogy/bib_guid/guideres/

HALS, Handbook on Latin American Studies
http://lcweb2.loc.gov/hlas/

Heraldry
http://www.loc.gov/rr/genealogy/bib_guid/herald.html

Hispanic Reading Room
http://lcweb.loc.gov/rr/hispanic/

Immigrant Arrivals
http://www.loc.gov/rr/genealogy/bib_guid/immigrant/

International Genealogical Research
http://www.loc.gov/rr/genealogy/bib_guid/foreign.html

Irish Genealogy
http://www.loc.gov/rr/genealogy/bib_guid/england.html

Liberia Maps, 1830–1870
http://memory.loc.gov/ammem/gmdhtml/libhtml/libhome.html

Life Histories
http://memory.loc.gov/ammem/wpaintro/wpahome.html

Local History and Genealogy Room
http://lcweb.loc.gov/rr/genealogy/

National Union Catalog of Manuscript Collections (NUCMC)
http://lcweb.loc.gov/coll/nucmc/nucmc.html

Native Americans, Pacific Northwest
http://memory.loc.gov/ammem/award98/wauhtml/aipnhome.html

Nebraska Photographs and Letters
http://memory.loc.gov/ammem/award98/nbhihtml/pshome.html

Nevada, Ranching Culture
http://memory.loc.gov/ammem/ncrhtml/crhome.html

Newspaper and Periodical Reading Room
http://lcweb.loc.gov/global/ncp/ncp.html

Newspapers, Links, U.S. and Worldwide
http://lcweb.loc.gov/rr/news/extnewsp.html

New York City, Films, 1898–1906
http://memory.loc.gov/ammem/papr/nychome.html

Norwegian American Genealogical Research
http://www.loc.gov/rr/genealogy/bib_guid/norway.html

Preservation
http://lcweb.loc.gov/preserv/preserve.html

Prints and Photographs Reading Room
http://lcweb.loc.gov/rr/print/

Puerto Rico Resources
http://memory.loc.gov/ammem/prhtml/prhome.html

Russian Task Force
http://lcweb2.loc.gov/frd/tfrquery.html

San Francisco Earthquake, Films
http://memory.loc.gov/ammem/papr/sfhome.html

Scottish Genealogy
http://www.loc.gov/rr/genealogy/bib_guid/scotland.html

Spanish-American War Films
http://memory.loc.gov/ammem/sawhtml/sawhome.html

Special Collections Department, Index
http://lcweb.loc.gov/spcoll/spclhome.html

Surnames
http://www.loc.gov/rr/genealogy/bib_guid/surnames.html

Telephone and City Directories
http://www.loc.gov/rr/genealogy/bib_guid/telephon.html

Texas Border Photographs
http://memory.loc.gov/ammem/award97/txuhtml/runyhome.html

Today in History
http://lcweb2.loc.gov/ammem/today/today.html

Vietnam POW/MIA Index
http://lcweb2.loc.gov/pow/powhome.html

Welsh Genealogy
http://www.loc.gov/rr/genealogy/bib_guid/wales.html

WPA, Life History Manuscripts
http://lcweb2.loc.gov/ammem/wpaintro/wpahome.html

E X T R A O R D I N A R Y   S I T E
One of the Most Extraordinary Web Sites Online

National Archives and Records Administration
http://www.archives.gov

African American Resources
http://www.archives.gov/research_room/genealogy/research_topics/african_american_research.html

Genealogy Research
http://www.archives.gov/research_room/genealogy/

Immigration Records
http://www.archives.gov/research_room/genealogy/research_topics/immigration.html

Military Records
http://www.archives.gov/research_room/genealogy/research_topics/military.html

National Personnel Records Center, Civilian Records Facility
http://www.archives.gov/facilities/mo/st_louis/civilian_personnel_records.html

National Personnel Records Center, Military Records Facility
http://www.archives.gov/facilities/mo/st_louis/military_personnel_records.html

Native American Records
http://www.archives.gov/research_room/genealogy/research_topics/native_american_records.html

Regional Facilities Directory
http://www.archives.gov/facilities/index.html

U.S. Census Bureau
http://www.census.gov

Washington, DC 20233   *E-mail   Genealogy@Census.GOV*

Age Search Service
http://www.census.gov/genealogy/www/agesearch.html

Availability of Census Records for Individuals
http://www.census.gov/prod/2000pubs/cff-2.pdf

Frequently Occurring Names
http://www.census.gov/genealogy/www/freqnames.html

Genealogy Guide
http://www.census.gov/genealogy/www/

Spanish Surname List from the 1990 Census
http://www.census.gov/genealogy/www/spanname.html

FLORIDA

STATE HOME PAGE

Florida Home Page
http://www.myflorida.com/myflorida/index.html

Office of Vital Statistics
http://www9.myflorida.com/Planning_eval/Vital_Statistics/

STATE ARCHIVES

Bureau of Archives and Records Management
http://www.dos.state.fl.us/dlis/barm/fsa.html

R.A. Gray Building   *Phone   (850) 245-6700*
500 South Bronough Street   *E-mail   barm@mail.dos.state.fl.us*
Tallahassee, FL 32399-0250

Afro-American Resources
http://www.dos.state.fl.us/dlis/barm/BlackExperience/blackexperience.html

Call and Brevard Family Papers
http://dlis.dos.state.fl.us/barm/CallBrevardPapers/Default.htm

Confederate Pension Application Records
http://dlis.dos.state.fl.us/barm/PensionFiles.html

Online Library Catalog
http://dlis.dos.state.fl.us/barm/rediscovery/default.asp

Spanish Land Grants
http://dlis.dos.state.fl.us/barm/SpanishLandGrants/Default.htm

Women's Historical Resources
http://dlis.dos.state.fl.us/barm/fsa/women%27sguide.htm

STATE LIBRARY

State Library of Florida
http://dlis.dos.state.fl.us/stlib/

R.A. Gray Building, Second Floor   *Phone   (904) 487-2651*
500 South Bronough   *Fax   (904) 488-2746*
Tallahassee, FL 32399-0250

Florida Vital Records
http://www.doh.state.fl.us/planning_eval/vital_statistics/index.html

Rosewood Bibliography
http://dlis.dos.state.fl.us/stlib/rosewood_bib.html

OTHER STATE SITES

University of Florida
http://www.ufl.edu/

P. K. Yonge Library of Florida History
http://web.uflib.ufl.edu/spec/pkyonge/

P.O. Box 117007   *Phone   (352) 392-0319*
208 Smathers Library
Gainesville, FL 32611-7001

East Florida Papers
http://web.uflib.ufl.edu/spec/pkyonge/eflapap.html

Manuscripts
http://web.uflib.ufl.edu/spec/manuscript/mnscrpt.html#General

Maps
http://web.uflib.ufl.edu/spec/pkyonge/fhmaps.html

Newspapers
http://web.uflib.ufl.edu/spec/pkyonge/newspap.html

Photograph Collection
http://web.uflib.ufl.edu/spec/pkyonge/picture.html

University of Miami
http://www.miami.edu/

Archives and Special Collections Department
http://www.library.miami.edu/archives/intro.html

Richter Library
Coral Gables, FL 33124

Aaron Thomas: The Caribbean Journal of a Royal Navy Seaman, 1798–1799
http://www.library.miami.edu/archives/thomas/index.html

Amos Beebe Eaton: A Soldier's Journal of the Second Seminole Indian War
http://www.library.miami.edu/archives/eaton/index.html

Calvin Shedd Papers: The Civil War in Florida: Letters of a New Hampshire Soldier
http://www.library.miami.edu/archives/shedd/index.htm

Caribbean Collection
http://www.library.miami.edu/archives/collections/carrib.html

Manuscript Collections
http://www.library.miami.edu/archives/papers/reposit.html

Photographs, Lanatern Slides
http://www.library.miami.edu/archives/Wooley/Local_Publish/index.html

GEORGIA

STATE HOME PAGE

Georgia Online Network
http://www.state.ga.us/

Vital Records Office
http://www.ph.dhr.state.ga.us/programs/vitalrecords/

STATE ARCHIVES

Georgia Department of Archives and History
http://www.sos.state.ga.us/archives/

330 Capitol Avenue, SE   *Phone*   *(404) 656-2397*
Atlanta, GA 30334   *E-mail* *reference@sos.state.ga.us*

African American Records
http://www.sos.state.ga.us/archives/rs/ethnic.htm#aa

Census Records
http://www.sos.state.ga.us/archives/rs/fcg.htm

Genealogical Resources
http://www.sos.state.ga.us/archives/ci/geneal.htm

Georgia Historical Records Advisory Board Newsletter. (Serial). Irregular.
(September 1995)– .
http://www.sos.state.ga.us/archives/ghrab/news/news.html

Georgia History
http://www.sos.state.ga.us/archives/index/qg.htm

Historical Resources, Organizations Directory
http://www.sos.state.ga.us/archives/ghrab/dir/dir.htm

Land Records
http://www.sos.state.ga.us/archives/rs/land.htm

Military Records
http://www.sos.state.ga.us/archives/rs/military.htm

Military Records, Civil War
http://www.sos.state.ga.us/archives/rs/cws.htm

Military Records, Georgia Land Lottery Grants to Revolutionary Veterans Index
http://www.sos.state.ga.us/archives/oe/rv_summary.htm

Passports to the Cherokee and Creek Nations
http://www.sos.state.ga.us/archives/rs/passports.htm

Vital Records, Births and Deaths
http://www.sos.state.ga.us/archives/rs/gbdr.htm

Vital Records, Pre-1900 Marriage Records
http://www.sos.state.ga.us/archives/rs/dmg.htm

STATE HISTORICAL SOCIETY

Georgia Historical Society
http://www.georgiahistory.com/

501 Whitaker Street
Savannah, GA 31401

Georgia Historical Markers
http://www.georgiahistory.com/Markers.htm

OTHER STATE SITES

Archdiocese of Atlanta
http://www.archatl.com

Archives of the Archdiocese of Atlanta
http://www.archatl.com/offices/archives/

The Catholic Center	*Phone*	*(404) 885-7203*
680 West Peachtree Street, NW	*Fax*	*(404) 885-7230*
Atlanta, GA 30308-1984	*E-mail*	*abritton@archatl.com*

Georgia Bulletin: Official Newspaper of the Archdiocese of Atlanta. (Serial). Weekly. (January 4, 1963)– .
http://www.archatl.com/gabulletin/gb-year.html

Parish Profiles
http://www.archatl.com/parishes/index_bydate.html

Atlanta History Center
http://www.atlhist.org/

130 West Paces Ferry Road, NW	*Phone*	*(404) 814-4040*
Atlanta, GA 30305-1366	*Fax*	*(404) 814-4175*

Atlanta History Timeline
http://www.atlhist.org/archives/html/timeline.htm

HAWAII

STATE HOME PAGE

Hawaii State Government Home Page
http://www.hawaii.gov/

Vital Records
http://www.state.hi.us/doh/records/

STATE ARCHIVES

Hawaii State Archives
http://www.state.hi.us/dags/archives/welcome.html

Department of Accounting	*Phone*	*(808) 586-0329*
and General Services	*Fax*	*(808) 586-0330*
Kekauluohi Building		
Iolani Palace Grounds		
Honolulu, HI 96813		

Online Catalog
http://statearchives.lib.hawaii.edu/

STATE LIBRARY

Hawaii State Public Library System (HSPLS)
http://www.hcc.hawaii.edu/hspls/

Hawaii State Library	*Phone*	*(808) 586-3535*
478 South King Street		
Honolulu, HI 96813-2901		

Directory of HSPLS Libraries
http://www.hcc.hawaii.edu/hspls/dirlibs.html

STATE HISTORICAL SOCIETY

Hawaiian Historical Society
http://www.hawaiianhistory.org/

560 Kawaiahao Street	*Phone*	*(808) 537-6271*
Honolulu, HI 96813	*Fax*	*(808) 537-6271*
	E-mail	*bedunn@lava.net*

Chronology of Hawaii
http://www.hawaiianhistory.org/ref/chron.html

Hawaiiana: Historical Bibliography. (Serial). Annual. (1995–1998).
http://www.hawaiianhistory.org/biblio/bibmain.html

Hawaiian Journal of History. (Serial). Annual. Table of Contents. Vol. 1 (1967)– .
http://www.hawaiianhistory.org/pubs/hjhlist.html

Hawaiian Journal of History. (Serial). Annual. Index. Vols. 26–30 (1992–1996).
http://www.hawaiianhistory.org/pubs/hjh26_30.pdf

Hawaiian Journal of History. (Serial). Annual. Index. Vols. 31–35 (1997–2001).
http://www.hawaiianhistory.org/pubs/hjh31_35.pdf

Historical Records Repositories in Hawaii
http://www.hawaiianhistory.org/recrep.html

Library Services
http://www.hawaiianhistory.org/libmain.html

OTHER STATE SITES

University of Hawaii at Manoa
http://www.hawaii.edu/

Special Collections Department
http://www2.hawaii.edu/~speccoll/

Hamilton Library, 5th Floor	*Phone* (808) 956-8264
2550 The Mall	*Fax* (808) 956-5968
Honolulu, HI 96822	*E-mail* *speccoll@hawaii.edu*
	jimc@hawaii.edu

'Aina in History Bibliography
http://www2.hawaii.edu/~speccoll/hawaiiaina.html

Genealogy Resources
http://www2.hawaii.edu/~speccoll/hawaiigenealogy.html

Hawaiian Collection
http://www2.hawaii.edu/~speccoll/hawaii.html

Hawaii War Records Depository
http://libweb.hawaii.edu/hwrd/HWRD_html/HWRD_welcome.htm

Local Identity in Hawaii
http://www2.hawaii.edu/~speccoll/hawaiilocal.html

Newspaper Collection, Hawaiian Language Newspapers
http://www2.hawaii.edu/~ruthh/newsbib.html

Newspaper Collection, Online Newspapers
http://libweb.hawaii.edu/uhmlib/databases/electronic_resources.html

Pacific Collection
http://www2.hawaii.edu/~speccoll/pacific.html

Trust Territory, Pacific Archives
http://128.171.57.100/ttp/ttpi.html

Written Record of Hawaii's Women
http://libweb.hawaii.edu/libdept/womenbib/index.html

IDAHO

STATE HOME PAGE

Idaho Home Page
http://www.state.id.us/

Bureau of Vital Records and Health Statistics
http://www2.state.id.us/dhw/health/des_programs_health.htm#vital%20stats

STATE LIBRARY

Idaho State Library
http://www.lili.org/isl/

325 West State Street   *Phone   (208) 334-2150*
Boise, ID 83702   *Fax   (208) 334-4016*
                                E-mail   Webteam@isl.state.id.us

Directory of Idaho Libraries
http://www.lili.org/isl/il1a.htm

STATE GENEALOGICAL SOCIETY

Idaho Genealogical Society
http://www.lili.org/idahogenealogy/

P.O. Box 1854   *Phone   (208) 384-0542*
Boise, ID 83701-1854

Elmore County, Genealogical Toolkit
http://www.lili.org/idahogenealogy/ElmoreCoToolkit.htm

Idaho Genealogical Society Quarterly. (Serial). Quarterly. Table of Contents.
Current Issue.
http://www.lili.org/idahogenealogy/Win2001TC.htm

OTHER STATE SITES

University of Idaho
http://www.uidaho.edu/

Special Collections and Archives Department
http://www.lib.uidaho.edu/special-collections/

P.O. Box 442351   *Phone   (208) 885-7951*
Moscow, ID 83844-2351   *Fax   (208) 885-6817*
                               E-mail   tabraham@uidaho.edu

Archives
http://www.lib.uidaho.edu/special-collections/Archives/

Digital Memories (Online Collections)
http://www.lib.uidaho.edu/special-collections/dm/dgtlcurr.htm

Ethnic Collections
http://www.lib.uidaho.edu/special-collections/ethnicity.htm

Genealogy, Idaho
http://www.lib.uidaho.edu/special-collections/genealgl.htm

Manuscripts
http://www.lib.uidaho.edu/special-collections/Manuscripts/

Photograph Collection
http://www.lib.uidaho.edu/special-collections/Historical.Photographs.html

Repositories of Primary Sources
http://www.uidaho.edu/special-collections/Other.Repositories.html

University of Idaho, Bibliography
http://www.lib.uidaho.edu/special-collections/History.Bibliography.html

Women, a Guide to Resources
http://www.lib.uidaho.edu/special-collections/women.htm

ILLINOIS

STATE HOME PAGE

State of Illinois Home Page
http://www.state.il.us/

Division of Vital Records
http://www.idph.state.il.us/vital/vitalrec.htm

Illinois Adoption Registry
http://www.idph.state.il.us/vital/iladoptreg.htm

STATE ARCHIVES

Illinois State Archives
http://www.sos.state.il.us/departments/archives/archives.html

Margaret Cross Norton Building	*Phone*	*(217) 782-3492*
Capitol Complex	*Fax*	*(217) 524-3930*
Springfield, IL 62756		

Abraham Lincoln Documents
http://www.sos.state.il.us/departments/archives/lincoln.html

African American Online Database, Servitude and Emancipation Records Database, 1722–1863

    http://www.sos.state.il.us/cgi-bin/archives/servitude.s

African American Resources

    http://www.sos.state.il.us/departments/archives/research_series/rseries5.html

Census Records, Federal

    http://www.sos.state.il.us/departments/archives/research_series/rseries4.html

Census Records, State

    http://www.sos.state.il.us/departments/archives/research_series/rseries5.html

Chicago Police Department Homicide Index, 1870–1930

    http://www.cyberdriveillinois.com/departments/archives/homicide.html

Cook County Coroner's Inquest Records Index, 1872–1911

    http://www.cyberdriveillinois.com/departments/archives/cookinqt.html

Descriptive Inventory of the Archives, 2nd edition

    http://www.sos.state.il.us/departments/archives/isaholdings.html

Genealogical Resources

    http://www.sos.state.il.us/departments/archives/services.html

Land Records

    http://www.sos.state.il.us/departments/archives/research_series/rseries1.html

Land Records, Online Database, Public Domain Land Sales

    http://www.sos.state.il.us/departments/archives/data_lan.html

Local Governmental Records

    http://www.sos.state.il.us/departments/archives/irad/iradholdings.html

Marriage Records Online Index, 1763–1900

    http://www.sos.state.il.us/departments/archives/marriage.html

Military Records

    http://www.sos.state.il.us/departments/archives/research_series/rseries3.html

Military Records, Online Databases

    http://www.sos.state.il.us/departments/archives/databases.html

Military Records, Online Databases, Blackhawk War

    http://www.sos.state.il.us/departments/archives/blkhawk.html

Military Records, Online Databases, Burial Sites, as of 1929

    http://www.sos.state.il.us/departments/archives/honorroll.html

Military Records, Online Databases, Civil War

    http://www.sos.state.il.us/departments/archives/datcivil.html

Military Records, Online Databases, Civil War, Missouri Units

    http://www.sos.state.il.us/departments/archives/missouri.html

Military Records, Online Databases, Civil War, U.S. Navy
http://www.sos.state.il.us/departments/archives/ilnavy.html

Military Records, Online Databases, Mexican War
http://www.sos.state.il.us/departments/archives/mexwar.html

Military Records, Online Databases, Soldiers and Sailors Home Residents, 1887–1916
http://www.sos.state.il.us/departments/archives/quincyhome.html

Military Records, Online Databases, Spanish-American War
http://www.sos.state.il.us/departments/archives/spanam.html

Military Records, Online Databases, War of 1812
http://www.sos.state.il.us/departments/archives/war1812.html

Military Records, Online Databases, Winnebago War
http://www.sos.state.il.us/departments/archives/winebago.html

Probate Records
http://www.sos.state.il.us/departments/archives/research_series/rseries2.html

Teacher Document Packets
http://www.sos.state.il.us/departments/archives/docpacks.html

STATE LIBRARY

Illinois State Library
http://www.sos.state.il.us/library/isl/isl.html

300 South Second Street   *Phone*   *(217) 785-5600*
Springfield, IL 62701-1796   *(800) 665-5576 in Illinois*
                                   TDD   *(217) 524-1137*

Digital Imaging in Illinois
http://www.sos.state.il.us/library/digital/digital.html

Illinois Authors
http://www.sos.state.il.us/library/isl/reading/il_auth.html

Illinois Digital Archives
http://eli.sls.lib.il.us/ida/

Illinois Library Directory
http://www.sos.state.il.us/library/lib_dir/lib_dir.html

Map Collection
http://www.sos.state.il.us/library/isl/ref/islmaps.html

Map Collection: A Checklist of the Illinois State Library's Complete Holdings of Illinois County Land Ownership Maps and Atlases
http://www.sos.state.il.us/library/isl/ref/plats/index.html

Map Collection: Checklist of County Traffic and Highway Maps
http://www.sos.state.il.us/library/isl/ref/county_hwy.html

Map Collection: Large-Scale Topographic Quadrangles of Illinois
http://www.sos.state.il.us/library/isl/ref/lstopo_quads.html

Map Collection: Location Guide to the General Land Office (GLO) Survey Plats
http://www.sos.state.il.us/library/isl/ref/glo/glolocguide.html

Virtual Illinois Online Library Catalog (Holdings of over 600 Illinois Libraries)
http://www.vic.lib.il.us/

STATE GENEALOGICAL SOCIETY

Illinois State Genealogical Society
http://www.rootsweb.com/~ilsgs/

P.O. Box 10195   Phone   (217) 789-1968
Springfield, IL 62791-0195

Cemetery Location Project
http://www.rootsweb.com/~ilsgs/ilcemeteries/ilcemetery.html

Illinois Genealogical Society Quarterly. (Serial). Quarterly. Index. (1968–1999).
http://www.rootsweb.com/~ilsgs/quarterly-index.html

STATE HISTORICAL SOCIETY

Illinois State Historical Society
http://www.historyillinois.org/

210 1/2 S. Sixth   Phone   (217) 525-2781
Springfield, IL 62701-1503   Fax   (217) 525-2783
                                        E-mail   ishs@eosinc.com

Historical Markers Program
http://www.historyillinois.org/

OTHER STATE SITES

Chicago Historical Society
http://www.chicagohistory.org/

Library   Phone   (312) 642-6400
Clark Street at North Avenue   Fax   (312) 266-2077
Chicago, IL 60614-6099

Archives and Manuscripts
http://www.chicagohistory.org/collections/archives.html

Illinois Newspaper Project
http://www.chicagohistory.org/collections/newspaper.html

Library
http://www.chicagohistory.org/collections/collections.html

Online Projects
http://www.chicagohistory.org/projects.html

Prints and Photographs
http://www.chicagohistory.org/collections/prints.html

OUTSTANDING SITE

Newberry Library
http://www.newberry.org/

60 West Walton Street   *Phone   (312) 255-3512*
Chicago, IL 60610-3305   *Fax   (312) 255-3658*
                                 E-mail   genealogy@newberry.org

---

African American Resources
http://www.newberry.org/nl/genealogy/L3gabout.html

Alabama Genealogy
http://www.newberry.org/nl/genealogy/L3gabout.html

Arkansas Genealogy
http://www.newberry.org/nl/genealogy/L3gabout.html

Biographical Resources
http://www.newberry.org/nl/genealogy/L3gabout.html

Bohemian Genealogy
http://www.newberry.org/nl/genealogy/L3gabout.html

British Genealogy
http://www.newberry.org/nl/genealogy/L3gabout.html

Canadian Genealogy
http://www.newberry.org/nl/genealogy/L3gabout.html

Cherokee Genealogy
http://www.newberry.org/nl/genealogy/L3gabout.html

Chicago Genealogy Sources
http://www.newberry.org/nl/genealogy/L3gabout.html

City Directories
http://www.newberry.org/nl/genealogy/L3gabout.html

Connecticut Genealogy
http://www.newberry.org/nl/genealogy/L3gabout.html

Delaware Genealogy
http://www.newberry.org/nl/genealogy/L3gabout.html

Family Research Collections
http://www.newberry.org/nl/genealogy/L3gabout.html

Friends of Genealogy (FOG)
http://www.newberry.org/nl/genealogy/L3gfriends.html

Germanic Genealogy
http://www.newberry.org/nl/genealogy/L3gabout.html

Hispanic Genealogy
http://www.newberry.org/nl/genealogy/L3gabout.html

Illinois Genealogy
http://www.newberry.org/nl/genealogy/L3gabout.html

Illinois Newspapers
http://www.newberry.org/nl/genealogy/L3gabout.html

Indiana Genealogy
http://www.newberry.org/nl/genealogy/L3gabout.html

Iowa Genealogy
http://www.newberry.org/nl/genealogy/L3gabout.html

Irish Genealogy
http://www.newberry.org/nl/genealogy/L3gabout.html

Italian Genealogy
http://www.newberry.org/nl/genealogy/L3gabout.html

Jewish Genealogy
http://www.newberry.org/nl/genealogy/L3gabout.html

Kentucky Genealogy
http://www.newberry.org/nl/genealogy/L3gabout.html

Library Online Catalog
http://www.newberry.org/nl/collections/virtua.html

Louisiana Genealogy
http://www.newberry.org/nl/genealogy/L3gabout.html

Maine Genealogy
http://www.newberry.org/nl/genealogy/L3gabout.html

Maps
http://www.newberry.org/nl/collections/mapoverview.html

Massachusetts Genealogy
http://www.newberry.org/nl/genealogy/L3gabout.html

Michigan Genealogy
http://www.newberry.org/nl/genealogy/L3gabout.html

Military Resources
    http://www.newberry.org/nl/genealogy/L3gabout.html

Missouri Genealogy
    http://www.newberry.org/nl/genealogy/L3gabout.html

New Hampshire Genealogy
    http://www.newberry.org/nl/genealogy/L3gabout.html

New Jersey Genealogy
    http://www.newberry.org/nl/genealogy/L3gabout.html

New York Genealogy
    http://www.newberry.org/nl/genealogy/L3gabout.html

North Carolina Genealogy
    http://www.newberry.org/nl/genealogy/L3gabout.html

Ohio Genealogy
    http://www.newberry.org/nl/genealogy/L3gabout.html

Pennsylvania Genealogy
    http://www.newberry.org/nl/genealogy/L3gabout.html

Polish Genealogy
    http://www.newberry.org/nl/genealogy/L3gabout.html

Rhode Island Genealogy
    http://www.newberry.org/nl/genealogy/L3gabout.html

Royal Lineages
    http://www.newberry.org/nl/genealogy/L3gabout.html

Teaching Genealogy
    http://www.newberry.org/nl/genealogy/L3gservices.html

Vermont Genealogy
    http://www.newberry.org/nl/genealogy/L3gabout.html

Virginia Genealogy
    http://www.newberry.org/nl/genealogy/L3gabout.html

Wisconsin Genealogy
    http://www.newberry.org/nl/genealogy/L3gabout.html

North Park College
    http://www.northpark.edu/

Archives and Special Collections
    http://campus.northpark.edu/library/archives/index.htm
    3225 W. Foster Avenue   *Phone*   *(773) 244-6224*
    Chicago, IL 60625-4895   *Fax*   *(773) 244-4891*
    Archives and Special Collections
    http://campus.northpark.edu/library/archives/default.htm

Covenant Archives
http://campus.northpark.edu/library/archives/cahl.htm

St. Ansgarius Church Records, 1849–1971
http://campus.northpark.edu/library/archives/saagc_mss/saagc_mss45.htm

Swedish American Archives, of Greater Chicago
http://campus.northpark.edu/library/archives/saagc.htm

Southern Illinois University
http://www.lib.siu.edu/

Special Collections Department
http://www.lib.siu.edu/spcol/

Morris Library   *Phone   (618) 453-2516*
Carbondale, IL 62901-6632   *Fax   (618) 453-3451*

American Conference for Irish Studies, Newsletter. (Serial). (Winter 1995–Spring 1996).
http://www.lib.siu.edu/projects/irish/resource.htm

First Presbyterian Church Records, Carbondale, Illinois, 1850–1970
http://www.lib.siu.edu/spcol/manus_guide.htm#F

Manuscript Collections
http://www.lib.siu.edu/spcol/manuscripts.htm

Swenson Swedish Immigration Center
http://www2.augustana.edu/administration/swenson/index.htm

Augustana College   *Phone   (309) 794-7204*
639 38th Street   *Fax   (309) 794-7443*
Rock Island, IL 61201-2296 *E-mail sag@augustana.edu*

Archives, Organizational and Lodge Records
http://www2.augustana.edu/administration/swenson/Archives/LR.html

Archives, Personal Papers
http://www2.augustana.edu/administration/swenson/Archives/PP.html

Fellowship, Dagmar and Nils William Olsson Fellowship
http://www2.augustana.edu/administration/swenson/research.html

Library
http://www2.augustana.edu/administration/swenson/library.html

Microfiche Collection
http://www2.augustana.edu/administration/swenson/svar.html

Parish Records
http://www.augustana.edu/administration/swenson/svarcats.html

Swedish American Genealogical Research
http://www2.augustana.edu/administration/swenson/genealogy.html

INDIANA

STATE HOME PAGE

Indiana State Home Page
http://www.state.in.us/

Vital Records
http://www.state.in.us/isdh/bdcertifs/birth_and_death_certificates.htm

STATE ARCHIVES

Indiana State Archives
http://www.in.gov/icpr/archives/

State Library Building   *Phone*   *(317) 232-3660*
140 North Senate Avenue   *Fax*   *(317) 233-1085 or 232-0002*
Indianapolis, IN 46204

African American Resources
http://www.in.gov/icpr/archives/family/afam.html

African Americans, Vigo County Registry 1853–1854
http://www.in.gov/icpr/archives/databases/vigo_reg.html

Civil War
http://www.in.gov/icpr/archives/databases/civilwar/resource.html

Civil War, Telegraph Communications of Governor Oliver P. Morton
http://www.in.gov/icpr/archives/databases/civilwar/morton.html

Collections Guide
http://www.in.gov/icpr/archives/subject/

Fort Wayne Online Database
http://www.in.gov/icpr/archives/databases/land/fwnames.html

Genealogy Resources
http://www.in.gov/icpr/archives/family/index.html

Historical Societies Directory
http://www.in.gov/icpr/archives/featured/loclsocs.html

Hoosier Homestead Award Online Database
http://www.in.gov/serv/icpr_homestead

Indiana Soldiers and Sailors Children's Home Records Online Index
http://www.in.gov/icpr/archives/databases/issch/index.html

Land Records, Online Index
http://www.in.gov/icpr/archives/databases/land/land_off.html

Naturalization Records
http://www.in.gov/icpr/archives/family/nat.html

Naturalization Records Online Index
http://www.in.gov/serv/icpr_naturalization

Photographs, Aerial
http://www.in.gov/icpr/archives/featured/photogra/aerial.html

Posey County Circuit Court Records Online Index
http://www.in.gov/icpr/archives/databases/posey/index.html

Prison Records, Index to Statements of Life Prisoners
http://www.in.gov/icpr/archives/databases/crime_pr.html

STATE LIBRARY

Indiana State Library
http://www.statelib.lib.in.us/

140 North Senate Avenue
Indianapolis, IN 46204

Phone	*(317) 232-3670*	*Reference*
	(317) 232-3689	*Genealogy*
	(317) 232-3668	*IN Division*
	(317) 232-3671	*Manuscripts*
	(317) 232-3664	*Newspapers*
Fax	*(317) 232-3728*	
TDD	*(317) 232-7763*	
E-mail	*cfaunce@statelib.lib.in.us*	*Manuscripts*

Cemetery Directory
http://199.8.200.90:591/cemetery.html

Centennial Indiana, 1816–1916
http://www.statelib.lib.in.us/WWW/INDIANA/centennial/centennial.html

Genealogy
http://www.statelib.lib.in.us/WWW/INDIANA/GENEALOGY/genmenu.HTML

Indiana Library Directory
http://199.8.200.90:591/indlibdata.html

Indiana Section
http://www.statelib.lib.in.us/WWW/INDIANA/INMENU.HTML

Marriage Records Online Index, Pre-1850
http://www.statelib.lib.in.us/www/indiana/genealogy/mirr.html

Newspaper Collection
http://www.statelib.lib.in.us/WWW/INDIANA/newspaper.HTML

Newspaper Holdings, by County
http://www.statelib.lib.in.us/WWW/INDIANA/NEWSPAPER/HOLD.HTML

Photograph, Online Collection, by County
http://www.statelib.lib.in.us/WWW/INDIANA/counties/county.html

World War II Serviceman Online Index
http://199.8.200.90:591/wwii.html

STATE HISTORICAL SOCIETY

Indiana Historical Society
http://www.indianahistory.org/

Indiana State Library and   Phone   *(317) 234-0321*
    Historical Building   Fax   *(317) 234-0168*
450 West Ohio Street
Indianapolis, IN 46202-3299

Collections
http://www.indianahistory.org/library/library.php?page=2

Indiana's County Historians
http://www.indianahistory.org/resources.php?page=22

Indiana Historical Topics
http://www.indianahistory.org/library/library.php?page=46

Library
http://www.indianahistory.org/index.php?page=6

Library, Online Catalog
http://157.91.92.2/

Naturalization Records
http://www.indianahistory.org/library/library.php?page=34

OUTSTANDING SITE

Indiana Historical Bureau
http://www.statelib.lib.in.us/www/ihb/ihb.html

140 North Senate Avenue,   Phone   *(317) 232-2535*
    Room 408   Fax   *(317) 232-3728*
Indianapolis, IN 46204-2296   E-mail   *ihb@statelib.lib.in.us*

African Americans, Bibliography
http://www.statelib.lib.in.us/www/ihb/publications/aabib.html

African Americans, Indiana Emigrants to Liberia
http://www.statelib.lib.in.us/www/ihb/publications/inemigrants.html

Bibliography, Indiana History
http://www.statelib.lib.in.us/www/ihb/publications/histbib.html

Bibliography of Indiana Resources
http://www.statelib.lib.in.us/WWW/ihb/histbib.html

Girl Scouting in Indiana
  http://www.statelib.lib.in.us/www/ihb/publications/tiharch-mar97.html

Indiana Governors, Bibliography
  http://www.statelib.lib.in.us/www/ihb/govportraits/govbib.html

Indiana Governors' Portraits
  http://www.statelib.lib.in.us/www/ihb/govportraits/index.html

Indiana Historian. (Serial). Subject Index.
  http://www.statelib.lib.in.us/www/ihb/publications/tihtop.html

Indiana Historical Markers
  http://www.statelib.lib.in.us/www/ihb/marklist.html

Indiana History Bulletin. (Serial). Suspended. Vol. 69, No. 3–Vol. 70, No. 4
(September 1998–December 1999).
  http://www.statelib.lib.in.us/www/ihb/publications/index.html

Indiana History Bulletin. (Serial). Suspended. Index. Vol. 64–Vol. 69 (1993–1998).
  http://www.statelib.lib.in.us/www/ihb/publications/index.html

Native American Resources, Bibliography
  http://www.statelib.lib.in.us/www/ihb/publications/nabib.html

Northwest Ordinance of 1787, Bibliography
  http://www.statelib.lib.in.us/www/ihb/publications/nwordbib.html

Spanish-American War
  http://www.statelib.lib.in.us/www/ihb/publications/tiharch-sep98.html

OTHER STATE SITES

Allen County Public Library
  http://www.acpl.lib.in.us

Fred J. Reynolds Historical Genealogy Department
  http://www.acpl.lib.in.us/genealogy/whoweare.html
  900 Webster Street   *Phone   (260) 424-7241*
  Fort Wayne, IN 46801

Fort Wayne and Allen County Obituary Index, 1841–1900
  http://www.acpl.lib.in.us/genealogy/acres.html

Online Library Catalog
  http://catalog.acpl.lib.in.us/uhtbin/cgisirsi/

Photographs, Fort Wayne Digital Photograph Collection
  http://www.acpl.lib.in.us/readers_services/index.html

Youth and Genealogy
  http://www.acpl.lib.in.us/genealogy/youthgen.html

Indiana University-Purdue University at Fort Wayne

Department of History
> http://www.ipfw.edu/hist/

> *Classroom—Medical 209*
> *2101 East Coliseum Blvd.*
> *Fort Wayne, IN 46805-1499*

Fort Wayne Biography
> http://www.ipfw.edu/ipfwhist/indiana/fwbiog.htm

Fort Wayne History
> http://www.ipfw.edu/ipfwhist/ftwayne/fwresour.htm

Indiana Biography
> http://www.ipfw.edu/ipfwhist/indiana/biog.htm

OUTSTANDING SITE

St. Joseph County Public Library
http://sjcpl.lib.in.us/homepage/

304 South Main Street   *Phone*   *(574) 282-4621*
South Bend, IN 46601   *E-mail*   *m.waterson@gomail.sjcpl.lib.in.us*

African American Resources for St. Joseph County
> http://sjcpl.lib.in.us/homepage/LocalHist/community.html

Genealogy
> http://sjcpl.lib.in.us/homepage/LocalHist/Genealogy.html

German American Heritage Research
> http://sjcpl.lib.in.us/homepage/LocalHist/german.html

Hispanic American Genealogical Research
> http://sjcpl.lib.in.us/homepage/LocalHist/hispanicher.html

Hungarian American Heritage Research
> http://sjcpl.lib.in.us/homepage/LocalHist/hungarian.html

Jewish Heritage Research
> http://sjcpl.lib.in.us/homepage/LocalHist/jewish.html

Local History and Genealogy Services
> http://www.sjcpl.lib.in.us/homepage/LocalHist/LocalHistory.html

Necrology Index
> http://sjcpl.lib.in.us/homepage/LocalHist/Necrology.html

Newspapers, Microfilm
> http://www.sjcpl.lib.in.us/homepage/LocalHist/NewspapersMF.html

Online Library Catalog
http://www.sjcpl.lib.in.us/online.html

Polish-American Heritage Research
http://sjcpl.lib.in.us/homepage/LocalHist/polishher.html

Post Office Mural, Area History
http://www.sjcpl.lib.in.us/LocalHist/sbhistory.html

Revolutionary War Research
http://sjcpl.lib.in.us/homepage/LocalHist/revwar.html

St. Joseph County Research
http://www.sjcpl.lib.in.us/homepage/LocalHist/research1.html

South Bend Tribune. (Serial). Index, (1990)– .
http://sjcpl.lib.in.us/Databases/TribIndexFindLinks.html/

Vietnam and Korean Wars Online Index
http://sjcpl.lib.in.us/VietnamFile/

World War II Online Database
http://sjcpl.lib.in.us/WWIIFile/

Society of Indiana Archivists
http://cawley.archives.nd.edu/sia/

Indiana State Archives   *E-mail   Cawley.1@nd.edu*
315 West Ohio
Indianapolis, IN 46202

From Attic to Archives: First Steps to Setting Up Your Archives
http://cawley.archives.nd.edu/sia/attic.html

Guide to the Indiana Sesquicentennial Manuscript Project
http://cawley.archives.nd.edu/sia/ism.htm

Indiana Archives Repositories
http://cawley.archives.nd.edu/sia/guide/reposito.htm

University of Notre Dame
http://www.nd.edu/

Rare Books and Special Collections
http://www.rarebooks.nd.edu/

102 Hesburgh Library   *Phone   (574) 631-5636*
Notre Dame, IN 46556   *Fax   (574) 631-6772*
                                    E-mail   Library.rarebook.1@nd.edu

Civil War Manuscript Collection
http://www.rarebooks.nd.edu/collections/manuscripts/american_civil_war/

Irish Map Collection
http://www.rarebooks.nd.edu/collections/map/ireland/

Irish Rebellion of 1798 Collection
    http://www.rarebooks.nd.edu/collections/pamphlet/irish/

Parish History Collection
    http://archives1.archives.nd.edu/PARISHES.HTM

University Archives
    http://www.nd.edu/~archives/

IOWA

STATE HOME PAGE

Iowa State Home Page
    http://www.state.ia.us

Bureau of Vital Records
    http://www.idph.state.ia.us/pa/vr.htm

STATE LIBRARY

State Library of Iowa
    http://www.silo.lib.ia.us/

East 12th and Grand	*Phone*	*(515) 281-4102*
Des Moines, IA 50319	*Fax*	*(515) 281-3384*
		(515) 281-6191

Iowa Library Directory
    http://www.silo.lib.ia.us/explore.htm

Iowa Online Card Catalog
    http://www.silo.lib.ia.us/lib-cat.html

STATE GENEALOGICAL SOCIETY

Iowa Genealogical Society
    http://www.iowagenealogy.org/

P.O. Box 7735	*Phone*	*(515) 276-0287*
Des Moines, IA 50322-7735	*Fax*	*(515) 727-1824*
	E-mail	*igs@iowagenealogy.org*

County Chapters
    http://www.iowagenealogy.org/county.htm

German Interest Group
    http://www.iowagenealogy.org/GIGPage.htm

Library
    http://www.iowagenealogy.org/library.htm

Native American Records
    http://www.iowagenealogy.org/NaAmRsrc.htm

STATE HISTORICAL SOCIETY

State Historical Society of Iowa
http://www.iowahistory.org/

600 East Locust   *Phone*   *(515) 281-5111*
Des Moines, IA 50319-0290

Historic Sites Program
http://www.iowahistory.org/sites/index.html

Iowa Battle Flags
http://www.iowaflags.org/

Library
http://www.iowahistory.org/library/index.html

Local Government Records
http://www.iowahistory.org/archives/research_collections/local_government_records/local_government_records.html

OTHER STATE SITES

Iowa State University
http://www.iastate.edu/

Special Collections Department
http://www.lib.iastate.edu/spcl/

Parks Library, Room 403   *Phone*   *(319) 294-6672*
Ames, IA 50011

Archives and Manuscripts
http://www.lib.iastate.edu/spcl/collections/index.html

The Road I Grew Up On, Virtual Tour
http://www.lib.iastate.edu/spcl/road/road.html

University Archives Name Index
http://www.lib.iastate.edu/spcl/arch/name.html

University of Iowa
http://www1.arcade.uiowa.edu/

Special Collections Department
http://www1.arcade.uiowa.edu/spec-coll/

100 Main Library   *Phone*   *(319) 335-5921 Archives*
Iowa City, IA 52242-1420

Books at Iowa. (Serial). Bi-annual. Ceased. Table of Contents and Index.
(1964–1996).
http://www.lib.uiowa.edu/spec-coll/bai/books_at_iowa.htm

Ingham Native American Collection
http://www.lib.uiowa.edu/spec-coll/Bai/gibson.htm

Iowa Land Records
http://www.lib.uiowa.edu/spec-coll/Bai/swierenga.htm

Iowa Women's Archives Holdings
http://www.lib.uiowa.edu/iwa/

Library Online Catalog
http://infohawk.uiowa.edu:4545/ALEPH

Manuscript Collection
http://www.lib.uiowa.edu/spec-coll/framefin.html

Railroadiana
http://www.lib.uiowa.edu/spec-coll/Bai/hofsommer.htm

University of Northern Iowa
http://www.uni.edu

Collection Management and Special Services
http://www.library.uni.edu/cmss/

Rod Library, 3rd Floor   *Phone   (319) 273-6307*
Cedar Falls, IA 50613-3675   *Fax   (319) 273-2913*
                                  E-mail   Gerald.Peterson@uni.edu

Collections Guide
http://www.uni.edu/petersog/collguid.html

County Histories Collection
http://www.library.uni.edu/indexuni/

Historic Newspaper Collection
http://www.uni.edu/petersog/msc24nws.html

University History Index
http://www.library.uni.edu/indexuni/

KANSAS

STATE HOME PAGE

State of Kansas Home Page
http://www.accesskansas.org/

Office of Vital Statistics
http://www.kdhe.state.ks.us/vital/

STATE HISTORICAL SOCIETY

OUTSTANDING SITE

Kansas State Historical Society
http://www.kshs.org/

6425 SW Sixth Avenue
Topeka, KS 66615-1099

Phone   (785) 272-8681
Fax   (785) 272-8682
TTY   (785) 272-8683
E-mail   user@hspo.wpo.state.ks.us
Archives@hspo.wpo.state.ks.us
Referenc@hspo.wpo.state.ks.us

African American Biographies
www.kshs.org/research/collections/documents/bibliographies/ethnic/african_american.htm#bios

African Americans in Kansas and the West
http://www.kshs.org/research/collections/documents/bibliographies/ethnic/african_american.htm

African American Newspapers
http://www.kshs.org/research/collections/documents/bibliographies/ethnic/african_american.htm
#newspapers

Bibliographies
http://www.kshs.org/research/collections/documents/bibliographies/index.htm

Biography
http://www.kshs.org/people/index.htm

Biography, Notable Kansans
http://www.kshs.org/people/index.htm

Census Holdings
http://www.kshs.org/genealogists/census/index.htm

City Directories
http://www.kshs.org/genealogists/directories/index.htm

Civil War Resources
http://www.kshs.org/genealogists/military/recscivil.htm

County Histories
http://www.kshs.org/research/collections/documents/bibliographies/counties/index.htm

Genealogy
http://www.kshs.org/genealogists/index.htm

Governors of Kansas
http://www.kshs.org/people/governors.htm

Guide to Kansas Research Resources
    http://www.kshs.org/research/collections/resourceguide.pdf

Index to Kansas Military Pension Cards, 1861–1900
    http://www.kshs.org/research/collections/documents/personalpapers/findingaids/pensionindex.htm

Jews in Kansas
    http://www.kshs.org/research/collections/documents/bibliographies/ethnic/jew.htm

Kansas G.A.R. Necrology Index
    http://www.kshs.org/genealogists/military/gar/garindex.htm

Kansas Heritage Magazine. (Serial). Table of Contents. Vol. 4, No. 1 (Spring 1996)– .
    http://www.kshs.org/publicat/heritage/index.htm

Kansas History: A Journal of the Central Plains. (Serial). Quarterly. Table of Contents. Vol. 1 (1978)– .
    http://www.kshs.org/publicat/history/index.htm

Kansas Preservation. (Serial). Bi-monthly. Full-text. Vol. 23, No. 2 (March/April 2001)– .
    http://www.kshs.org/resource/kpnews.htm

Land Records
    http://www.kshs.org/genealogists/land/index.htm

Library
    http://www.kshs.org/research/index.htm

Library Online Catalog
    http://www.kshs.org/research/collections/documents/opac/opac1.htm

Manuscripts Collection
    http://www.kshs.org/research/collections/index.htm

Map Collection
    http://www.kshs.org/research/collections/documents/maps/moremaps.htm

Military Records
    http://www.kshs.org/genealogists/military/sources.htm

National and State Register of Historical Properties
    http://www.kshs.org/tourists/landmarks.htm

Native American Census Rolls
    http://www.kshs.org/genealogists/culture_ethnic/Native%20American/indian_census.htm

Native American Genealogy Resources
    http://www.kshs.org/genealogists/culture_ethnic/Native%20American/indian.htm

Native Americans in Kansas
    http://www.kshs.org/shop/books/booklist_native_americans.htm

Newspapers
    http://www.kshs.org/research/collections/documents/newspapers/labor.htm

Photographs
  http://www.kshs.org/research/collections/documents/photos/index.htm

Researcher's Guide to Local Government Records
  http://www.kshs.org/genealogists/localgovt/microfilm/sedgwick.htm

State Archives
  http://www.kshs.org/research/collections/documents/govtrecords/index.htm

Telephone Directories
  http://www.kshs.org/genealogists/directories/index.htm

This Day in Kansas History
  http://www.kshs.org/research/timeline/thisday/

Topeka State Hospital Cemetery Online Index
  http://www.kshs.org/genealogists/vital/topekastatehospitalcemetery.htm

World War I
  http://www.kshs.org/genealogists/military/recswwiarchives.htm

World War II
  http://www.kshs.org/research/collections/documents/bibliographies/military/wwiibib.htm

OTHER STATE SITES

E X T R A O R D I N A R Y   S I T E
One of the Most Extraordinary Web Sites Online
University of Kansas

Kansas Collection
http://www.kancoll.org/

Spencer Research Library,	*Phone*	*(913) 864-4274*
Room 220	*E-mail*	*lhnelson@raven.cc.ukans.edu*
Lawrence, KS 66045-2800		*husker@sky.net*
		susancs@awod.com
Thomas R. Smith Map Collection	*Phone*	*(913) 864-4420*
Level 1, Anschutz Library	*Fax*	*(913) 864-5380*
	E-mail	*maps-ref@ukans.edu*
Kansas Heritage Center for Family	*E-mail*	*lhnelson@ukanaix.cc.ukans.edu*
and Local History. Kansas Data		*chinn@ctrvax.vanderbilt.edu*
and Links		

Articles, Essays on Kansas History
  http://www.kancoll.org/articles/index.html

Bibliography, A–L
http://www.kancoll.org/research/kanhistory.a-l

Bibliography, M–Z
http://www.kancoll.org/research/kanhistory.m-z

Bibliography of Kansas Dissertations and Theses
http://www.kancoll.org/research/theses.htm

Biography, Kansas
http://www.kancoll.org/research/kanbiog.html

County Organization Dates
http://history.cc.ukans.edu/heritage/research/coorgdat.html

eBook Collection
http://kuhttp.cc.ukans.edu/carrie/kancoll/books/

eContent
http://kuhttp.cc.ukans.edu/carrie/kancoll/articles/

Gazeteer of Kansas Towns
http://www.ukans.edu/heritage/towns/hdkt/hdkt.html

Jewish Agricultural Communities in Frontier Kansas
http://www.kancoll.org/books/harris/

Kansas Heritage Center for Family and Local History
http://www.ukans.edu/heritage/khis/119/index.html

Kansas Historical Quarterly. (Serial). Mostly Full-text. Vol. 1, No. 1 (November 1931)– .
http://www.kancoll.org/khq/index.html

Kansas Pioneers Project
http://skyways.lib.ks.us/kansas/genweb/pioneers/index.html

Kansas POWs in Texas 1863–1865
http://www.ku.edu/heritage/research/campford.html

Maps
http://history.cc.ukans.edu/carrie/kancoll/graphics/maps/

Methodists in Kansas
http://history.cc.ukans.edu/heritage/um/um.html

Native Americans, a Bibliography
http://www.kancoll.org/research/kanindians.txt

Orphan Trains
http://www.rootsweb.com/~neadoptn/Orphan.htm

Post Card Collections
http://www.kancoll.org/galwin.htm

Railroads, a Kansas Bibliography
http://www.kancoll.org/research/kanrails.htm

Society for Spanish and Portuguese Historical Studies
http://www.cc.ukans.edu/~iberia/ssphs/ssphs_main.html

Voices, KanColl's Online Magazine. (Serial). Vol. 1, No.1 (December 1996)– .
http://www.kancoll.org/voices_2001/0701news.htm

KENTUCKY

STATE HOME PAGE

Kentucky State Page
http://kentucky.gov/

Office of Vital Statistics
http://publichealth.state.ky.us/vital.htm

STATE LIBRARY AND ARCHIVES

OUTSTANDING SITE

Kentucky Department for Libraries and Archives
http://www.kdla.state.ky.us/

300 Coffee Tree Road   *Phone*   *(502) 564-8300*
P.O. Box 537   *E-mail*   *minder@a1.kdla.state.ky.us*
Frankfort, KY 40602-0537

Archives Reading Room   *Phone*   *(502) 564-8704*

African American Sources
http://www.kdla.net/links/blackhis.htm

Annual Report. (Serial). Annual. Current Issue. Full-text.
http://www.kdla.net/intro/annualreport00.pdf

Census Records
http://www.kdla.net/arch/kentcens.htm

Civil War Records
http://www.kdla.net/arch/civil.htm

Friends of the Kentucky Public Archives
http://www.kdla.net/pubrec/friends.htm

Governors of Kentucky
    http://www.kdla.net/arch/Govbio2.htm

Guide to Archives and Manuscripts Resources
    http://cuadranew.kdla.net/marcaty.htm

Kentucky Guide Project
    http://www.kdla.state.ky.us/arch/guidwebe.htm

Kentucky State Archives
    http://www.kdla.state.ky.us/arch/reseroom.htm

Land Records
    http://www.kdla.net/arch/land.htm

Lieutenant Governors of Kentucky
    http://www.kdla.net/links/ltgovs2.htm

Library Directory of Kentucky Libraries
    http://www.kdla.net/libserv/publdir.htm

Native American Resources
    http://www.kdla.net/links/native_amer.htm

Naturalization Records
    http://www.kdla.net/arch/naturali.htm

Online Archives Catalog
    http://www.kdla.state.ky.us/cuadra/welcome.htm

State Historical Records Advisory Board
    http://www.kdla.net/pubrec/strecadv.htm

State Publications Online
    http://www.kdla.net/arch/pubson.htm

Vital Records
    http://www.kdla.net/arch/vital.htm

STATE GENEALOGICAL SOCIETY

Kentucky Genealogical Society
    http://www.kygs.org/

P.O. Box 153   *E-mail   kygs@aol.com*
Frankfort, KY 40602

Bluegrass Roots. (Serial). Quarterly. Table of Contents. Vol. 1, No. 1 (Fall 1976)– .
    http://www.kygs.org/backissu.htm

Landon Wills, in Memoriam
    http://www.kygs.org/landon.htm

STATE HISTORICAL SOCIETY

Kentucky Historical Society
http://www.kyhistory.org/

100 West Broadway	*Phone (502) 564-1792*
P.O. Box 1792	*Fax (502) 696-3846*
Frankfort, KY 40602-1792	

Cemetery Records Online Database
http://catalog.kyhistory.org/help/Cemetery_Database.htm

Civil Rights Oral History Project
http://www.kyhistory.org/Programs/KOHC/KOHC_Civil_Rights.htm

Kentucky Encyclopedia Online
http://catalog.kyhistory.org/help/Ky_Ency_Online.htm

Kentucky Oral History Commission Records
http://www.kyhistory.org/Programs/KOHC/KOHC_Home.htm

Kentucky Virtual Library
http://www.kyvl.org

Online Library Catalog
http://catalog.kyhistory.org/

OTHER STATE SITES

Eastern Kentucky University
http://www.eku.edu/

Special Collections and Archives
http://www.library.eku.edu/SCA/

Crabbe Library, Room 126	*Phone (859) 622-1792*
521 Lancaster Avenue	*Fax (859) 622-1174*
Richmond, KY 40475-3121	*E-mail archives@eku.edu*

Eastern Kentucky University History
http://www.library.eku.edu/SCA/history.htm

Family Files
http://www.library.eku.edu/SCA/familyfiles.htm

Manuscript Collections
http://www.library.eku.edu/SCA/invent.htm

Maps
http://www.library.eku.edu/SCA/maps.htm

Oral History Collection
http://www.library.eku.edu/SCA/invent.htm

OUTSTANDING SITE

Kentucky Biography Project
http://www.rootsweb.com/~kygenweb/kybiog/

OUTSTANDING SITE

University of Kentucky
http://www.uky.edu/

Special Collections and Archives
http://www.uky.edu/Libraries/Special/

Margaret I. King Library   Phone   (859) 257-8611
Lexington, KY 40506

Kentucky Place Names
http://www.uky.edu/KentuckyPlaceNames/

Kentucky Vital Records Online Indexes
http://ukcc.uky.edu/~vitalrec/

Oral History Program
http://www.uky.edu/Libraries/Special/oral_history/

LOUISIANA

STATE HOME PAGE

Info Louisiana
http://www.state.la.us/

Vital Records Registry
http://oph.dhh.state.la.us/recordsstatistics/vitalrecords/index.html

STATE ARCHIVES

Louisiana State Archives
http://www.sec.state.la.us/archives/archives/archives-index.htm

Archives and Records Section   Phone   (504) 342-3389
Essen Lane   Fax   (504) 342-3547
P.O. Box 94125
Baton Rouge, LA 70804-9125

Confederate Pension Applications Online Database Index
http://www.sec.state.la.us/archives/gen/cpa-index.htm

History of the Archives
http://www.sec.state.la.us/archives/archives/archives-historical.htm

Le Comité des Archives de la Louisiane (Friends of the Archives Group)
http://www.sec.state.la.us/archives/archives/archives-comite.htm

Le Raconteur. (Serial). 3/year. Index. Vol. 4 (1984)– .
http://www.sec.state.la.us/archives/archives/arch-5b.htm

Le Raconteur. (Serial). 3/year. Table of Contents. Vol. 4, No. 1 (1984)– .
http://www.sec.state.la.us/archives/archives/arch-5a.htm

Louisiana Governors
http://sec.state.la.us/gov-1.htm

Research Library
http://www.sec.state.la.us/archives/archives/archives-library.htm

This Month in Louisiana History
http://sec.state.la.us/museums/osc/month/month.htm

STATE LIBRARY

Louisiana State Library
http://www.state.lib.la.us/

760 North Third Street   *Phone*   *(225) 342-4914*
P.O. Box 131   *Fax*   *(225) 342-2791*
Baton Rouge, LA 70821-0131   *E-mail*   *ladept@pelican.state.lib.la.us*

Louisiana Genealogical Societies
http://www.state.lib.la.us/Dept/LaSect/societies.htm

Louisiana Section
http://www.state.lib.la.us/Dept/LaSect/index.htm

Searching for Your Louisiana Ancestors . . . *And All That Jazz!*
http://www.state.lib.la.us/Dept/LaSect/searchin.htm

OTHER STATE SITES

Historic New Orleans Collection
http://www.hnoc.org/
533 Royal Street
New Orleans, LA 70130

Williams Research Center   *Phone*   *(504) 598-7171*
410 Chartres Street   *Fax*   *(504) 598-7168*
New Orleans, LA 70130   *E-mail*   *wrc@hnoc.org*

Historic New Orleans Collections Quarterly. (Serial). Quarterly. Full-text. Vol. 17, No. 4 (Fall 1999)– .
   http://www.hnoc.org/hnocpubs.htm

Manuscripts
   http://www.hnoc.org/

Louisiana Archives and Manuscripts Association
   http://nutrias.org/lama/lama.htm
   P.O. Box 51213
   New Orleans, LA 70151-1213

Louisiana Repositories on the Web
   http://nutrias.org/lama/louarch.htm

Newsletter. (Serial). Full-text. (Fall 1996)– .
   http://nutrias.org/lama/fall96.htm

Louisiana State University Libraries
   http://www.lsu.edu/

Special Collections Department
   http://www.lib.lsu.edu/special/
      Hill Memorial Library, Room 201   *E-mail   notvfp@unix1.sncc.lsu.edu*
      Baton Rouge, LA 70803-3300

Louisiana and Lower Mississippi Valley Collections
   http://www.lib.lsu.edu/special/frames/llmvc.html

EXTRAORDINARY SITE

One of the Most Extraordinary Web Sites Online—
Best Example of Online Web Site by a Large Public Library

New Orleans Public Library
http://www.nutrias.org/

City Archives and Louisiana Division Special Collections
   http://nutrias.org/~nopl/spec/speclist.htm
   219 Loyola Avenue
   New Orleans, LA 70112-2044

African American Resource Center
   http://nutrias.org/~nopl/info/aarcinfo/aarcinfo.htm

African American Resources
    http://nutrias.org/~nopl/guides/black.htm

Architecture and Allied Arts. (Serial). Ceased. Index. Vol. 1, No. 1 (July 1905–January 1913).
    http://nutrias.org/~nopl/info/louinfo/aart/aartintro.htm

Census, 1850. Hints
    http://nutrias.org/~nopl/info/louinfo/louinfo5.htm

Census, 1860–1920
    http://nutrias.org/~nopl/info/louinfo/census2.htm

City Archives and Special Collections
    http://nutrias.org/~nopl/inv/invlist.htm

City Directories
    http://nutrias.org/~nopl/info/louinfo/citydir.htm

Digging Up Roots in the Mud Files: Sources for Family History Research in the Orleans Parish Civil Court Records
    http://nutrias.org/~nopl/inv/cdcdemo/text2.htm

Guide to African American Genealogical Research in New Orleans and Louisiana
    http://nutrias.org/~nopl/info/aarcinfo/guide.htm

Guide to Genealogical Materials, NOPL
    http://nutrias.org/~nopl/guides/genguide/ggcover.htm

How to Research the History of Your House (or Other Building) in New Orleans
    http://nutrias.org/~nopl/guides/house/title.htm

Manuscript Collections
    http://nutrias.org/~nopl/mss/mss.htm

Map Collection
    http://nutrias.org/~nopl/maps/maps.htm

Naturalization Records
    http://nutrias.org/~nopl/info/louinfo/louinfo4.htm

Newspapers, New Orleans
    http://nutrias.org/~nopl/info/louinfo/npfilm.htm

Newspapers, *Daily Picayune.* (Serial). New Orleans Death Index. (1837–1857; 1870).
    http://nutrias.org/~nopl/info/louinfo/deaths/deaths.htm

Newspapers, *Daily Picayune.* (Serial). New Orleans Marriage Index. (1837–1857).
    http://nutrias.org/~nopl/info/louinfo/newsmarr/newsmarr.htm

Notable African Amerians from Louisiana
    http://nutrias.org/~nopl/info/aarcinfo/notabl2.htm

Online, Digital Collections
http://nutrias.org/~nopl/spec/pamphlets/pamphlets.htm

Orleans Parish Civil and Criminal Court Records
http://nutrias.org/~nopl/inv/courts.htm

Orleans Parish Government Records Finding Aids
http://nutrias.org/~nopl/inv/opp.htm

Photograph Collection
http://nutrias.org/~nopl/photos/photolist.htm

Street Name Changes
http://nutrias.org/~nopl/facts/streetnames/namesa.htm

OUTSTANDING SITE

Tulane University
http://www.tulane.edu

Special Collections Department
http://specialcollections.tulane.edu/

Tilton Memorial Library   Phone   *(504) 865-5685*
6823 St. Charles Avenue   Fax   *(504) 865-5761*
New Orleans, LA 70118-5682   E-mail   *meneray@tulane.edu*

Amistad Research Center
http://www.tulane.edu/~amistad/

Family History Collections
http://www.tulane.edu/~lmiller/FamilyHistory.html

Louisiana Collection
http://www.tulane.edu/~lmiller/LaCollection.html

Manuscripts Department
http://www.tulane.edu/~lmiller/ManuscriptsHome.html

Maps
http://www.tulane.edu/~lmiller/Maps2.html

Military Records
http://www.tulane.edu/~lmiller/Military.html

Southern Jewish Archives
http://www.tulane.edu/~lmiller/JewishStudiesIntro.html

World War I Research
http://www.tulane.edu/~lmiller/WWI.htm

MAINE

STATE HOME PAGE

Maine State Home Page
http://www.state.me.us/

Office of Vital Records
http://www.state.me.us/dhs/bohodr/ovrpage.htm

STATE ARCHIVES

Maine State Archives
http://www.state.me.us/sos/arc/

84 State House Station   Phone   *(207) 287-5795*
Augusta, ME 04333-0084   Fax   *(207) 287-5739*

Genealogy Resources
http://www.state.me.us/sos/arc/geneology/homepage.html

Judicial Records
http://www.state.me.us/sos/arc/archives/judicial/judicial.htm

Land Office Records
http://www.state.me.us/sos/arc/archives/land1.htm

Legislative Records
http://www.state.me.us/sos/arc/archives/legislat/legislat.htm

Maine State Agencies, a Guide to Their Records
http://www.state.me.us/sos/arc/guide/guidintr.htm

Military Records
http://www.state.me.us/sos/arc/archives/military/military.htm

Preserving Your Collections, a Planning and Resource Manual
http://www.state.me.us/sos/arc/files/PRESMAN1.DOC

Vital Records, Deaths, Online Index. 1960–1996
http://thor.dafs.state.me.us/pls/archives/archdev.death_archive.search_form

Vital Records, Marriages, Online Index. (1892–1866; 1976–1996).
http://thor.dafs.state.me.us/pls/archives/archdev.marriage_archive.search_form

STATE LIBRARY

Maine State Library
http://www.state.me.us/msl/index.html

State House Station #64   Phone   *(207) 287-5600*
Augusta, ME 04333   Fax   *(207) 287-5615*
                                   E-mail   *slgnich@state.me.us*
                                            sldwhit@state.me.us

Maine Library Directory

http://msl1.ursus.maine.edu/statsnew/searchn.cfm

Maine Memo. (Serial). Vol. 20, No. 1 (January 1998)– .

http://mainelibraries.org/mainememo/

STATE HISTORICAL SOCIETY

Maine Historical Society

http://www.mainehistory.org/home.html

485 Congress Street   *Phone   (207) 774-1822*
Portland, ME 04101   *Fax   (207) 775-4301*
                                                E-mail   info@mainehistory.org

Library

http://www.mainehistory.org/about.html#famhist

Maine History Museum

http://www.mainehistory.org/about.html#gallery

OTHER STATE SITES

University of Maine

http://www.umaine.edu/

Special Collections Department

http://www.library.umaine.edu/speccoll/

5729 Fogler Library   *Phone   (207) 581-1686*
Orono, ME 04469-5729   *Fax   (207) 581-1653*
                                                E-mail   spc@umit.maine.edu

Maine Folklife Center
   University of Maine
5773 South Stevens Hall
Orono, ME 04469-5773

Archives Database

http://www.library.umaine.edu/speccoll/archives.htm

Canadian Studies Collection

http://www.ume.maine.edu/~canam/library.html

Census

http://www.library.umaine.edu/reference/guides/genecensus.htm

Census, Canadian

http://www.library.umaine.edu/reference/guides/censuscanada.htm

Maine Collection

http://www.library.umaine.edu/speccoll/mainecol.htm

Maine Folklife Center

http://www.umaine.edu/folklife/

Maine Folklife Newsletter. (Serial). Semi-annual. Vol. 4, No. 1 (Spring 1998)– .
http://www.umaine.edu/folklife/Arcives.htm

Maine Manuscripts
http://www.library.umaine.edu/speccoll/manucol.htm

Maine Newpapers
http://www.library.umaine.edu/speccoll/newspapers.htm

Manuscripts
http://www.library.umaine.edu/speccoll/manulist.htm

Online Library Catalog
http://www.library.umaine.edu/speccoll/ursus.htm

MARYLAND

STATE HOME PAGE

Maryland Electronic Capitol
Maryland State Home Page
http://www.mec.state.md.us/

Vital Statistics Administration
http://mdpublichealth.org/vsa/

STATE ARCHIVES

Maryland State Archives
http://www.mdarchives.state.md.us/

350 Rowe Boulevard   *Phone*   *(410) 260-6400*
Annapolis, MD 21401-1686   *(800) 235-4045 in Maryland*
                                        Fax   *(410) 974-3895*
                                        E-mail *archives@mdarchives.state.md.us*

Admiralty Court Records, Online
http://www.mdarchives.state.md.us/msa/speccol/sc4600/sc4646/html/title.html

African American Resources
http://www.mdarchives.state.md.us/msa/refserv/html/afro.html

Archives of Maryland. Full-text
http://www.mdarchives.state.md.us/megafile/msa/speccol/sc2900/sc2908/html/index.html

Biographical Resources
http://www.mdarchives.state.md.us/msa/refserv/html/bioinfo.html

Boundary Records Index, 1720–1985
http://www.mdarchives.state.md.us/msa/refserv/staghist/serdesc/html/s1474.html

Cemetery Records
http://www.mdarchives.state.md.us/msa/refserv/genealogy/html/graves.html

Census, Anne Arundel County, 1870 Census Index
http://www.mdarchives.state.md.us/msa/refserv/quickref/html/allssi1526.html

Census, Anne Arundel County, 1880 Census Index
http://www.mdarchives.state.md.us/msa/stagser/s1500/s1525/html/ssi1525.html

Census Records
http://www.mdarchives.state.md.us/msa/refserv/html/census.html

Checklist of Indexes
http://www.mdarchives.state.md.us/msa/refserv/html/checklst.html

Church Records
http://speccol.mdarchives.state.md.us/msa/speccol/catalog/religion/cfm/index.cfm

County History Information
http://www.mdarchives.state.md.us/msa/refserv/html/counties.html

Early Settlers of Maryland, Supplement
http://www.mdarchives.state.md.us/msa/refserv/staghist/serdesc/html/s1503.html

Electronic, Online Indexes
http://www.mdarchives.state.md.us/msa/refserv/html/quickref.html

Genealogy
http://www.mdarchives.state.md.us/msa/refserv/genealogy/html/genstart.html

Government House
http://www.mdarchives.state.md.us/msa/homepage/html/govhouse.html

Government Records
http://www.mdarchives.state.md.us/msa/refserv/html/series.html#county

Land Records
http://www.mdarchives.state.md.us/msa/refserv/genealogy/html/land.html

Maps
http://www.mdarchives.state.md.us/msa/speccol/maps/html/collect.html

Maryland Board of Public Works Online Database, 1875–1981
http://www.mdarchives.state.md.us/msa/refserv/staghist/serdesc/html/s1473.html

Maryland Day
http://www.mdarchives.state.md.us/msa/homepage/html/educ.html#celebrat

Maryland Manual
http://www.mdarchives.state.md.us/msa/mdmanual/html/mmtoc.html

Maryland Place Names
http://www.mdarchives.state.md.us/msa/refserv/quickref/html/placenames.html

Medical Care in the City of Baltimore, 1752–1919
http://www.mdhistoryonline.net/mdmedicine/cfm/index.cfm

Military Records
   http://www.mdarchives.state.md.us/msa/refserv/genealogy/html/militrec.html

National Guard Service Index, 1888–1933
   http://www.mdarchives.state.md.us/msa/refserv/quickref/html/mdguard.html

Naturalization Records
   http://www.mdarchives.state.md.us/msa/refserv/genealogy/html/immigrat.html

Newspapers, Maryland Newspaper Project
   http://speccol.mdarchives.state.md.us/msa/speccol/catalog/newspapers/cfm/index.cfm

Probate Records
   http://www.mdarchives.state.md.us/msa/refserv/genealogy/html/probate.html

Roman Catholic Church Records
   http://www.mdarchives.state.md.us/msa/refserv/html/catholic.html

Understanding Church Records
   http://www.mdarchives.state.md.us/msa/refserv/html/churchguide.html

Understanding Maryland Records
   http://www.mdarchives.state.md.us/msa/refserv/html/mdrecords.html

Vital Records
   http://www.mdarchives.state.md.us/msa/refserv/html/vitalrec.html

Vital Records, Baltimore Death Index (1875–1880)
   http://www.mdarchives.state.md.us/msa/refserv/quickref/html/allssi1483a.html

Vital Records, Baltimore Death Index (1943–1949)
   http://www.mdarchives.state.md.us/msa/refserv/quickref/html/allssi1483b.html

Women Legislators of Maryland Collection, Online
   http://www.mdarchives.state.md.us/msa/speccol/4492/html/0000.html

STATE HISTORICAL SOCIETY

Maryland Historical Society
   http://www.mdhs.org/
   201 West Monument Street   *Phone   (410) 685-3750*
   Baltimore, MD 21201   *Fax   (410) 385-2105*

Baltimore Album Quilts
   http://www.mdhs.org/online/quilt_exhibit.html

Baltimore Architecture, Then and Now
   http://www.mdhs.org/library/baltarch/archhome.html

Library
   http://www.mdhs.org/explore/library.html

Mapping Maryland
http://www.mdhs.org/library/MappingMD/mmhpg.html

Maritime Historical Collection
http://www.mdhs.org/explore/maritime/

Maryland Firsts
http://www.mdhs.org/library/MDfirsthome.html

Photographs, Maryland in Focus
http://www.mdhs.org/library/MDfocHP.html

OTHER STATE SITES

University of Maryland, College Park
http://www.umd.edu/

Marylandia and Rare Book Department
http://www.lib.umd.edu/RARE/index.html

McKeldin Library   *Phone   (301) 405-9212*
College Park, MD 20742

African American Resources
http://www.lib.umd.edu/RARE/MarylandCollection/MDResourceGuide/AfAmResources.html

Archives and Manuscripts Department
http://www.lib.umd.edu/ARCV/arcvmss/arcvmss.html

Baltimore Architecture
http://www.lib.umd.edu/RARE/MarylandCollection/MDResourceGuide/BaltArch.html

Baltimore News American. (Serial). Photo Collection.
http://www.lib.umd.edu/RARE/MarylandCollection/NewsAmerican/NewsAmerican.html

Census
http://www.lib.umd.edu/RARE/census.html

City Directories
http://www.lib.umd.edu/RARE/MarylandCollection/MDResourceGuide/CityDir.html

Maps
http://www.lib.umd.edu/GOV/mapcoll.html

Maps, Sanborn Map Guide
http://www.lib.umd.edu/RARE/MarylandCollection/MDResourceGuide/Sanborn.html

Maryland State Publications
http://www.lib.umd.edu/RARE/MarylandCollection/StatePubs.html

Newspapers
http://www.lib.umd.edu/RARE/MarylandCollection/MDNewspapers.html

Women's History
http://www.lib.umd.edu/RARE/MarylandCollection/MDResourceGuide/wommdhistory.html

MASSACHUSETTS

STATE HOME PAGE

Commonwealth of Massachusetts Home Page
http://www.mass.gov/portal/index.jsp

Registry of Vital Records and Statistics
http://www.state.ma.us/dph/bhsre/rvr/rvr.htm

STATE ARCHIVES

Massachusetts State Archives
http://www.state.ma.us/sec/arc/arcidx.htm

220 Morrissey Boulevard   *Phone*   *(617) 727-2816*
Boston, MA 02125   *Fax*   *(617) 288-4429*
                                     E-mail   *archives@sec.state.ma.us*

Collections Guide
http://www.state.ma.us/sec/arc/arccol/colidx.htm

Family History
http://www.state.ma.us/sec/arc/arcgen/genidx.htm

Land Records, Registry of Deeds
http://www.state.ma.us/sec/rod/rodidx.htm

Maps, PDF Files
http://www.state.ma.us/sec/cis/cismap/mapidx.htm

Massachusetts Maps
http://www.state.ma.us/sec/cis/cismap/mapidx.htm

STATE LIBRARY

Massachusetts Board of Library Commissioners
http://www.mlin.lib.ma.us/flash3.html

648 Beacon Street   *Phone*   *(617) 267-9400*
Boston, MA 02215   *(800) 952-7403 in Massachusetts*
                               Fax   *(617) 421-9833*
                               E-mail   *info@mlin.lib.ma.us*

OTHER STATE SITES

American Antiquarian Society
http://www.americanantiquarian.org/

185 Salisbury Street   *Phone*   *(508) 755-5221*
Worcester, MA 01609-1634   *Fax*   *(508) 754-9069*
                                  E-mail   *library@mwa.org*

Biography Collections
http://www.americanantiquarian.org/biography.htm

Canadiana
http://www.americanantiquarian.org/canadiana.htm

Cemetery Art, Photographs
http://www.americanantiquarian.org/gravestones.htm

City Directories
http://www.americanantiquarian.org/directories.htm

Genealogy
http://www.americanantiquarian.org/genealogy.htm

Guide, Under Its Generous Dome
http://www.americanantiquarian.org/alphaindex.htm

Hawaiian Collection
http://www.americanantiquarian.org/hawaiian.htm

Local, County, and State Histories
http://www.americanantiquarian.org/localhist.htm

Maps and Atlases
http://www.americanantiquarian.org/maps.htm

Newspapers
http://www.americanantiquarian.org/newspapers.htm

Portraits
http://www.americanantiquarian.org/portraits.htm

Western Americana
http://www.americanantiquarian.org/western.htm

OUTSTANDING SITE

Historical Records of Dukes County, Massachusetts
http://www.vineyard.net/vineyard/history/

RR2 Box 247   *E-mail   cbaer@vineyard.net*
Vineyard Haven, MA 02568

Maps and Photographs
http://www.vineyard.net/vineyard/history/photmaps.htm

Martha's Vineyard Genealogy
http://www.vineyard.net/vineyard/history/gene.htm

Portuguese Genealogy Project
http://www.vineyard.net/vineyard/history/mvpgp/index.html

Tisbury Cemeteries
http://www.vineyard.net/vineyard/history/cemetery/cemlist.htm

Vital Records, Online Indexes
http://www.vineyard.net/vineyard/history/lists.htm

What Is the Correct Name of Martha's Vineyard?
http://www.vineyard.net/vineyard/history/banks1na.htm

Natick Historical Society and Museum
http://www.ixl.net/~natick/

58 Eliot Street   *Phone   (508) 647-4841*
South Natick, MA 01760   *E-mail   eliot@ixl.net*

Annals of Elm Bank, the Cheney Estate
http://www.ixl.net/~natick/ElmBank.html

Natick History
http://www.ixl.net/~natick/Natick_History_Brief.html

Natick Manufacturing
http://www.ixl.net/~natick/Business_and_Industry.html

MICHIGAN

STATE HOME PAGE

Michigan State Government
http://www.michigan.gov/gov

Division for Vital Records and Health Statistics
http://www.michigan.gov/mdch/1,1607,7-132-4645---,00.html

GENDIS, Genealogical Death Indexing System. Index (1867–1884)
http://www.mdch.state.mi.us/PHA/OSR/gendis/

STATE ARCHIVES

OUTSTANDING SITE

State Archives of Michigan
http://www.michigan.gov/hal/0,1607,7-160-17445_19273_19313---,00.html

Michigan Library and Historical   *Phone   (517) 373-1408*
Center   *Fax   (517) 241-1658*
717 West Allegan Street
Lansing, MI 48918-1805

Census Records, Special
http://www.michigan.gov/documents/mhc_sa_circular45_49971_7.pdf

Census Records, State
http://www.michigan.gov/documents/mhc_sa_circular45_49971_7.pdf

Civil War Manuscripts
http://www.michigan.gov/documents/mhc_sa_circular20_49709_7.pdf

County Clerks Genealogy Directory
http://www.michigan.gov/hal/0,1607,7-160-17449_18635_20736---,00.html

Court Records
http://www.michigan.gov/documents/mhc_sa_circular37_49972_7.pdf

Diaries, Journals
http://www.michigan.gov/hal/0,1607,7-160-18835_18897-56325--,00.html

Land Records
http://www.michigan.gov/documents/mhc_sa_circular02_49679_7.pdf

Manuscripts
http://www.michigan.gov/documents/mhc_sa_circular55_50000_7.pdf

Military, Local Records
http://www.michigan.gov/documents/mhc_sa_circular27_50001_7.pdf

Military, Post-War Records
http://www.michigan.gov/documents/mhc_sa_circular07_49691_7.pdf

Military, War Records
http://www.michigan.gov/documents/mhc_sa_circular04_49684_7.pdf

Naturalization Records
http://www.michigan.gov/hal/0,1607,7-160-17449_18635_20684---,00.html

Newspapers
http://www.michigan.gov/hal/0,1607,7-160-17449_18643---,00.html

Photographs
http://www.michigan.gov/documents/mhc_sa_circular31_50007_7.pdf

Probate Records
http://www.michigan.gov/documents/mhc_sa_circular06_49689_7.pdf

Railroad Records
http://www.michigan.gov/documents/mhc_sa_circular13_49702_7.pdf

School Records
http://www.michigan.gov/documents/mhc_sa_circular11_49700_7.pdf

Vital Records
http://www.michigan.gov/documents/mhc_sa_circular19_49707_7.pdf

Women, Records on
http://www.michigan.gov/documents/mhc_sa_circular35_50019_7.pdf

STATE LIBRARY

Library of Michigan
http://www.michigan.gov/hal/0,1607,7-160-17445_19270---,00.html

Abrams Foundation Historical Collection: Genealogy and Local History
http://www.michigan.gov/hal/0,1607,7-160-17449_18635_18648---,00.html

P.O. Box 30007	*Phone (517) 373-1300*
717 West Allegan Street	*(517) 373-1580*
Lansing, MI 48909-7507	*E-mail info@libofmich.lib.mi.us*

Bibliography
http://www.libofmich.lib.mi.us/genealogy/basictitles.html

Census, 1870 Online Index
http://www.michigan.gov/hal/0,1607,7-160-17449_18635_20683---,00.html

Diaries and Autobiographies
http://www.michigan.gov/documents/mhc_sa_circular61_49967_7.pdf

Fur Trade
http://www.michigan.gov/hal/0,1607,7-160-18835_18897_20856-56336--,00.html

Library Directory, Michigan Libraries
http://www.michigan.gov/hal/0,1607,7-160-18835_18891---,00.html

Library Online Catalog
http://opac.libofmich.lib.mi.us/screens/opacmenu.html

Lighthouses
http://www.michigan.gov/hal/0,1607,7-160-17449_18638_21818---,00.html

Lumbering
http://www.michigan.gov/documents/mhc_sa_circular28_49999_7.pdf

Maps
http://www.michigan.gov/hal/0,1607,7-160-17449_18642-56864--,00.html

Native Americans
http://www.michigan.gov/documents/mhc_sa_circular30_50002_7.pdf

Newspapers, Michigan Newspaper Project
http://www.michigan.gov/hal/0,1607,7-160-17449_18643-49361--,00.html

STATE HISTORICAL SOCIETY

Michigan Historical Center
http://www.michigan.gov/hal/0,1607,7-160-15481_19268_20822-57624--,00.html

Michigan Department of State	*Phone (517) 373-3559*
717 West Allegan Street	
Lansing, MI 48918-1805	

Historic Preservation Office
http://www.michigan.gov/hal/0,1607,7-160-17445_19273_19318---,00.html

Michigan History Magazine. (Serial). Bi-monthly. Some Full-text. Table of Contents. (March/April 1973)– .
http://www.michiganhistorymagazine.com/

Museums
http://www.michigan.gov/hal/0,1607,7-160-17445_19273_19306---,00.html

State Archaeologist
http://www.michigan.gov/hal/0,1607,7-160-17445_19273_19325---,00.html

OTHER STATE SITES

Detroit Public Library
http://www.detroit.lib.mi.us/

Burton Historical Collection   *Phone*   *(313) 833-1480*
5201 Woodward Avenue   *E-mail* *dporemba@detroit.lib.mi.us*
Detroit, MI 48202

African American Inventors Database
http://www.detroit.lib.mi.us/glptc/aaid/index.asp

Burton Historical Collection
http://www.detroit.lib.mi.us/burton/

Map Collection
http://www.detroit.lib.mi.us/map/

Municipal Reference Library
http://www.detroit.lib.mi.us/mrl/special_collections.htm

Photograph Collection
http://www.detroit.lib.mi.us/burton/photos/using_photos.htm

Michigan Technological University
http://www.lib.mtu.edu/jrvp/index.htm

MTU Archives and Copper Country Historical Collections
http://www.lib.mtu.edu/mtuarchives/mtuarchives.htm

J. R. Van Pelt Library   *Phone*   *(906) 487-2508*
1400 Townsend Drive   *Fax*   *(906) 487-2357*
Houghton, MI 49931-1295   *E-mail* *copper@mtu.edu*

Archives History
http://www.lib.mtu.edu/mtuarchives/history.htm

Brockway Family Collection
http://www.lib.mtu.edu/mtuarchives/ms010brockwaydiary.htm

Cemetery Records
http://www.lib.mtu.edu/mtuarchives/ms027.htm

Cornwall, England Genealogical Collection
http://www.lib.mtu.edu/mtuarchives/ross.htm

Cornwall, England Vital Records Indexes
http://www.lib.mtu.edu/mtuarchives/ms007.htm

County Records
http://www.lib.mtu.edu/mtuarchives/statearchives.htm

Guide to Researching Michigan Copper Mining Companies
http://www.lib.mtu.edu/mtuarchives/miningcompanyhistory.htm

Map Collection
http://www.lib.mtu.edu/govdocs/maps.htm

Mining History Association
http://www.mg.mtu.edu/mining/mining/hist.htm

Quincy Mining Company Collection
http://www.lib.mtu.edu/mtuarchives/ms001-intro.htm

University of Michigan–Dearborn
http://www.umd.umich.edu/

4901 Evergreen Road
Dearborn, MI 48128-1491

Armenian Research Center
http://www.umd.umich.edu/dept/armenian/

Holocaust Survivor Oral History Project
http://holocaust.umd.umich.edu/

EXTRAORDINARY SITE
One of the Most Extraordinary Web Sites Online

University of Michigan—Dearborn
http://www.umd.umich.edu/

Bentley Historical Library	*Phone*	*(734) 764-3482*
1150 Beal Avenue	*Fax*	*(734) 936-1333*
Ann Arbor, MI 48109-2113	*E-mail*	*bentley.ref@umich.edu*
William L. Clements Library	*Phone*	*(734) 764-2347*
909 S. University Avenue	*Fax*	*(734) 647-0716*
Ann Arbor, MI 48109-1190	*E-mail*	*clements.library@umich.edu*
Special Collections Library	*Phone*	*(734) 764-9377*
711 Harlan Hatcher Graduate	*Fax*	*(734) 764-9368*
Library	*E-mail*	*special.collections@umich.edu*
Ann Arbor, MI 48109-1205		

African American Organizations and Leaders
    http://www.umich.edu/~bhl/bhl/mhchome/afro_org.htm

Church Histories Collection
    http://www.umich.edu/~bhl/bhl/mhchome/denomhis.htm

Civil War Collection
    http://www.clements.umich.edu/Schoff.html

Civil War Collection, Name Index
    http://www.clements.umich.edu/Webguides/Schoff/ScGuidesA.html

Clements Library History
    http://www.clements.umich.edu/History.html

Collections
    http://www.clements.umich.edu/Collections.html

Detroit Collections
    http://www.umich.edu/~bhl/bhl/mhchome/detroit/dettp.htm

Genealogy
    http://www.umich.edu/~bhl/bhl/refhome/genie.htm

Land Ownership Maps and Records
    http://www.umich.edu/~bhl/bhl/mhchome/atlases.htm

Local History Collection
    http://www.umich.edu/~bhl/bhl/mhchome/localhis.htm

Making of America Project
    http://moa.umdl.umich.edu/

Manuscripts Division
    http://www.clements.umich.edu/Manuscripts.html

Map Division
    http://www.clements.umich.edu/Maps.html

Michigan Historical Collections
    http://www.umich.edu/~bhl/bhl/mhchome/mhchome.htm

Newspaper Collection
    http://www.umich.edu/~bhl/bhl/mhchome/news/newspapr.htm

Photographs Division
    http://www.clements.umich.edu/Photos.html

Special Collections
    http://www.lib.umich.edu/spec-coll/collections.html

Women's History Project
    http://www.clements.umich.edu/Gurls/Gurl.html

MINNESOTA

STATE HOME PAGE

North Star! Minnesota Government Information and Services
http://www.state.mn.us/

Minnesota Department of Health, Vital Records
http://www.health.state.mn.us/divs/chs/data/bd_1.htm

STATE HISTORICAL SOCIETY

Minnesota Historical Society
http://www.mnhs.org/

345 Kellogg Blvd. West   *Phone*   *(651) 296-2143*
St. Paul, MN 55102-1906

African American Research
http://www.mnhs.org/library/collections/manuscripts/african.html

African American Stories
http://www.mnhs.org/school/classroom/africam.html

Asian Americans
http://www.mnhs.org/library/collections/manuscripts/african.html

Building and House History
http://www.mnhs.org/library/tips/bldghistory/bldghistory.html

Cemetery Research
http://www.mnhs.org/about/publications/techtalk/TechTalkNovember1996.pdf

City and Telephone Directories
http://www.mnhs.org/library/about/e5.html

Episcopalian Church Records
http://www.mnhs.org/library/collections/manuscripts/epis.html

Genealogy
http://www.mnhs.org/library/tips/family/family.html

Historical Societies and Organizations in Minnesota
http://www.mnhs.org/preserve/mho/index.html

History Center Museum
http://www.mnhs.org/places/historycenter/index.html

Lutheran Church Records
http://www.mnhs.org/library/collections/manuscripts/lutheran.html

Manuscripts
http://www.mnhs.org/library/collections/manuscripts/manuscripts.html

"Minnesota eBooks: Local History Books on the World Wide Web," by Thomas Jay Kemp

http://www.mnhs.org/market/mhspress/mnhistmag/ebooks.html

Minnesota Place Names Index

http://mnplaces.mnhs.org/index.cfm

Minnesota State Archives

http://www.mnhs.org/preserve/records/index.html

Naturalization Records

http://www.mnhs.org/library/about/e2.html

Organizational Records

http://www.mnhs.org/library/collections/manuscripts/org.html

Preservation

http://www.mnhs.org/preserve/treasures/index.html

Preserving Digital Data

http://www.mnhs.org/preserve/records/digitalinfo.html

Preserving Newspapers

http://www.mnhs.org/about/publications/techtalk/TechTalkMarch1997.pdf

Preserving, Storing Photographic Material

http://www.mnhs.org/preserve/records/photographs.html

School District Records

http://www.mnhs.org/preserve/records/infoleaf2.pdf

Township Records

http://www.mnhs.org/preserve/records/infoleaf1.pdf

Vital Records, Index to Death Certificates, 1908–1955

http://people.mnhs.org/dci/Search.cfm

OTHER STATE SITES

OUTSTANDING SITE

University of Minnesota Libraries
http://www1.umn.edu/

Immigration History Research Center (IHRC)

http://www1.umn.edu/ihrc/

311 Andersen Library	*Phone*	*(612) 625-4800*
222-21st Avenue S.	*Fax*	*(612) 626-0018*
Minneapolis, MN 55455-0439	*E-mail*	*ihrc@tc.umn.edu*

African American Collection and Guide
http://special.lib.umn.edu/rare/givens/

African American Genealogy Research
http://wilson.lib.umn.edu/reference/afr-gene.html

African American Newspapers, Published in Minnesota
http://special.lib.umn.edu/rare/givens/bibliography.html#newspapers

African American Research
http://wilson.lib.umn.edu/reference/afrobibl.html

Albanian American Collection
http://www1.umn.edu/ihrc/albanian.htm#top

Armenian American Collection
http://www1.umn.edu/ihrc/armenian.htm#top

Belarusan American Collection
http://www1.umn.edu/ihrc/byelorus.htm#top

British Periodicals, Nineteenth Century
http://mh.cla.umn.edu/britper.html

Carpatho-Rusin American Collection
http://www1.umn.edu/ihrc/carpatho.htm#top

Croatian American Collection
http://www1.umn.edu/ihrc/croatian.htm#top

Czech American Collection
http://www1.umn.edu/ihrc/croatian.htm#top

Estonian American Collection
http://www1.umn.edu/ihrc/estonian.htm#top

Finnish American Collection
http://www1.umn.edu/ihrc/finnish.htm#top

Genealogical Sources at the IHRC
http://www1.umn.edu/ihrc/family.htm#top

Greek American Collection
http://www1.umn.edu/ihrc/greek.htm#top

Hungarian American Collection
http://www1.umn.edu/ihrc/hungaria.htm#top

Immigration History Research Center News. (Serial). Full-text. Vol. 14, Nos. 2/3 (Spring-Summer 1999)– .
http://www1.umn.edu/ihrc/news.htm#newsletter

Italian American Collection
http://www1.umn.edu/ihrc/italian.htm#top

James Ford Bell Library, an Annotated Catalog of Original Source Materials Relating to the History of European Expansion, 1400–1800. Full-text.
http://www.bell.lib.umn.edu/cat/Catalog.html

Jewish American Collection
http://www1.umn.edu/ihrc/eej.htm#top

Latvian American Collection
http://www1.umn.edu/ihrc/latvian.htm#top

Lithuanian American Collection
http://www1.umn.edu/ihrc/lithuani.htm#top

Manuscripts Division
http://special.lib.umn.edu/manuscripts/

Near Eastern American Collection
http://www1.umn.edu/ihrc/neareast.htm#top

Polish American Collection
http://www1.umn.edu/ihrc/polish.htm#top

Romanian American Collection
http://www1.umn.edu/ihrc/romanian.htm#top

Russian American Collection
http://www1.umn.edu/ihrc/russian.htm#top

Serbian American Collection
http://www1.umn.edu/ihrc/serbian.htm#top

Slovak American Collection
http://www1.umn.edu/ihrc/slovak.htm#top

Slovene American Collection
http://www1.umn.edu/ihrc/slovene.htm#top

Special Collections
http://mh.cla.umn.edu/speccoll.html

Ukranian American Collection
http://www1.umn.edu/ihrc/ukrainia.htm#top

University of St. Thomas Libraries
http://www.lib.stthomas.edu/

Department of Special Collections	*Phone*	*(651) 962-5467*
O'Shaughnessy-Frey Library,	*Fax*	*(651) 962-5406*
Mail #5004	*E-mail*	*amkenne1@stthomas.edu*
2115 Summit Avenue		
St. Paul, MN 55105-1096		

Bach-Dunn Collection of Luxembourgiana
http://www.lib.stthomas.edu/special/bachdunn.htm

Celtic Collection
> http://www.lib.stthomas.edu/special/celtic.htm

French Memoir Collection
> http://www.lib.stthomas.edu/special/french_memoir.htm

Manuscript Collections
> http://www.lib.stthomas.edu/special/manuscript/index.html

University Archives
> http://www.lib.stthomas.edu/special/archives/intro_uarchive.htm

MISSISSIPPI

STATE HOME PAGE

Mississippi State Government Home Page
> http://www.ms.gov/

State Department of Health
> http://www.msdh.state.ms.us/msdhsite/index.cfm/4,0,109,html

STATE LIBRARY

Mississippi Library Commission
> http://www.mlc.lib.ms.us

1221 Ellis Avenue	*Phone (601) 961-4111*
P.O. Box 10700	*Fax (601) 354-6257*
Jackson, MS 29289-0700	*E-mail mlcref@mail.mlc.lib.ms.us*

Directory of Mississippi Libraries
> http://www.mlc.lib.ms.us/directory_of_mississippi_libraries/

OTHER STATE SITES

University of Mississippi
> http://www.olemiss.edu/

Department of Archives and Special Collections
> http://www.olemiss.edu/depts/general_library/files/archives/index.html

John D. Williams Library	*Phone (662) 915-7091*
University, MS 38677	

Civil Rights Collections
> http://www.olemiss.edu/depts/general_library/files/archives/guides/civilrights.html

Civil War Collections
> http://www.olemiss.edu/depts/general_library/files/archives/guides/women.html

Electronic Journals
http://www.olemiss.edu/depts/general_library/files/ejournals.html

Women's Studies Collections
http://www.olemiss.edu/depts/general_library/files/archives/guides/women.html

---

OUTSTANDING SITE

University of Southern Mississippi
http://www.usm.edu/

Manuscripts and Archives Department
http://www.lib.usm.edu/~archives/

McCain Library and Archives	*Phone* (601) 266-4345
P.O. Box 5148	*Fax* (601) 266-4409
Hattiesburg, MS 39406-5148	*E-mail spcol@lib.usm.edu*

African American Genealogy
http://www.lib.usm.edu/%7Espcol/msana/msanapath_gen_african.htm

Biography, Mississippi
http://www.lib.usm.edu/%7Espcol/msana/msanapath_miss_pple.htm

Biography, Vertical File Index Headings
http://www.lib.usm.edu/%7Espcol/msana/msanavert_NameA.htm

Center for Oral History and Cultural Heritage
http://www-dept.usm.edu/%7Eocach/

Church Record Collections
http://www.lib.usm.edu/~archives/subj-chu.htm

City Directories
http://www.lib.usm.edu/%7Espcol/msana/city%20direct.html

Civil Rights Collection
http://www.lib.usm.edu/~archives/subj-cr.htm

Civil Rights in Mississippi Digital Archive
http://www.lib.usm.edu/~spcol/digi/collections.htm

Civil Rights in Mississippi Documentation Project
http://www-dept.usm.edu/~mcrohb/

Digitization Resources Online
http://www.lib.usm.edu/~spcol/digi/online.htm

Genealogy Collections
http://www.lib.usm.edu/%7Espcol/msana/msanacoll_gen.htm

Governors of Mississippi
    http://www.lib.usm.edu/%7Espcol/msana/msanapath_miss_gov.htm

Hattiesburg, Mississippi, Bibliography
    http://www.lib.usm.edu/%7Espcol/msana/msanapath_hbrg_bib.htm

Hattiesburg, Mississippi, Collection
    http://www.lib.usm.edu/~archives/subj-hat.htm

Historical Collections
    http://www.lib.usm.edu/~archives/subj-his.htm

History of University of Southern Mississippi Sources
    http://www.lib.usm.edu/%7Espcol/msana/msanapath_miss_usm.htm

Jewish Collections
    http://www.lib.usm.edu/~archives/subj-jew.htm

Jews in the South
    http://www.lib.usm.edu/%7Espcol/msana/msanapath_south_jews.htm

Lumber Company Collections
    http://www.lib.usm.edu/~archives/subj-lum.htm

Manuscripts and Archives Department
    http://www.lib.usm.edu/~archives/

Military Records, Civil War Materials
    http://www.lib.usm.edu/~archives/subj-cw.htm

Military Records, Except Civil War
    http://www.lib.usm.edu/~archives/subj-war.htm

Mississippiana
    http://www.lib.usm.edu/%7Espcol/msana/

Mississippi Politics and Government Collection
    http://www.lib.usm.edu/~archives/subj-pol.htm

Natchez Trace
    http://www.lib.usm.edu/%7Espcol/msana/msanapath_miss_trace.htm

Native Americans Collection
    http://www.lib.usm.edu/~archives/subj-nat.htm

Organizational Records Collections
    http://www.lib.usm.edu/~archives/subj-org.htm

Railroad Collection
    http://www.lib.usm.edu/~archives/subj-rr.htm

Women
    http://www.lib.usm.edu/women.html

MISSOURI

STATE HOME PAGE

Missouri State Government Web Page
http://www.state.mo.us/

Bureau of Vital Records
http://www.health.state.mo.us/BirthAndDeathRecords/BirthAndDeathRecords.html

STATE ARCHIVES

Missouri State Archives
http://www.sos.state.mo.us/archives/

State Information Center   Phone   (573) 751-3280
600 West Main Street   Fax   (573) 526-7333
P.O. Box 1747   E-mail   archref@sosmail.state.mo.us
Jefferson City, MO 65102

African American Marriage Record, Example from 1865
http://www.sos.state.mo.us/archives/resources/africanamerican/intro.asp

Archives Online Catalog
http://msa.library.net/

Chronology of Missouri History
http://www.sos.state.mo.us/archives/history/timeline/timeline1.asp

County Map of Missouri
http://www.sos.state.mo.us/archives/pubs/archweb/map.asp

County Officials
http://www.sos.state.mo.us/BlueBook/0829-0846.pdf#p830

County Records
http://www.sos.state.mo.us/archives/localrecs/

Family History
http://www.sos.state.mo.us/archives/pubs/archweb/history.asp

Historical Listing of Missouri Public Officials
http://www.sos.state.mo.us/archives/history/historicallistings/historicallistings.asp

Judicial Records Program
http://www.sos.state.mo.us/archives/projects/judicialrecords.asp

Land Records Inventory Database
http://www.sos.state.mo.us/CountyInventory/index.asp

Local Records Preservation Program
http://www.sos.state.mo.us/archives/localrecs/program.asp

Military Records
http://www.sos.state.mo.us/archives/pubs/archweb/military.asp

Missouri History
http://www.sos.state.mo.us/archives/history/

Missouri Images from the Past: Teaching with Documents. Full-text
http://www.sos.state.mo.us/archives/education/teaching/modocs.asp

Origin of Missouri Counties
http://www.sos.state.mo.us/archives/history/counties.asp

Photographs
http://www.sos.state.mo.us/archives/resources/photo.asp

Provost Marshal Papers, 1861–1866
http://www.sos.state.mo.us/archives/provost/

St. Louis Circuit Court Case Files Project
http://www.sos.state.mo.us/archives/projects/stlcircuitcourt.asp

Vital Records
http://www.sos.state.mo.us/archives/resources/birthdeath/

World War I Military Service Cards Database
http://www.sos.state.mo.us/ww1/

OTHER STATE SITES

Kansas City Area Archivists
http://www.umkc.edu/KCAA/INDEX.HTM

Western Historical Manuscript	*Phone*	*(816) 235-1543*
Collection	*E-mail*	*WHMCKC@umkc.edu*
302 Newcomb Hall		
University of Missouri-Kansas City		
5100 Rockhill Road		
Kansas City, MO 64110-2499		

Directory of Kansas City Area Archives
http://www.umkc.edu/KCAA/KCAADIR/KCAADIR.HTM

Dusty Shelf. (Serial). Full-text. Vol. 15, No. 2 (1996)– .
http://www.umkc.edu/KCAA/DUSTYSHELF/DUSTY.HTM

Mid-Continent Public Library
http://www.mcpl.lib.mo.us/

Genealogy and Local History Department
http://www.mcpl.lib.mo.us/branch/ge/

317 W. 24 Highway	*Phone*	*(816) 252-7228*
Independence, MO 64050	*E-mail*	*ge@mcpl.lib.mo.us*

American Family Records Association [AFRA], Pedigree Charts. Online Database
http://www.mcpl.lib.mo.us/branch/ge/afra/

Charts and Worksheet Forms, Downloadable Forms
http://www.mcpl.lib.mo.us/branch/ge/forms/

Circulating Library, Catalogs
http://www.mcpl.lib.mo.us/branch/ge/heartland/

Microfiche Collection Catalog
http://www.mcpl.lib.mo.us/branch/ge/microfiche.htm

Microfilm Collection Catalog
http://www.mcpl.lib.mo.us/branch/ge/microfilm.htm

University of Missouri-Kansas City
http://www.umkc.edu/

Library
http://www.umkc.edu/lib/

302 Newcomb Hall   *Phone   (816) 235-1543*
5100 Rockhill Road   *E-mail   WHMCKC@smtpgate.umkc.edu*
Kansas City, MO 64110-2499

Collections Guide
http://www.umkc.edu/whmckc/Collections/cframe.htm

Kansas City Regional Histories Index
http://www.umkc.edu/whmckc/KCRHI/index.htm

Native Sons of Greater Kansas City Archives
http://www.umkc.edu/whmckc/Collections/NSA.HTM

A "Virtual Scrapbook" of Kansas City Regional History
http://www.umkc.edu/whmckc/Scrapbook/Scrapbook.htm

Western Historical Manuscript Collection
http://www.umkc.edu/whmckc/

MONTANA

STATE HOME PAGE

Montana State Home Page
http://www.state.mt.us/css/default.asp

Vital Statistics
http://vhsp.dphhs.state.mt.us/dph_l2.htm

STATE LIBRARY

Montana State Library
http://msl.state.mt.us/

1515 East 6th Avenue   *Phone   (406) 444-3115*
P.O. Box 201800
Helena, MT 59620-1800

Montana Public Libraries
http://msl.state.mt.us/slr/otherlbs.html

STATE HISTORICAL SOCIETY

Montana Historical Society
http://his.state.mt.us/Default.asp

225 North Roberts   *Phone   (406) 444-2694*
P.O. Box 201201   *Fax   (406) 444-2696*
Helena, MT 59620-1201

Collections
http://www.his.state.mt.us/departments/archives/archiv_4.html

Historic Preservation Office
http://his.state.mt.us/departments/shpo/index.html

Lewis and Clark Resources
http://www.discoveringmontana.com/MHSweb/lewisandclark/css/default.asp

Montana, the Magazine of Western History. (Serial). Quarterly. Index. (1951)– .
http://www.his.state.mt.us/departments/magazine/ReferenceIndex.asp

Montana State Archives
http://his.state.mt.us/departments/Library-Archives/index.html

OTHER STATE SITES

University of Montana
http://www.lib.umt.edu/

Archives and Special Collections
http://www.lib.umt.edu/guide/specialcollections.htm

Mansfield Library   *Phone   (406) 243-6866   Reference*
Missoula, MT 59812   *Fax   (406) 243-2060*
                             E-mail   archives@selway.umt.edu

History of the Mansfield Library
http://www.lib.umt.edu/gen/history.htm

Locating Out of Print Books
http://www.lib.umt.edu/guide/oldbooks.htm

Native American Resources
http://www.lib.umt.edu/guide/natamer.htm

Newspapers, Determining Authenticity and Value
http://www.lib.umt.edu/guide/oldpapers.htm

NEBRASKA

STATE HOME PAGE

Nebraska State Home Page
http://www.state.ne.us/

Vital Records, Nebraska Health and Human Services System
http://www.hhs.state.ne.us/ced/nevrinfo.htm

STATE LIBRARY

Nebraska Library Commission
http://www.nlc.state.ne.us/

The Atrium
1200 North Street, Suite 120
Lincoln, NE 68508-2023

Phone   (402) 471-2045
(800) 307-2665 in Nebraska
Fax   (402) 471-2083
E-mail   webspinner@neon.nlc.state.ne.us

Nebraska Library Directory
http://www.nlc.state.ne.us/libdir/libdir.html

NEVADA

STATE HOME PAGE

State of Nevada
http://silver.state.nv.us/

State Office of Vital Records and Statistics
http://health2k.state.nv.us/telephone_directory.htm

STATE LIBRARY AND ARCHIVES

OUTSTANDING SITE

Nevada State Library and Archives
http://dmla.clan.lib.nv.us/docs/nsla/

Nevada State Archives
http://dmla.clan.lib.nv.us/docs/nsla/archives/nsa.htm

100 N. Stewart Street   *Phone*   *(775) 684-3360*
Carson City, NV 89701-4285   *(775) 684-3330*

Bibliography of Nevada
http://dmla.clan.lib.nv.us/docs/nsla/services/nvbiblio.htm

Biographical Files, Vertical File Index
http://dmla.clan.lib.nv.us/docs/nsla/services/vertbios.htm

Carson County, Utah Territory
http://dmla.clan.lib.nv.us/docs/nsla/archives/archival/ccu.htm

Carson County, Utah Territory, First Record Book. Full-text
http://dmla.clan.lib.nv.us/docs/nsla/archives/1record/

County Recorders
http://dmla.clan.lib.nv.us/docs/nsla/services/recorders.htm

Genealogical Resources
http://dmla.clan.lib.nv.us/docs/nsla/services/genealres.htm

Governors' Biographies
http://dmla.clan.lib.nv.us/docs/nsla/archives/gov/govbib.htm

Governors' Records
http://dmla.clan.lib.nv.us/docs/nsla/archives/gov/govguide.htm

Local Governments Records
http://dmla.clan.lib.nv.us/docs/nsla/records/localgov.htm

Mining Claims
http://dmla.clan.lib.nv.us/docs/nsla/archives/mining.htm

Native Americans, Bibliography
http://dmla.clan.lib.nv.us/docs/nsla/fedpubs/nativebib.htm

Naturalization Records
http://dmla.clan.lib.nv.us/docs/nsla/archives/natural.htm

Nevada Executive Branch Agencies, History, Chronology
http://dmla.clan.lib.nv.us/docs/nsla/archives/archival/execbran.htm

Nevada Historical Markers
http://dmla.clan.lib.nv.us/docs/shpo/markers/

Nevada Library Directory
http://dmla.clan.lib.nv.us/docs/nsla/directory/

Nevada Myths
http://dmla.clan.lib.nv.us/docs/nsla/archives/myth/

Nevada Records. (Serial). Full-text. Vol. 1, No. 1 (June 1997)– .
http://dmla.clan.lib.nv.us/docs/dca/newsletters/rec.htm

Newspapers, *Carson Appeal.* (Serial). Index. (1865–66, 1879–80, 1881, 1885–86).
http://dmla.clan.lib.nv.us/docs/nsla/archives/appeal/appeal.htm

Newspapers, Holdings
http://dmla.clan.lib.nv.us/docs/nsla/services/news/news.htm

Newspapers, *Nevada Appeal.* (Serial). Obituary Index. 1996– .
http://dmla.clan.lib.nv.us/docs/nsla/services/obit96/obit96.htm

Newspapers, Nevada Newspaper Indexes
http://dmla.clan.lib.nv.us/docs/nsla/services/newsind.htm

Photograph Collections, Online
http://dmla.clan.lib.nv.us/docs/nsla/archives/photos.htm

Political History of Nevada
http://dmla.clan.lib.nv.us/docs/nsla/archives/political/main.htm

Supreme Court Justices, Official Memorials, Obituary Tributes
http://dmla.clan.lib.nv.us/docs/nsla/archives/archival/memorials/

Supreme Court Records
http://dmla.clan.lib.nv.us/docs/nsla/archives/archival/judbranch.htm

Territorial Records
http://dmla.clan.lib.nv.us/docs/nsla/archives/archival/nvterr.htm

Territorial, State, and County Records
http://dmla.clan.lib.nv.us/docs/nsla/archives/terr.htm

Vital Records
http://dmla.clan.lib.nv.us/docs/nsla/archives/birth.htm

STATE HISTORICAL SOCIETY

Nevada Historical Society
http://dmla.clan.lib.nv.us/docs/museums/reno/his-soc.htm

1650 North Virginia Street   *Phone   (775) 688-1190*
Reno, NV 89503

Biography Files Index; Russell McDonald Collection Index
http://dmla.clan.lib.nv.us/docs/museums/reno/russell/russell.htm

Manuscripts
http://dmla.clan.lib.nv.us/docs/museums/reno/msscoll.htm

Museums in Nevada
http://dmla.clan.lib.nv.us/docs/museums/reno/nvmuseum.htm

Native Americans, Virtual Exhibit
http://dmla.clan.lib.nv.us/docs/museums/reno/expeople/people.htm

Nevada Historical Society Quarterly. (Serial). Quarterly. Table of Contents. Vol. 43, No. 3 (Fall 2000)– .

> http://dmla.clan.lib.nv.us/docs/museums/reno/quarterly.htm

Photograph Collections

> http://dmla.clan.lib.nv.us/docs/museums/reno/photos.htm

OTHER STATE SITES

University of Nevada, Las Vegas

> http://www.unlv.edu/

Special Collections Department

> http://www.library.unlv.edu/speccol/index.html

4505 Maryland Parkway	*Phone*	*(702) 895-2234*
Box 457010	*Fax*	*(702) 895-2253*
University of Nevada, Las Vegas		
Las Vegas, NV 89154-7010		

Manuscript Collections

> http://www.library.unlv.edu/speccol/msspage.html

Nevada Women's Archives

> http://www.library.unlv.edu/women/index.html

Newspaper Collections

> http://www.library.unlv.edu/speccol/newspape.html

Oral History Collections

> http://www.library.unlv.edu/speccol/oralhist.html

Photograph Collections

> http://www.library.unlv.edu/speccol/photos.html

University Archives

> http://www.library.unlv.edu/speccol/univarch.html

University of Nevada, Reno

> http://www.unr.edu/

Special Collections Department

> http://www.library.unr.edu/specoll/

Getchell Library, Room 322	*Phone*	*(702) 784-6500 Ext. 327*
Reno, NV 89557-0044	*Fax*	*(702) 784-4529*
	E-mail	*specoll@unr.edu*

Manuscripts

> http://www.library.unr.edu/specoll/msscoll.html

Native Americans, Great Basin

> http://www.library.unr.edu/specoll/gbi.html

Nevada Women's Archives
http://www.library.unr.edu/specoll/womarchp.html

Photograph Collection
http://www.library.unr.edu/specoll/photos.html

NEW HAMPSHIRE

STATE HOME PAGE

Webster, New Hampshire, State Government Online
http://webster.state.nh.us/

Bureau of Vital Records
http://www.dhhs.state.nh.us/DHHS/BVR/default.htm

STATE ARCHIVES

New Hampshire Division of Records Management and Archives
http://www.state.nh.us/state/index.html

| *71 South Fruit Street* | *Phone* | *(603) 271-2236* |
| *Concord, NH 03301* | *Fax* | *(603) 271-2272* |

Civil War Records
http://www.state.nh.us/state/civil.html

Genealogy
http://www.state.nh.us/state/genealogy.html

Land Title Research
http://www.state.nh.us/state/land.html

STATE LIBRARY

New Hampshire State Library
http://www.state.nh.us/nhsl/

20 Park Street	*Phone*	*(603) 271-6823 Genealogy Desk*
Concord, NH 03301-6314	*Fax*	*(603) 271-2205*
	E-mail	*zmoore@finch.nhsl.lib.nh.us*

History and Genealogy Section
http://www.state.nh.us/nhsl/history/index.html

History of the State Library
http://www.state.nh.us/nhsl/nhslhistory.html

New Hampshire Newspaper Project
http://www.state.nh.us/nhsl/network/newstitle_1.html

STATE GENEALOGICAL SOCIETY

New Hampshire Society of Genealogists
http://nhsog.org/

P.O. Box 2316
Concord, NH 03302-2316

New Hampshire Old Graveyard Association, Master Burial Sites Index
http://nhsog.org/nhoga/index.htm

STATE HISTORICAL SOCIETY

New Hampshire Historical Society
http://www.nhhistory.org/

30 Park Street	*Phone*	*(603) 228-6688*
Concord, NH 03301-6304	*Fax*	*(603) 224-0463*
	E-mail	*nhhslib@aol.com*

Lesson Plans for Teachers
http://www.nhhistory.org/edu/lessonplans/intro.html

Manuscripts
http://www.nhhistory.org/libraryexhibits/manuscriptcollection/manuscript.html

Map Collection
http://www.nhhistory.org/libraryexhibits/maps/maps.html

Museum of New Hampshire History
http://www.nhhistory.org/museum.html

Online Library Catalog
http://nhhistory.library.net/

Tuck Library
http://www.nhhistory.org/library.html

OTHER STATE SITES

Dartmouth College
http://www.dartmouth.edu/

Baker Library
Rauner Special Collections Library
http://www.dartmouth.edu/~library/speccoll/

6065 Webster Hall	*Phone*	*(603) 646-0538*
Hanover, NH 03755-3590	*Fax*	*(603) 646-0447*
	E-mail	*Rauner.Reference@dartmouth.edu*

Alumni Records and Publications
http://www.dartmouth.edu/~cmdc/cdp/arch.alum.html

http://www.dartmouth.edu/~library/speccoll/specoll/FAQresearch.html

"Black Green," Early African American Students at Dartmouth
http://www.dartmouth.edu/~library/speccoll/

Daniel Webster: Dartmouth's Favorite Son
http://www.dartmouth.edu/~dwebster/

Dartmouth History
http://www.dartmouth.edu/~library/speccoll/specoll/shmenhistory.html

The Dartmouth Online. (Serial). "America's Oldest College Newspaper." (1993)– .
http://www.thedartmouth.com/

Dr. Gilman Frost Genealogical Collection
http://www.dartmouth.edu/~speccoll/specoll/FAQFrostCards.html

Hanover, New Hampshire, Town Records
http://www.dartmouth.edu/~speccoll/specoll/frequentlyusedholdings.html#hanover

Local History Collection
http://www.dartmouth.edu/~cmdc/cdp/arch.lochist.html

New Hampshire Manuscript Collection
http://www.dartmouth.edu/~cmdc/cdp/manu.nh.html

Photograph Collections
http://www.dartmouth.edu/~cmdc/cdp/arch.photorecs.html

EXTRAORDINARY SITE
One of the Most Extraordinary Web Sites Online—
Best Example of Online Web Site by a Small Public Library

Lane Memorial Library
http://www.hampton.lib.nh.us/

2 Academy Avenue   *Phone   (603) 926-3368*
Hampton, NH 03842   *Fax   (603) 926-1348*
                            E-mail   bteschek@hampton.lib.nh.us

---

Biographical Resources, Digital Resources
http://www.hampton.lib.nh.us/referenc/Biography/Hampton_Biographies/index.htm

Business History, Digital Resources
http://www.hampton.lib.nh.us/referenc/Hampton_Area_History/Businesses/

Cemetery Records, Digital Resources
http://www.hampton.lib.nh.us/referenc/Hampton_Area_History/Cemeteries/

Church Histories, Digital Resources
http://www.hampton.lib.nh.us/referenc/Hampton_Area_History/Churches/

Disasters, Digital Resources
http://www.hampton.lib.nh.us/referenc/Hampton_Area_History/Disasters/

Genealogy, Digital Resources
http://www.hampton.lib.nh.us/genealog/

Genealogy, Published Genealogies in the Collection
http://www.hampton.lib.nh.us/genealog/books.htm

Hampton, New Hampshire, Area Genealogical Digital Resources
http://www.hampton.lib.nh.us/referenc/Genealogy/Hampton_Genealogy/index.htm

Hampton, New Hampshire, Area Governmental History, Digital Resources
http://www.hampton.lib.nh.us/referenc/Hampton_Area_History/Government/

Hampton, New Hampshire, Area History Digital Resources
http://www.hampton.lib.nh.us/referenc/Hampton_Area_History/

Hampton, New Hampshire, Chronology, 1820–1975
http://www.hampton.lib.nh.us/hampton/history/holman/timeline.htm

Hampton Beach, New Hampshire, Digital Resources
http://www.hampton.lib.nh.us/referenc/Hampton_Area_History/Hampton_Beach/

Lane Library History, Digital Resources
http://www.hampton.lib.nh.us/library/lanehist.htm

Legends, Digital Resources
http://www.hampton.lib.nh.us/referenc/Hampton_Area_History/Legends/

Maps, Digital Resources
http://www.hampton.lib.nh.us/referenc/Hampton_Area_History/Maps/

Military Records, Digital Resources
http://www.hampton.lib.nh.us/referenc/Hampton_Area_History/Wars/

Newspapers, Hampton *Union, Herald Sunday,* and *Atlantic News.* (Serial). Index.
http://www.hampton.lib.nh.us/hampton/history.htm

Rev. Stephen Bachiller, Digital Resources
http://www.hampton.lib.nh.us/hampton/biog/bachilertoc.htm

School History, Digital Resources
http://www.hampton.lib.nh.us/referenc/Hampton_Area_History/Schools/

Transportation, Digital Resources
http://www.hampton.lib.nh.us/referenc/Hampton_Area_History/Transportation/

Travelogues, 19th- and Early 20th-Century Reports, Digital Resources
http://www.hampton.lib.nh.us/referenc/Hampton_Area_History/Travelogues/

Londonderry Project
http://jefferson.village.virginia.edu/~ensp482/erc2g/thesis/text/thshome.html

History of Londonderry
http://jefferson.village.virginia.edu/~ensp482/erc2g/thesis/text/thshome.html

OUTSTANDING SITE

The Old Man of the Mountains
http://www.mutha.com/oldmanmt.html

Cannon Mountain   *Phone   (603) 823-5563*
Franconia Notch, NH 03580

Historic Photographs
http://www.cs.dartmouth.edu/whites/photos/old/oldman.jpg

Photograph Collection
http://www.cs.dartmouth.edu/whites/old_man.html

OUTSTANDING SITE

University of New Hampshire
http://www.unh.edu/

Special Collections Department
http://www.izaak.unh.edu/specoll/

Nesmith Hall   *Phone   (603) 862-2714*
Durham, NH 03824

Civil War Collection
http://www.izaak.unh.edu/specoll/mancoll/civwar.htm

Genealogy Resources
http://www.izaak.unh.edu/specoll/mancoll/genealogy.htm

History, Colonial Collection
http://www.izaak.unh.edu/specoll/mancoll/earlyrep/home.htm

Lewis Stark, Early New Hampshire Imprints Collection
http://www.izaak.unh.edu/specoll/stark.htm

Manuscripts
http://www.izaak.unh.edu/specoll/mancoll.htm

New Hampshire History Collection
http://www.izaak.unh.edu/specoll/mancoll/durham.htm

Newspapers, Historical Collection
http://www.izaak.unh.edu/specoll/mancoll/nhnews.htm

Photographic Collections
http://www.izaak.unh.edu/specoll/mancoll/visual.htm

Shaker Materials
http://www.izaak.unh.edu/specoll/mancoll/shaker.htm

Town and Church Records
http://www.izaak.unh.edu/specoll/mancoll/townrecs.htm

University of New Hampshire Archives
http://www.izaak.unh.edu/archives/

University of New Hampshire Museum
http://www.izaak.unh.edu/museum/

World War II Collection
http://www.izaak.unh.edu/specoll/mancoll/WWII.htm

NEW JERSEY

STATE HOME PAGE

State of New Jersey Home Page
http://www.state.nj.us/

New Jersey Vital Records
http://www.state.nj.us/health/vital/vital.htm

STATE ARCHIVES

Division of Archives and Records Management
http://www.state.nj.us/state/darm/index.html

State Library Building   Phone   (609) 292-6260
225 West State Street, Level 2   Fax   (609) 396-2454
P.O. Box 307   E-mail   feedback@sos.state.nj.us
Trenton, NJ 08625-0307

STATE LIBRARY

New Jersey State Library
http://www.njstatelib.org/

Genealogy and Local History Collection
http://www.njstatelib.org/aboutus/SGIS/libgene.htm

185 West State Street   Phone   (609) 292-6274 Genealogy
P.O. Box 520   Fax   (609) 984-7901
Trenton, NJ 08625-0520   E-mail   rpreece@njstatelib.org

Afro-Americans in New Jersey History
    http://www.njstatelib.org/cyberdesk/digidox/digidox9.htm

Genealogy Resources for New Jersey
    http://www.njstatelib.org/cyberdesk/genealog.htm

History of New Jersey
    http://www.njstatelib.org/cyberdesk/gbgday1.htm#chronology

Legal Resources for New Jersey
    http://www.njstatelib.org/cyberdesk/law.htm#njlaw

Maps of New Jersey
    http://www.njstatelib.org/cyberdesk/gbgday1.htm#maps

New Jersey Libraries
    http://www2.njstatelib.org/njlib/ref/njlibs.htm

New Jersey Union List of Serials
    http://www2.njstatelib.org/njlib/njuls/index.htm

Online Library Catalog
    http://www.njstatelib.org/cyberdesk/newcat.htm

OTHER STATE SITES

Joint Free Public Library of Morristown and Morris Township
    http://www.jfpl.org/

1 Miller Road   *Phone*   *(973) 538-3473*
Morristown, NJ 07960   *E-mail*   *jochem@main.morris.org*

History Now (Digital Local History) Project
    http://www.jfpl.org/historynow/index.html

History of the Library
    http://www.jfpl.org/history.htm

Local History and Genealogy Department
    http://www.jfpl.org/gene.htm

Online Library Catalog
    http://web2.morris.org/

Thomas Nast Society
    http://www.jfpl.org/nast.htm

New Jersey Preservation Organizations
    http://www.preservationdirectory.com/preservationorganizations_nj.html

Newark Public Library

http://www.npl.org/

New Jersey Information Center   *Phone*   *(973) 733-7775*
3rd Floor, Main Library   *Fax*   *(973) 733-4870*
5 Washington Street
Newark, NJ 07102

New Jersey Information Center (Local History Material)

http://www.npl.org/Pages/Collections/njic.html

Princeton University

http://www.princeton.edu/index.shtml

Princeton University Library

http://infoshare1.princeton.edu:2003/

One Washington Road   *Phone*   *(609) 258-3184*
Princeton, NJ 08544-2098   *E-mail*   *mmsherry@princeton.edu*

Population Research Library

http://opr.princeton.edu/library/

21 Prospect Avenue   *Phone*   *(609) 258-4874*
Princeton, NJ 08544-2091   *E-mail*   *popindex@opr.princeton.edu*

Alumni Index, Graduate School, 1839–1998

http://www.princeton.edu/mudd/search/graduate.html

Alumni Index, Undergraduates, 1748–1920

http://www.princeton.edu/mudd/search/alumni.html

Commencement Records, 1748–

http://infoshare1.princeton.edu:2003/libraries/firestone/rbsc/finding_aids/commence.html

Delafield Family Papers

http://infoshare1.princeton.edu:2003/libraries/firestone/rbsc/aids/delafield.html

Maps, Historic

http://libserv3.princeton.edu/rbsc2/portfolio/hm/index.html

Maps, New Jersey Geological Survey Atlas Sheets

http://gisserver.princeton.edu/njgsatlas.html

Maps and Aerial Photographs, Princeton Campus

http://gisserver.princeton.edu/campusmaps.html

Nassau Hall Bible Society, 1813–1877

http://infoshare1.princeton.edu:2003/libraries/firestone/rbsc/finding_aids/bible.html

New Jerseyana

http://www.princeton.edu/~ferguson/h-mo-pr.html#njana

Office of Population Research

http://opr.princeton.edu/

Online Catalog
http://catalog.princeton.edu/cgi-bin/Pwebrecon.cgi?DB=localandPAGE=First

Population Index
http://popindex.princeton.edu/

Rare Books and Special Collections Department Guide
http://www.princeton.edu/~ferguson/handbook.html

University Archives
http://infoshare1.princeton.edu:2003/libraries/firestone/rbsc/finding_aids/archives.html

World War II, Letters and Diaries of Princetonians in Service
http://infoshare1.princeton.edu:2003/libraries/firestone/rbsc/finding_aids/letters.html

Seton Hall University
http://www.shu.edu/

Walsh Library
http://library.shu.edu/

Special Collections Center
http://library.shu.edu/SpecColl.htm

Walsh Library, First Floor   *Phone   (973) 761-9476*
400 South Orange Avenue   *E-mail   DeloziAl@shu.edu*
South Orange, NJ 07079-2696

New Jersey Catholic Historical   *Phone   (973) 275-2773*
*   Records Commission*   *E-mail   MahoneJo@shu.edu*
History Department
South Orange, NJ 07079-2696

Archdiocese of Newark
http://library.shu.edu/SpecColl-anc.htm

New Jersey Catholic Records Newsletter
http://library.shu.edu/catholicrec/njhrc.htm

NEW MEXICO

STATE HOME PAGE

State of New Mexico Home Page
http://www.state.nm.us/

New Mexico Vital Records
http://dohewbs2.health.state.nm.us/VitalRec/Birth%20Certificates.htm

STATE ARCHIVES

Commission on Public Records
State Archives and Records Center
http://www.nmcpr.state.nm.us/

1205 Camino Carlos Rey   *Phone   (505) 576-7908*
Santa Fe, NM 87505   *Fax   (505) 576-7909*

Genealogy
http://www.nmcpr.state.nm.us/archives/ancestors.htm

Quipu. (Serial). Quarterly. Vol. 4 (January 1999)– .
http://www.nmcpr.state.nm.us/pubs/publications_forms.htm

STATE LIBRARY

New Mexico State Library
http://www.stlib.state.nm.us/

1275 Camino Carlos Rey   *Phone   (505) 827-4083*
Santa Fe, NM 87501-2777   *Fax   (505) 827-3888*
                                   E-mail   Southwest@stlib.state.nm.us

Bibliography of New Mexico
http://www.stlib.state.nm.us/libraryservices/statepubs/bib.html

Biography, Clipping Files List
http://www.stlib.state.nm.us/libraryservices/statepubs/sg11.html

City Directories
http://www.stlib.state.nm.us/libraryservices/statepubs/sg3.html

Hitchhiker, Newsletter
http://www.stlib.state.nm.us/hiker2/oldhiker.html

New Mexico Library Directory
http://www.stlib.state.nm.us/libraryservices/lsmain.html

STATE GENEALOGICAL SOCIETY

New Mexico Genealogical Society
http://www.nmgs.org/

P.O. Box 8283   *E-mail   info@nmgs.org*
Albuquerque, NM 87198-8283

Catholic Church Records in New Mexico, Online Finding Aid
http://www.nmgs.org/Chrchs-intro.htm

Colfax County Marriages, 1889–1993, 1897–1901
http://www.nmgs.org/artcolmar.htm

Grant County Marriages, 1868–1872
http://www.nmgs.org/artGrantmar1868.htm

Grant County Marriages, 1909
http://www.nmgs.org/artGrantmar1909.htm

Grant County Marriages, 1910
http://www.nmgs.org/artGrantmar1910.htm

Luna County Marriages, 1909–1912
http://www.nmgs.org/artlunamar.htm

Mora County Guardianships, 1882–1885
http://www.nmgs.org/artmoraguard.htm

Mora County Marriages, 1875–1890
http://www.nmgs.org/artmrgs-mora.htm

New Mexico Genealogist. (Serial). Selected Articles, Full-text.
http://www.nmgs.org/znmgs.htm

Rio Arriba County Marriages, 1902–1904
http://www.nmgs.org/artmrgs-ra.htm

Valencia County Death Register, 1907–1909
http://www.nmgs.org/artVal-deaths.htm

Valencia County Probate Abstracts, 1882–1888
http://www.nmgs.org/artvalpro.htm

OTHER STATE SITES

OUTSTANDING SITE

Carnuél, New Mexico, and the Villages East of Albuquerque
http://home.earthlink.net/~carnuel/index.html

E-mail   carnuel@earthlink.net

Baptismal Records, Carnuél and Towns East of Albuquerque
http://home.earthlink.net/~carnuel/baptrec.html

Confirmations, 1876
http://home.earthlink.net/~carnuel/confrec.html

Marriages, 1726–1855
http://home.earthlink.net/~carnuel/marrec.html

Census, 1763. Land Grants
http://home.earthlink.net/~carnuel/1763set.html

Census, 1819. Land Grants
http://home.earthlink.net/~carnuel/1819Gen.html

Census, 1860
http://home.earthlink.net/~carnuel/1860Census.html

Census, 1870
http://home.earthlink.net/~carnuel/1870Census.html

Deaths, 1726–1776
http://home.earthlink.net/~carnuel/deathrec.html

New Mexico Magazine Online
http://www.nmmagazine.com/

Lew Wallace Building   *Phone   (505) 827-7447*
495 Old Santa Fe Trail
Santa Fe, NM 87501

Brief History of New Mexico
http://www.nmmagazine.com/features/nmhistory.html

Chronology of State History
http://www.nmmagazine.com/features/memorias.html

New Mexico State University
http://www.nmsu.edu/

Library
http://lib.nmsu.edu/index.html

Rio Grande Historical Collections
http://archives.nmsu.edu/

P.O. Box 30006   *Phone   (505) 646-3839*
Las Cruces, NM 88003-8006   *Fax   (505) 646-7477*
                      E-mail   archives@lib.nmsu.edu

Archivo General de Notarias del Estado de Durango, Mexico
http://archives.nmsu.edu/rghc/find.html

Archivos Históricos del Arzobispado de Durango (AHAD), Preliminary Guide
http://archives.nmsu.edu/rghc/durango/abtguide.html

Fabian Garcia, Pioneer Horticulturist
http://archives.nmsu.edu/rghc/exhibits/garcia.html

Genealogy Resources New Mexico State University Library
http://lib.nmsu.edu/resources/guides/other/geneal

Inventory of the Family History of the Alotees of Jicarilla Apaches, 1913
http://elibrary.unm.edu/oanm/NmLcU/nmlcu1%23ms378/

Las Cruces *Sun News*. (Newspaper). Index. (1995)– .
http://lib.nmsu.edu/resources/sunnews/intro.html

New Mexico State University Authors (Bibliography)
http://lib.nmsu.edu/depts/specol/authors.html

Newspapers, New Mexico Online Newspapers
http://lib.nmsu.edu/resources/papers.html#loc

Online Archive of New Mexico (Archival Finding Aids)
http://elibrary.unm.edu/oanm/

Online Library Catalog
http://libcat.nmsu.edu/webvoy.htm

Oral History Collections
http://archives.nmsu.edu/rghc/index/Oral.html

Photograph Collections
http://archives.nmsu.edu/rghc/photo/photos.html

Women, Southwestern Women, Books in the New Mexico State University Library
http://lib.nmsu.edu/resources/guides/swwomen/swwomen.html

University of Arizona

Special Collections Department
Library
P.O. Box 210055   *Phone*   *(520) 621-4345*
Tucson, AZ 85721-0055   *E-mail*   *stuartg@u.arizona.edu*

Archival Guides
http://www.library.arizona.edu/images/swja/findingaids/findingaids.htm

Arizona Jewish Pioneers
http://www.library.arizona.edu/images/swja/arizona.htm

Bibliography
http://www.library.arizona.edu/images/swja/suggreads.htm

Jewish Pioneers of the Southwest
http://www.library.arizona.edu/images/swja/pioneers.htm

Leona G. and David Bloom Southwest Jewish Archives
http://www.library.arizona.edu/images/swja/swjalist.html

Manuscript Collections
http://dizzy.library.arizona.edu/branches/spc/homepage/alphlist/alphlist.htm

New Mexico Jewish Pioneers
http://www.library.arizona.edu/images/swja/newmexico.htm

Southwest Jewish History. (Serial). Vol. 1 (Fall 1992–Winter 1995).
http://www.library.arizona.edu/images/swja/newsletter.html

Synagogues of the Southwest
http://www.library.arizona.edu/images/swja/synagogues.htm

West Texas Jewish Pioneers
http://www.library.arizona.edu/images/swja/westtexas.htm

University of New Mexico
http://www.unm.edu

Library
http://elibrary.unm.edu/

Center for Southwest Research
http://www.unm.edu/~cswrref/enghome.html

University of New Mexico Library   *Phone*   *(505) 277-6451*
Albuquerque, NM 87131-1466   *E-mail*   *cswrref@unm.edu*

Chaco Archives
http://www.unm.edu/~cswrref/engchac.html

Manuscripts Collection Guide
http://www.unm.edu/~cswrref/engmanuscripts.html

Online Library Catalog, LIBROS
http://libros.unm.edu/

Spanish Colonial Research Center
http://www.unm.edu/~cswrref/engscrc.html

University Archives
http://www.unm.edu/~unmarchv/unmarchv.html

NEW YORK

STATE HOME PAGE

New York State Home Page
http://www.state.ny.us/

Department of Vital Records
http://www.health.state.ny.us/nysdoh/consumer/vr.htm

STATE ARCHIVES

OUTSTANDING SITE

State Archives and Records Administration (SARA)
http://www.sara.nysed.gov/

New York State Archives   *Phone*   *(518) 474-8955*
New York State Education   *Fax*   *(518) 473-7573*
*   Department*
Albany, NY 12230

African American Records
http://www.sara.nysed.gov/

Canal Records
http://www.sara.nysed.gov/holding/aids/canal/content.htm

Corrections Department Records
http://www.sara.nysed.gov/holding/aids/correct/content.htm

Criminal Appeals, Trials, and Pardons
http://www.sara.nysed.gov/holding/fact/leaf9.htm

Genealogical Sources in SARA
http://www.sara.nysed.gov/holding/fact/genea-fa.htm

Guide to Records in the New York State Archives
http://www.sara.nysed.gov/pubs/guideabs.htm

Local Records, Microfilm
http://www.sara.nysed.gov/holding/fact/local-mi.htm

Military Records
http://www.sara.nysed.gov/holding/fact/genea-fa.htm

Native American Records
http://www.sara.nysed.gov/holding/aids/native/content.htm

Naturalization Records
http://www.sara.nysed.gov/holding/fact/natur-fa.htm

New York House of Refuge Records
http://www.sara.nysed.gov/holding/aids/school/content.htm

Photograph Collections
http://www.sara.nysed.gov/holding/aids/photo/content.htm

Probate Records
http://www.sara.nysed.gov/holding/fact/prob-fac.htm

Vital Records
http://www.sara.nysed.gov/holding/aids/native/content.htm

War Council, New York State
http://www.sara.nysed.gov/holding/aids/wwii/content.htm

Women, Records Pertaining to
http://www.sara.nysed.gov/holding/aids/native/content.htm

STATE LIBRARY

New York State Library
http://www.nysl.nysed.gov/

Empire State Plaza   *Phone*   *(518) 474-6282*
Cultural Education Center   *E-mail   refserv@unix2.nysed.gov*
Albany, NY 12230

Adoption Records
http://www.nysl.nysed.gov/genealogy/adopt.htm

African American Bibliographies
http://www.nysl.nysed.gov/genealogy/traceafr.htm

Cartography Collection
http://www.nysl.nysed.gov/mssc/maps.htm

Census Records
http://www.nysl.nysed.gov/genealogy/nyscens.htm

City Directories
http://www.nysl.nysed.gov/genealogy/citydir.htm

Daughters of the American Revolution Records
http://www.nysl.nysed.gov/genealogy/dar.htm

Gazetteer
http://www.nysl.nysed.gov/genealogy/fndplace.htm

Genealogy
http://www.nysl.nysed.gov/gengen.htm

Genealogy Card Indexes
http://www.nysl.nysed.gov/genealogy/cardind.htm

Loyalist Records
http://www.nysl.nysed.gov/genealogy/loyalist.htm

Manuscripts and Special Collections Department
http://www.nysl.nysed.gov/mssdesc.htm

Manuscripts Finding Aids
http://www.nysl.nysed.gov/msscfa/fa_toc.htm

New Netherland Project
http://www.nnp.org/

New York State Newspaper Project
http://www.nysl.nysed.gov/nysnp/

Vital Records
http://www.nysl.nysed.gov/genealogy/vitrec.htm

OTHER STATE SITES

OUTSTANDING SITE

New York Public Library
http://www.nypl.org/

Milstein Division of United States History, Local History, and Genealogy
http://www.nypl.org/research/chss/lhg/genea.html

5th Avenue and 42nd Street   *Phone   (212) 930-0828*
New York, NY 10018-2788

Schomburg Center for Research in Black Culture
http://www.nypl.org/research/sc/sc.html

515 Malcolm X Boulevard   *Phone   (212) 491-2200*
New York, NY 10037-1801

Biographical Sources
http://www.nypl.org/research/chss/grd/resguides/biog.html

Digital Schomburg, Nineteenth-Century African American Women Writers
http://digital.nypl.org/schomburg/writers_aa19/

Digital Schomburg, Nineteenth-Century Images of African Americans
http://digital.nypl.org/schomburg/images_aa19/

Fernando Ortiz Collection: A Bibliography of Afro-Cuban Material
http://digital.nypl.org/schomburg/ortiz/ortizfront.htm

Genealogy Research
http://www.nypl.org/research/chss/lhg/research.html

Manuscripts and Archives Division
http://www.nypl.org/research/chss/spe/rbk/mss.html

Map Division
http://www.nypl.org/research/chss/map/map.html

Mormon History
http://www.nypl.org/research/chss/grd/resguides/mormon.html

Obituaries
http://www.nypl.org/research/chss/grd/resguides/obit.html

Slavic and Baltic Division
http://www.nypl.org/research/chss/slv/slav.balt.html

Spanish-American War Records
http://www.nypl.org/research/chss/grd/resguides/spanamerwar/index.html

State University of New York, Oswego
http://www.oswego.edu/

Penfield Library
http://www.oswego.edu/library/

Special Collections Department
http://www.oswego.edu/library/archives/index.html

7060 State Route 104   *E-mail   archives@oswego.edu*
Oswego, NY 13126

Local History Collection
http://www.oswego.edu/library/archives/LocalHistory.html

Oswego County Historical Society Journal. (Serial). Index. (1899–1977).
http://www.oswego.edu/library/archives/ochsj.html

Oswego County Newspaper Index, 1820–1855+
http://www.oswego.edu/library/archives/newspp.html

NORTH CAROLINA

STATE HOME PAGE

North Carolina Home Page
http://www.sips.state.nc.us/nchome.html

North Carolina Center for Health Statistics, How to Request Vital Records
http://www.schs.state.nc.us/SCHS/certificates/

Roster of North Carolina Registrars of Deeds
http://www.iog.unc.edu/organizations/regdeeds/rod.htm

STATE ARCHIVES

OUTSTANDING SITE

North Carolina Division of Archives and History
http://www.ah.dcr.state.nc.us/

109 East Jones Street
Raleigh, NC 27601-2807

Phone   (919) 733-3952
Fax   (919) 733-1354
E-mail   archives@ncmail.net

Mailing Address:
4614 Mail Service Center
Raleigh, NC 27699-4614

County Records
http://www.ah.dcr.state.nc.us/sections/archives/arch/county.htm

Friends of the Archives
http://www.ah.dcr.state.nc.us/affiliates/foa/foa.htm

Genealogical Research
http://www.ah.dcr.state.nc.us/sections/archives/arch/gen-res.htm

Historic Preservation, Local Commissions
http://www.hpo.dcr.state.nc.us/commstaf.htm

Manuscripts, Guide to Finding Aids
http://www.ah.dcr.state.nc.us/sections/archives/arch/FindingAids/findaids.htm

Military Records
http://www.ah.dcr.state.nc.us/sections/archives/arch/military.htm

National Register of Historic Places in North Carolina
http://www.hpo.dcr.state.nc.us/nrhome.htm

North Carolina Historical Commission
http://www.ah.dcr.state.nc.us/nc-hist-com.htm

STATE LIBRARY

North Carolina State Library
http://statelibrary.dcr.state.nc.us/

Genealogical Services Department	*Phone*	*(919) 733-2222*
109 East Jones Street	*Fax*	*(919) 733-5679*
Raleigh, NC 27601-2807		

Mailing Address:
4647 Mail Service Center
Raleigh, NC 27699-4647

County History
http://statelibrary.dcr.state.nc.us/iss/gr/counties.htm

Genealogy, Getting Started
http://statelibrary.dcr.state.nc.us/iss/gr/starting.htm

North Carolina Genealogical Research Guide, Tar Heel Tracks
http://statelibrary.dcr.state.nc.us/iss/gr/tracks.htm

Online Library Catalog
http://statelibrary.dcr.state.nc.us/catalog.htm

STATE GENEALOGICAL SOCIETY

North Carolina Genealogical Society
http://www.rootsweb.com/~ncgs/index.html
P.O. Box 22
Greenville, NC 27835-0022

North Carolina Genealogical and Historical Societies
http://www.rootsweb.com/~ncgs/local.html

OTHER STATE SITES

Appalachian State University
http://www.appstate.edu/

Belk Library
http://www.library.appstate.edu/

Special Collections Department
http://www.library.appstate.edu/lib/archives/specialcollections.html

P.O. Box 32026   *Phone   (704) 262-4041*
Boone, NC 28608-2026   *Fax   (704) 262-2553*
                                                     E-mail   hayfj@appstate.edu

Appalachian Studies Bibliography
http://www.library.appstate.edu/appcoll/apsbib.html

Melungeon History, Research, and Resources
http://www.library.appstate.edu/appcoll/research_aids/Melungeons.html

Methodism in Western North Carolina
http://www.library.appstate.edu/appcoll/research_aids/methodism.html

Migration from Appalachia, Central Appalachians in Midwestern Cities
http://www.library.appstate.edu/appcoll/research_aids/migration.html

Native Americans of the Southeast
http://www.library.appstate.edu/appcoll/research_aids/native_americans.html

Online Library Catalog
http://www.library.appstate.edu/appcoll/research_aids/native_americans.html

Rutherford County Resources
http://www.library.appstate.edu/appcoll/research_aids/Rutherford.html

W. L. Eury Appalachian Collection
http://www.library.appstate.edu/appcoll/

Women, Life Narratives of Women in Appalachian North Carolina
http://www.library.appstate.edu/appcoll/research_aids/women_narratives.html

Charlotte, Mecklenburg County Public Library
http://www.plcmc.lib.nc.us/

310 N. Tryon Street   *Phone   (704) 336-2980*
Charlotte, NC 28202   *E-mail   ncr@plcmc.org*

Carolina Room
http://www.plcmc.lib.nc.us/libLoc/mainCarolina.htm

Mary Brevard Alexander Howell Papers
http://www.plcmc.lib.nc.us/libLoc/howell.htm

Online Library Catalog
http://www.plcmc.lib.nc.us/catalog/default.htm

Surname and Biography Files
http://www.plcmc.lib.nc.us/libLoc/mainCarolinaSurnames.htm

East North Carolina University
http://www.ecu.edu/

J. Y. Joyner Library
http://www.lib.ecu.edu/

East Fifth Street	*Phone*	*(252) 328-6601*
Greenville, NC 27858-4353	*Fax*	*(252) 328-4348*
	E-mail	*yorkm@mail.ecu.edu*

Census Indexes
http://www.lib.ecu.edu/NCCollPCC/Oldcensu.htm

Daily Reflector (Newspaper). Index. (1882–1906).
http://www.lib.ecu.edu/NCCollPCC/ERindxabt.htm

Genealogy Collection
http://www.lib.ecu.edu/NCCollPCC/genealogy.html

Manuscript Collection Guide
http://www.lib.ecu.edu/SpclColl/aidslist.html

Newspaper Clipping File
http://www.lib.ecu.edu/NCCollPCC/clipping.html

Newspapers, North Carolina
http://www.lib.ecu.edu/NCCollPCC/newspapers.html

North Carolina Collection
http://www.lib.ecu.edu/NCCollPCC/ncchome.htm

North Carolina Periodical Index
http://www.lib.ecu.edu/NCCollPCC/scope2.html

Photo Archives
http://www.lib.ecu.edu/NCCollPCC/PCCweb/RKphoto/Archives.html

Pitt County Compendium, Resources for Genealogists
http://www.lib.ecu.edu/NCCollPCC/PCCweb/PCChome.html

Pitt's Past. County History Column in the *Greenville Times* (Newspaper). (1983–1999).
http://www.lib.ecu.edu/NCCollPCC/PittPast.html

Old Buncombe County Genealogical Society
http://www.obcgs.com/

Innsbruck Mall	*E-mail OBCGS@buncombe.main.nc.us*
85 Tunnel Road, Suite 22	
Asheville, NC 28805	

Mailing Address:
P.O. Box 2122
Asheville, NC 28802-2122

Cemetery Records, Index
http://www.obcgs.com/cemeteries.htm

Family Bible Records, Index
http://www.obcgs.com/bibles.html

Marriage Records, Index
http://www.obcgs.com/wedindx.htm

Probate Records, Abstracts
http://www.obcgs.com/wills.htm

Revolutionary War Pension Records
http://www.obcgs.com/revolution.htm

Society of North Carolina Archivists
http://www.rtpnet.org/~snca/

P.O. Box 20448   *E-mail   paul_kiel@ncsu.edu*
Raleigh, NC 27619

North Carolina Archivist. (Newsletter). Full-text. (1996)– .
http://www.rtpnet.org/~snca/publica.htm

E X T R A O R D I N A R Y   S I T E
One of the Most Extraordinary Web Sites Online
University of North Carolina at Chapel Hill
http://www.unc.edu/

Library
http://www.lib.unc.edu/

Manuscripts Department
http://www.lib.unc.edu/mss/index.html

CB 3926 Wilson Library   *Phone*   *(919) 962-1345*
Chapel Hill, NC 27514-8890   *Fax*   *(919) 962-9354*
                                      E-mail *archives@email.unc.edu*

North Carolina Collection
http://www.lib.unc.edu/ncc/index.html

CB 3930 Wilson Library   *Phone*   *(919) 962-1172*
Chapel Hill, NC 27514-8890   *E-mail* *nccref@email.unc.edu*

University Archives
http://www.lib.unc.edu/mss/uars/index.html

CB 3926 Wilson Library   *Phone*   *(919) 962-0043*
Chapel Hill, NC 27514-8890   *Fax*   *(919) 962-4452*
                                      E-mail *archives@email.unc.edu*

African American Documentary Resources in North Carolina
http://www.upress.virginia.edu/epub/pyatt/

The Church in the Southern Black Community
http://docsouth.unc.edu/church/index.html

Documenting the American South
http://docsouth.unc.edu/

First-Person Narratives
http://docsouth.unc.edu/fpn/fpn.html

Library of Southern Literature
http://docsouth.unc.edu/southlit/southlit.html

Manuscripts, Online Finding Aids
http://www.lib.unc.edu/mss/finding.html

North American Slave Narratives
http://docsouth.unc.edu/neh/neh.html

North Carolina and the Great War
http://docsouth.unc.edu/wwi/index.html

North Carolina Experience, Beginnings to 1940
http://docsouth.unc.edu/nc/index.html

Southern Historical Collections
http://www.lib.unc.edu/mss/shcgl.html

Southern Homefront, 1861–1865
http://docsouth.unc.edu/imls/index.html

NORTH DAKOTA

STATE HOME PAGE

North Dakota Home Page
http://www.state.nd.us/

North Dakota Cities
http://discovernd.com/government/city.html

North Dakota Counties
http://discovernd.com/government/county.html

North Dakota Vital Records
http://www.vitalnd.com/

STATE HISTORICAL SOCIETY

State Historical Society of North Dakota
http://www.state.nd.us/hist/index.html

612 East Boulevard Avenue	*Phone*	*(710) 328-2666*
Bismarck, ND 58505-0830	*Fax*	*(710) 328-3710*
	E-mail	*histsoc@state.nd.us*

State Archives and State Research Library
http://www.state.nd.us/hist/sal.htm

Phone	*(710) 328-2091*
Fax	*(710) 328-3710*
E-mail	*archives@state.nd.us*

State Historical Records Advisory Board
http://www.state.nd.us/hist/shrab.htm

Phone	*(710) 328-2668*
E-mail	*ccmail.gnewborg@ranch.state.nd.us*

Biography Files, North Dakota Pioneers
http://www.state.nd.us/hist/infwpa.htm

Census
http://www.state.nd.us/hist/infcens.htm

Church Records
http://www.state.nd.us/hist/infomilitary.htm

Genealogical Resources
http://www.state.nd.us/hist/infgen.htm

History
http://www.state.nd.us/hist/history.htm

Land Records
http://www.state.nd.us/hist/infland.htm

Military Records
http://www.state.nd.us/hist/infomilitary.htm

Naturalization Records
http://www.state.nd.us/hist/infnat.htm

Newspapers
http://www.state.nd.us/hist/infnews.htm

North Dakota History, Journal of the Northern Plains (Serial). Table of Contents. Vol. 63, No. 1 (Winter 1996)– .
http://www.state.nd.us/hist/ndh.htm

Oral Histories
http://www.state.nd.us/hist/infoh.htm

Photo Collections
   http://www.state.nd.us/hist/infphot.htm

Plains Talk. Newsletter.
   http://www.state.nd.us/hist/Plainstalk.htm

Vital Records
   http://www.state.nd.us/hist/infvit.htm

OTHER STATE SITES

North Dakota State University
   http://www.ndsu.nodak.edu/

North Dakota State University Libraries
   http://www.lib.ndsu.nodak.edu/

| *P.O. Box 5599* | *Phone* | *(701) 231-8886* |
| *Fargo, ND 58105-5599* | *Fax* | *(701) 231-7138* |

Germans from Russia Heritage Collection
   http://www.lib.ndsu.nodak.edu/gerrus/

| | *Phone* | *(701) 231-8416* |
| | *Fax* | *(701) 231-7138* |

Institute for Regional Studies
   http://www.lib.ndsu.nodak.edu/ndirs/

	Phone	*(701) 231-8914*
	Fax	*(701) 231-7138*
	E-mail	*archives@www.lib.ndsu.nodak.edu*

Bibliography, Germans from Russia
   http://www.lib.ndsu.nodak.edu/grhc/info/bibliography/index.html

Biography and Genealogy Collections
   http://www.lib.ndsu.nodak.edu/reference/ndakotahist.html

Cass County, North Dakota, Marriage Records
   http://www.lib.ndsu.nodak.edu/ndirs/collections/manuscripts/casscounty/index.html

Census, 1885 Census Index
   http://www.lib.ndsu.nodak.edu/ndirs/bio&genealogy/dakterr1885census.html

Census Records
   http://www.lib.ndsu.nodak.edu/ndirs/bio&genealogy/ndfed&terrcensus.html

Family Reunions, Germans from Russia
   http://www.lib.ndsu.nodak.edu/grhc/outreach/reunion/index.htm

German Villages and Maps
   http://www.lib.ndsu.nodak.edu/grhc/history_culture/maps_villages/index.html

History, Germans from Russia
   http://www.lib.ndsu.nodak.edu/grhc/history_culture/history/index.html

Naturalization Records Index
http://www.lib.ndsu.nodak.edu/ndirs/bio&genealogy/ndnatrecords.html

Newspaper Articles about Germans from Russia, Full-text
http://www.lib.ndsu.nodak.edu/grhc/media/newspapers/index.html

North Dakota Biography Index
http://www.lib.ndsu.nodak.edu/ndirs/bio&genealogy/ndbioindex.html?PHPSESSID=
e1dc463e36f631ebdb2a2910bcbbe8ee

Obituary Index, *Fargo Forum,* (1985–1995)
http://www.lib.ndsu.nodak.edu/ndirs/bio&genealogy/forumobits.html

University Archives
http://www.lib.ndsu.nodak.edu/archives/

World War II Veterans, NDSU
http://www.lib.ndsu.nodak.edu/archives/WW2/index.html

University of North Dakota
http://www.und.nodak.edu/

Chester Fritz Library
http://www.und.edu/dept/library/

P.O. Box 9000	*Phone*	*(701) 777-4629*	*Reference*
Grand Forks, ND 58202		*(701) 777-4625*	*Special Collections*
	Fax	*(701) 777-3319*	
	E-mail	*library@mail.und.nodak.edu*	

Family History and Genealogy Room
http://www.und.edu/dept/library/Collections/Famhist/home.html

Family History and Genealogy Room, Guide to Collections
http://www.und.nodak.edu/dept/library/Collections/Famhist/fhguide.html#church

Norwegian Bygdebøker
http://www.und.nodak.edu/dept/library/Collections/Famhist/bygdebok.html

Special Collections Department
http://www.und.edu/dept/library/Collections/spk.html

OHIO

STATE HOME PAGE

Ohio Home Page
http://www.state.oh.us/

Ohio Department of Health
http://www.odh.state.oh.us/

STATE ARCHIVES

See: Ohio Historical Society

STATE LIBRARY

State Library of Ohio
http://winslo.state.oh.us/

65 South Front Street	*Phone (614) 644-7061*
Columbus, OH 43215-0334	*Fax (614) 644-7004*
	E-mail chordusk@mail.slonet.ohio.gov

Genealogy Services
http://winslo.state.oh.us/services/genealogy/index.html

Online Library Catalog
http://slonet.state.oh.us/

Public Library Directory, Ohio
http://statserver.slonet.state.oh.us/libstats/html/reports/lib_dir.cfm

Vital Records, Guide to Birth and Death Records, by County
http://winslo.state.oh.us/services/genealogy/slogenebir.html

STATE GENEALOGICAL SOCIETY

Ohio Genealogical Society
http://www.ogs.org/

713 South Main Street	*Phone (419) 522-9077*
P.O. Box 2625	*E-mail ogs@ogs.org*
Mansfield, OH 44907-1644	

Directory of Ohio Genealogical Society Chapters
http://www.ogs.org/chap.htm

Miami Valley Genealogical Index
http://www.ogs.org/datahome.htm

STATE HISTORICAL SOCIETY

Ohio Historical Society
http://www.ohiohistory.org/

1982 Velma Avenue	*Phone (614) 297-2300*
Columbus, OH 43211-2497	*E-mail ohsrefwinslo.ohio.gov*

Ohio State Archives
http://www.ohiohistory.org/resource/statearc/

Archives and Library	*Phone (614) 297-2510*
1982 Velma Avenue	*E-mail ohsref@winslo.ohio.gov*
Columbus, OH 43211-2497	

African American Experience in Ohio
http://dbs.ohiohistory.org/africanam/

Audiovisual Collections Guides (Photographs, Videos, etc.)
http://www.ohiohistory.org/resource/audiovis/

Census Records in Ohio
http://www.ohiohistory.org/resource/archlib/census.html

Civil War Collections, Online
http://www.ohiohistory.org/resource/database/civilwar.html

County Courthouses in Ohio
http://www.ohiohistory.org/resource/archlib/cthouse.html

Death Certificate Index, 1913–1937
http://www.ohiohistory.org/dindex/search.cfm

Encyclopedia of Ohio History, *Ohio History Central* Online
http://www.ohiokids.org/ohc/

Genealogical Resources
http://www.ohiohistory.org/resource/archlib/gensource.html

Governors of Ohio, 1803–1971
http://www.ohiohistory.org/onlinedoc/ohgovernment/governors/index.html

Historic Preservation Office
http://www.ohiohistory.org/resource/histpres/

Land Records in Ohio
http://www.ohiohistory.org/resource/archlib/landentr.html

Local Government Records Program
http://www.ohiohistory.org/resource/lgr/

Marriage Records in Ohio
http://www.ohiohistory.org/resource/archlib/marriag1.html

Military, *Fight for Colors: Ohio Battle Flag Collection at the Ohio Historical Society*
http://www.ohiohistory.org/etcetera/exhibits/fftc/index.cfm

National Register of Historic Places, Ohio
http://www.ohiohistory.org/resource/database/histpres.html

Naturalization Records in Ohio
http://www.ohiohistory.org/resource/archlib/natural.html

Newspapers at the Ohio Historical Society
http://www.ohiohistory.org/resource/database/news.html

Newspaper Index to Ohio Newspapers, 1793–1996
http://dbs.ohiohistory.org/newspaper/home.cfm

Ohio Association of Historical Societies and Museums
http://www.ohiohistory.org/resource/oahsm/

Ohio History Day
http://www.ohiohistory.org/resource/edserv/ohd/index.html

Online Collection Catalog
http://www.ohiohistory.org/occ/menu.html

Primary Sources for Teachers, Online
http://www.ohiohistory.org/resource/database/histpres.html

State Agency and Department Records, Guides, and Finding Aids
http://www.ohiohistory.org/resource/statearc/agencies/

War of 1812, Ohio Rosters
http://www.ohiohistory.org/resource/database/rosters.html

OTHER STATE SITES

Bowling Green State University
http://www.bgsu.edu/

Jerome Library
http://www.bgsu.edu/colleges/library/

Center for Archival Collections
http://www.bgsu.edu/colleges/library/cac/cac.html
Jerome Library, 5th Floor
Bowling Green, OH 43403-0175

Historical Collections for the Great Lakes
http://www.bgsu.edu/colleges/library/hcgl/hcgl.html

Bowling Green State University	*Phone*	*(419) 372-9612*
Jerome Library, Sixth Floor	*Fax*	*(419) 372-9600*
Bowling Green, OH 43403	*E-mail*	*rgraham@bgnet.bgsu.net*

Rutherford B. Hayes Presidential Library
http://www.rbhayes.org/library.htm

Spiegel Grove	*Phone*	*(419) 332-2081*
Fremont, OH 43420	*Fax*	*(419) 332-4952*
	E-mail	*hayeslib@rbhayes.org*

African American Collections
http://www.bgsu.edu/colleges/library/cac/multibib.html

Archival Chronicle. (Serial). 3/year. Vol. 7, No. 1 (March 1988)– .
http://www.bgsu.edu/colleges/library/cac/chron.html

BG News Online Index. (Serial). Index. (June 1985)– .
http://129.1.59.220/bgnews.htm

Church Records Manuscript Collections
http://www.bgsu.edu/colleges/library/cac/churchco.html

Civil War, 23rd Ohio Volunteer Infantry
http://www.rbhayes.org/ovi.htm

Diary, Rutherford B. Hayes Online Diary
http://www.ohiohistory.org/onlinedoc/hayes/index.cfm

Family Manuscript Collections
http://www.bgsu.edu/colleges/library/cac/family.html

Great Lakes Vessel Images Online Database
http://www.bgsu.edu/colleges/library/hcgl/vessel.html

Historical Collections of the Great Lakes Manuscript Collections
http://www.bgsu.edu/colleges/library/hcgl/cklist.html

Local Government Records Guide
http://www.bgsu.edu/colleges/library/cac/lrintro.html

Manuscript Collections Guides
http://www.bgsu.edu/colleges/library/cac/collhome.html#bibliography

Manuscript Collections, Rutherford B. Hayes Library
http://www.rbhayes.org/mssfind/msstop.htm

Military, Civil War Manuscript Collections
http://www.bgsu.edu/colleges/library/cac/civilwar.html

Military, Spanish-American War Manuscript Collections
http://www.bgsu.edu/colleges/library/cac/warbib.html#spanish

Military, World War I Manuscript Collections
http://www.bgsu.edu/colleges/library/cac/warbib.html#war1

Military, World War II Manuscript Collections
http://www.bgsu.edu/colleges/library/cac/warbib.html#war2

Native American Collections
http://www.bgsu.edu/colleges/library/cac/multibib.html

Newspaper Collections Guide
http://www.bgsu.edu/colleges/library/cac/intro.html

Northwest Ohio Quarterly. (Serial). Table of Contents. (1992)–.
http://www.bgsu.edu/colleges/library/nwoq/nwoq.html

Online Library Catalog
http://maurice.bgsu.edu/

Photograph Collection Guide
http://www.bgsu.edu/colleges/library/cac/photobib.html

Sandusky County, Ohio, Obituary Index, 1830– .
http://index.rbhayes.org/

University Archives
http://www.bgsu.edu/colleges/library/cac/uarchive.html

Wood County Obituary Index, (1870)– .
http://129.1.59.220/obits.htm

Kent State University
http://www.kent.edu/

Kent State Library
http://www.library.kent.edu/

Special Collections Department
http://speccoll.library.kent.edu/

Main Library, 12th Floor	*Phone (330) 672-2270*
Kent, OH 44242	

Annunciation Greek Orthodox Church (Akron, Ohio) Records, 1926–1997
http://speccoll.library.kent.edu/

Regional Historical Collections
http://speccoll.library.kent.edu/

Trinity Lutheran Church Records (Kent, Ohio), 1884–1978
http://speccoll.library.kent.edu/

University Archives
http://speccoll.library.kent.edu/

Oberlin College
http://www.oberlin.edu/

Oberlin College Library
http://www.oberlin.edu/library/libncollect/mudd.html

Special Collections Department
http://www.oberlin.edu/library/libncollect/special.html

Mudd Center	*Phone (440) 775-8285 Ext. 264 or 230*
148 West College Street	*Fax (440) 775-8739*
Oberlin, OH 44074-1532	*E-mail ed.vermue@oberlin.edu*

Architectural Records Guide
http://www.oberlin.edu/~archive/WWW_files/arch_records_intro.html

Congregational Church Records, 1834–1995
http://www.oberlin.edu/~archive/WWW_files/first_church_t.html

Newspaper Indexes; Index to *Lorain County News, Oberlin Weekly News,* and *Oberlin News,* 1860–1917.
http://www.oberlin.edu/library/news_sources/dobnews.html

Oberlin College Archives
http://www.oberlin.edu/~archive/OCA_homepage.html

Oberlin Community Records
http://www.oberlin.edu/~archive/Oberlin_community_records.html

Oberlin History Bibliography, 1833–1992
http://www.oberlin.edu/archive/resources/oberlin/index.html

Personal Papers
http://www.oberlin.edu/~archive/holdings/finding/RG30/index.html

Women's History Sources
http://www.oberlin.edu/archive/resources/women/index.html

Ohio University
http://www.ohiou.edu/

Ohio University Library
http://www.library.ohiou.edu/index.htm

Archives and Special Collections
http://www.library.ohiou.edu/libinfo/depts/archives/index.htm

Vernon R. Alden Library	*Phone*	*(740) 593-2710*
Park Place	*Fax*	*(740) 593-0138*
Athens, OH 45701-2978	*E-mail*	*gbain1@ohiou.edu*

Genealogical Resources in the Ohio University Libraries
http://www.library.ohiou.edu/libinfo/depts/archives/geninfo.htm

Local Government Records
http://www.library.ohiou.edu/libinfo/depts/archives/local.htm

Manuscript Collections Guide
http://www.library.ohiou.edu/libinfo/depts/archives/mssindex.htm

University Archives
http://www.library.ohiou.edu/libinfo/depts/archives/ouarch.htm

Wright State University
http://www.wright.edu/

Paul Laurence Dunbar Library
http://www.libraries.wright.edu/

Special Collections Department
http://www.libraries.wright.edu/special/

3640 Colonel Glenn Highway	*Phone*	*(937) 775-2092*
Dayton, OH 45435	*Fax*	*(937) 775-2356*
	E-mail	*archive@wsuol2.wright.edu*

African American Records
http://www.libraries.wright.edu/special/manuscripts/afamer.html

Auglaize County Records
http://www.libraries.wright.edu/special/gov_records/auglaize.html

Champaign County Records
http://www.libraries.wright.edu/special/gov_records/champaign.html

Church Records
  http://www.libraries.wright.edu/special/manuscripts/churches.html

Civil War Collection
  http://www.libraries.wright.edu/special/manuscripts/civwar.html

Clark County Records
  http://www.libraries.wright.edu/special/gov_records/clark.html

Darke County Records
  http://www.libraries.wright.edu/special/gov_records/darke.html

Greene County Records
  http://www.libraries.wright.edu/special/gov_records/greene.html

Local Government Records
  http://www.libraries.wright.edu/special/gov_records/

Logan County Records
  http://www.libraries.wright.edu/special/gov_records/logan.html

Medical, Physicians' Records
  http://www.libraries.wright.edu/special/manuscripts/locmed.html

Mercer County Records
  http://www.libraries.wright.edu/special/gov_records/mercer.html

Miami County Records
  http://www.libraries.wright.edu/special/gov_records/miami.html

Montgomery County Records
  http://www.libraries.wright.edu/special/gov_records/montgomery.html

Preble County Records
  http://www.libraries.wright.edu/special/gov_records/preble.html

Shelby County Records
  http://www.libraries.wright.edu/special/gov_records/shelby.html

Women's Collection
  http://www.libraries.wright.edu/special/manuscripts/women.html

OKLAHOMA

STATE HOME PAGE

Oklahoma State Home Page
  http://www.state.ok.us/

Vital Records Service
  http://www.health.state.ok.us/program/vital/brec.html

STATE LIBRARY

Oklahoma Department of Libraries
http://www.odl.state.ok.us/

200 Northeast 18th Street   *Phone   (405) 521-2502*
Oklahoma City, OK 73105-3298

Oklahoma State Archives and Records Management
http://www.odl.state.ok.us/oar/index.htm

Phone   (405) 522-3579
Fax   (405) 522-3582
*   (405) 521-8803   Records Center*
E-mail   cbittle@oltn.odl.state.ok.us

Aerial Photograph Collection
http://www.odl.state.ok.us/oar/resources/aerial.htm

Confederate Pension Records Index
http://www.odl.state.ok.us/oar/docs/pension.pdf

Genealogy in the Archives
http://www.odl.state.ok.us/oar/resources/genealogy.htm

Land Records
http://www.odl.state.ok.us/oar/land-records/index.htm

Maps, Historical
http://www.odl.state.ok.us/oar/resources/maps.htm

Oklahoma Almanac. (Serial). Current Issue.
http://www.odl.state.ok.us/almanac/index.htm

Oklahoma Historical Records Advisory Board
http://www.odl.state.ok.us/oar/administration/ohrab.htm

Oklahoma Libraries
http://www.odl.state.ok.us/oklibs.htm

Surveyors' Field Notes
http://www.odl.state.ok.us/oar/resources/surveyors.htm

STATE GENEALOGICAL SOCIETY

Oklahoma Genealogical Society
http://www.rootsweb.com/~okgs/

P.O. Box 12986
Oklahoma City, OK 73157-2986

Online Records
http://www.rootsweb.com/~okgs/records.htm

STATE HISTORICAL SOCIETY

Oklahoma Historical Society

http://www.ok-history.mus.ok.us/

2100 North Lincoln Blvd.   Phone   (405) 522-5209
Oklahoma City, OK 73105-4997   Fax   (405) 521-2492
                                  E-mail   mrarchives@ok-history.mus.ok.us

Archives Division

http://www.ok-history.mus.ok.us/arch/archindex.htm

Archives, Friends of the Oklahoma Historical Society Archives

http://www.ok-history.mus.ok.us/arch/friends.htm

Native American Archives Directory

http://www.ok-history.mus.ok.us/arch/indianrc/indfront.html

Newspaper Archives

http://www.ok-history.mus.ok.us/arch/newsarch.htm

Oral History Collections

http://www.ok-history.mus.ok.us/arch/ohcol.htm

Photographic Archives

http://www.ok-history.mus.ok.us/arch/photocol.htm

OTHER STATE SITES

Cherokee Heritage Center

http://www.cherokeeheritage.org

P.O. Box 515   Phone   (888) 999-6007
Tahlequah, OK 74465-0515   Fax   (918) 456-6165
                            E-mail   info@cherokeeheritage.org
                                     genealogy@CherokeeHeritage.org

Certificates of Degree of Indian Blood (CDIB) and Tribal Memberships

http://www.cherokeeheritage.org/gen_cdibtm.html

Genealogy

http://www.cherokeeheritage.org/genealogy.html

Library

http://www.cherokeeheritage.org/gen_library.html

Oklahoma State University

http://pio.okstate.edu/

Library, Special Collections Department

http://www.library.okstate.edu/scua/index.htm

204 Edmon Law Library   Phone   (405) 744-6311
Stillwater, OK 74078-1071   Fax   (405) 744-7579
                            E-mail   lib-scua@okstate.edu

Collections
> http://www.library.okstate.edu/scua/collalph.html

Online Library Catalog
> http://osucatalog.library.okstate.edu/

Women's Archives Guide
> http://www.library.okstate.edu/scua/women/women.htm

University of Tulsa
> http://www.utulsa.edu/

McFarlin Library
> http://www.lib.utulsa.edu/

Special Collections Department
> http://www.lib.utulsa.edu/Speccoll/

2933 East 6th Street   *Phone   (918) 631-2880*
Tulsa, OK 74104-3123   *Fax   (918) 631-5022*
                              E-mail   lori-curtis@utulsa.edu

Manuscripts and Correspondence Collections
> http://www.lib.utulsa.edu/Speccoll/native_american.htm

Native American Collections
> http://www.lib.utulsa.edu/Speccoll/native_american.htm

Newspaper Collections
> http://www.lib.utulsa.edu/Speccoll/histnew0.htm

Oklahoma Collections
> http://www.lib.utulsa.edu/Speccoll/oklahoma.htm

Photograph Collections
> http://www.lib.utulsa.edu/Speccoll/histpho0.htm

Tulsa Collections
> http://www.lib.utulsa.edu/Speccoll/tulsa.htm

University of Tulsa Collections
> http://www.lib.utulsa.edu/Speccoll/university_of_tulsa.htm

World War I Collection
> http://www.lib.utulsa.edu/Speccoll/ww100000.htm

OREGON

STATE HOME PAGE

Oregon Online
> http://www.oregon.gov/

Oregon Blue Book. (Serial). Annual. Current Issue.
http://bluebook.state.or.us/

Center for Health Statistics and Vital Records
http://www.ohd.hr.state.or.us/chs/certif/certfaqs.htm

STATE ARCHIVES

Oregon State Archives
http://arcweb.sos.state.or.us/

800 Summer Street, NE   *Phone   (503) 373-0701*
Salem, OR 97310   *Fax   (503) 373-0953*
                                   E-mail   reference.archives@state.or.us

Adoption Records
http://arcweb.sos.state.or.us/adoption.html

Census Records
http://arcweb.sos.state.or.us/census.html

County Historical Records Guide
http://arcweb.sos.state.or.us/county/cphome.html

County Histories
http://arcweb.sos.state.or.us/provisionalguide/CountyHistories.html

Highlights of the Archives
http://arcweb.sos.state.or.us/50th/50thintro.html

Land Records
http://arcweb.sos.state.or.us/land.html

Military Records
http://arcweb.sos.state.or.us/milit.html

National Register of Historic Places, Oregon
http://arcweb.sos.state.or.us/shpo/shpodefault.html

Naturalization Records
http://arcweb.sos.state.or.us/natural.html

OR-ROOTS Listserv
http://arcweb.sos.state.or.us/listserv_roots.html

Personal Name Online Index to Oregon Records
http://159.121.115.13/databases/searchgeneal.html

Portland Birth Index, 1881–1900
http://sos-venus.sos.state.or.us:8080/arc_prod/web_search_birth_index.search

Portland Death Index, 1881–1917
http://sos-venus.sos.state.or.us:8080/arc_prod/web_search_death_index.search

Probate Records
http://arcweb.sos.state.or.us/prob.html

Provisional and Territorial Records, Maps, and Documents
http://arcweb.sos.state.or.us/provisionalguide/provisionaltable.html

Territorial Records Guide
http://arcweb.sos.state.or.us/territ.html

Vital Records
http://arcweb.sos.state.or.us/vital.html

STATE LIBRARY

Oregon State Library
http://www.osl.state.or.us/home/

State Library Building   *Phone*   *(503) 378-4243*
250 Winter Street, NE   *E-mail*   *susan.niggli@state.or.us*
Salem, OR 97310-3950

Genealogy Room
http://www.osl.state.or.us/lib/gs.jpg

Oregon Library Directory
http://www.osl.state.or.us/home/libdev/index.html

Oregon Index, Newspapers, etc.
http://www.osl.state.or.us/home/orind.html

State Library History and Overview
http://www.osl.state.or.us/lib/osls.html

OTHER STATE SITES

Genealogical Forum of Oregon, Inc.
http://www.gfo.org/

P.O. Box 42567   *Phone*   *(503) 963-1932*
Portland, OR 97242- 0567   *Fax*   *(561) 325-7676*
                             E-mail   *Info@gfo.org*

Multnomah County Marriage Records
http://www.gfo.org/multcomar.htm

Oregon Genealogical Libraries and Collections
http://www.gfo.org/orlibs.html

Passenger Lists Research
http://www.gfo.org/repsngrlists.htm

Types of Oregon Records
http://www.gfo.org/torrec.htm

University of Oregon
http://darkwing.uoregon.edu/

University of Oregon Library
http://libweb.uoregon.edu/

Special Collections and University Archives
http://libweb.uoregon.edu/speccoll/

1299 University of Oregon   *Phone*   *(541) 346-3068*
Eugene, OR 97403-1299   *Fax*   *(541) 346-1882*

Manuscripts
http://libweb.uoregon.edu/speccoll/mss/index.html

Newspaper Indexes, Online. *Register Guard; Eugene Weekly*
http://www.ci.eugene.or.us/plweb-cgi/fastweb.exe?searchform+rg_view

Photograph Collections
http://libweb.uoregon.edu/speccoll/photo/photo.html

University Archives
http://libweb.uoregon.edu/speccoll/archives/index.html

PENNSYLVANIA

STATE HOME PAGE

Pennsylvania PowerPort
http://www.state.pa.us/PAPower/

Division of Vital Records
http://www.health.state.pa.us/vitalrecords/vital_records_information.htm

STATE ARCHIVES

State Archives of Pennsylvania
http://www.phmc.state.pa.us/bah/dam/overview.htm?secid=31

Pennsylvania Historical and Museum Commission
http://www.phmc.state.pa.us/

350 North Street   *Phone*   *(717) 783-3281*
P.O. Box 1026   *E-mail*   *webmaster@state.pa.us*
Harrisburg, PA 17108-1026

Archives, ARIAS Online Digital Documents
http://www.digitalarchives.state.pa.us/

Census Records
http://www.phmc.state.pa.us/bah/dam/census.htm

County Records
> http://www.phmc.state.pa.us/bah/dam/usecorec.htm

Historical Marker Program
> http://www.phmc.state.pa.us/bah/DOH/hmp.asp?secid=18

Land Office
> http://www.phmc.state.pa.us/bah/dam/landrec.htm

Military Records
> http://www.phmc.state.pa.us/bah/dam/milit2.htm

Mine Records
> http://www.phmc.state.pa.us/bah/dam/mines.htm

Naturalization Records
> http://www.phmc.state.pa.us/bah/dam/naturali.htm

Passenger Lists of German Passengers
> http://www.phmc.state.pa.us/bah/dam/ships.htm

Pennsylvania History
> http://www.phmc.state.pa.us/bah/pahist/overview.asp?secid=31

Prison Records
> http://www.phmc.state.pa.us/bah/dam/prison.htm

Railroad Records
> http://www.phmc.state.pa.us/bah/dam/parrvcards.htm

State Historical Records Advisory Board
> http://www.phmc.state.pa.us/bah/DARMS/shrab/shrab1.htm

Vital Records
> http://www.phmc.state.pa.us/bah/dam/vitalsta.htm

STATE LIBRARY

State Library of Pennsylvania
> http://www.statelibrary.state.pa.us/libraries/site/

P.O. Box 1601	*Phone*	*(717) 783-5950*
Commonwealth and Walnut Streets	*Fax*	*(717) 783-2070*
Harrisburg, PA 17105-1601	*E-mail*	*payne@shrsys.hslc.org*

STATE GENEALOGICAL SOCIETY

Genealogical Society of Pennsylvania
> http://www.libertynet.org/gspa/

215 South Broad Street, 7th Floor	*Phone*	*(215) 545-0391*
Philadelphia, PA 19144	*Fax*	*(215) 545-0936*
	E-mail	*gsppa@aol.com*

Collection Holdings

http://www.libertynet.org/gspa/library.html

Milton Rubincam Collection, Index

http://www.libertynet.org/gspa/RubinInd.html

STATE HISTORICAL SOCIETY

Historical Society of Pennsylvania

http://www.hsp.org/

1300 Locust Street	*Phone (215) 732-6201*
Philadelphia, PA 19107-5699	*Fax (215) 732-2680*
	E-mail hsppr@aol.com

OTHER STATE SITES

Athenaeum

http://www.philaathenaeum.org/

219 South 6th Street	*Phone (215) 925-2688*
Philadelphia, PA 19106-3794	*Fax (215) 925-3755*
	E-mail laverty@PhilaAthenaeum.org

Collections Guide

http://www.philaathenaeum.org/libcollections.html

Online Library Catalog

http://pacl-iol2.auto-graphics.com/wp2000/signin.asp?cid=pacl&lid=PAT&mode=P

Philadelphia Architects and Buildings Catalog

http://www.philadelphiabuildings.org/pab/

Balch Institute for Ethnic Studies

http://www.balchinstitute.org/

18 South 7th Street	*Phone (215) 925-8090*
Philadelphia, PA 19106	*Fax (215) 925-4392*
	E-mail info@BalchInstitute.org

Guide to Manuscripts

http://www.balchinstitute.org/manuscript_guide/html/contents.html

Online Library Catalog

http://www.auto-graphics.com/cgipac/mmx/bai

Biographical Dictionary of Pennsylvania Legislators (BDOPL)

http://www.bdopl.com/bdopl/home.html

Temple University	*Phone (215) 204-3406*
917 Gladfelter Hall (025-24)	*Fax (215) 204-5891*
12th Street and Berks Mall	*E-mail info@bdopl.com*
Philadelphia, PA 19122	

BDOPL Biographical Index
http://www.bdopl.com/bdopl/bdind.html

Carnegie Library of Pittsburgh
http://alphaclp.clpgh.org/CLP/

4400 Forbes Avenue   *Phone*   *(412) 622-3114*
Pittsburgh, PA 15213   *E-mail   padept@alphaclp.clpgh.org.*

African American Genealogy
http://www.carnegielibrary.org/locations/pennsylvania/genealogy/afroamerican.html

Archaeology in Pittsburgh
http://www.carnegielibrary.org/locations/pennsylvania/history/archae.html

Architecture, How to Trace the Genealogy of Your Home
http://www.carnegielibrary.org/locations/pennsylvania/history/househistories.html

Genealogy Resources, Pennsylvania
http://www.carnegielibrary.org/locations/pennsylvania/how2.html

Obituary Notices Index
http://www.carnegielibrary.org/locations/pennsylvania/genealogy/deathnotices.html

Orphanages, a Directory of Orphanages in Allegheny County and Some Adjacent Counties
http://www.carnegielibrary.org/locations/pennsylvania/orphanages/

Pittsburgh, How to Spell Pittsburgh
http://www.carnegielibrary.org/exhibit/hname.html

Pittsburgh in 1816
http://www.carnegielibrary.org/locations/pennsylvania/history/pgh1816.html

Special Collections Department
http://www.carnegielibrary.org/locations/oliver/

World War I, Soldiers Index
http://www.carnegielibrary.org/locations/pennsylvania/genealogy/wwi.html

The Free Library of Philadelphia
http://www.library.phila.gov/

1901 Vine Street   *Phone   (215) 686-5322*
Philadelphia, PA 19103

Biographies, Autobiographies, and Diaries
http://www.library.phila.gov/ssh/genealogy/biography.htm

Birth Records
http://www.library.phila.gov/ssh/genealogy/birth.htm

Census
http://www.library.phila.gov/ssh/genealogy/census.htm

Death Records
http://www.library.phila.gov/ssh/genealogy/death.htm

Directories
http://www.library.phila.gov/ssh/genealogy/directory.htm

Genealogies, Published and Unpublished
http://www.library.phila.gov/ssh/genealogy/genealogies.htm

Government and Law Records
http://www.library.phila.gov/ssh/genealogy/gov.htm

Marriage Records
http://www.library.phila.gov/ssh/genealogy/marriage.htm

Military Records
http://www.library.phila.gov/ssh/genealogy/military.htm

Newspapers and Indexes
http://www.library.phila.gov/ssh/genealogy/newspapers.htm

Passenger and Naturalization Records
http://www.library.phila.gov/ssh/genealogy/passenger.htm

Probate and Land Records
http://www.library.phila.gov/ssh/genealogy/deed.htm

Published Pennsylvania Archives
http://www.library.phila.gov/ssh/genealogy/pupaar.htm

Haverford College
http://www.haverford.edu/

Magill Library
www.haverford.edu/library

Special Collections Department
http://www.haverford.edu/library/special/

370 Lancaster Avenue   *Phone   (610) 896-1161*
Haverford, PA 19041-1392   *E-mail   jbertole@haverford.edu*

Friends Historical Association
http://www.haverford.edu/library/fha/fha.html

E-mail   fha@haverford.edu

Archives, Finding Aids
http://www.haverford.edu/library/special/aids/

Family Papers
http://www.haverford.edu/library/special/collections/quaker-familypapers.html

Genealogical Resources
http://www.haverford.edu/library/special/genealogy.html

Photograph Collections
http://www.haverford.edu/library/special/collections/photo.html

Quaker Meeting and Other Records
http://www.haverford.edu/library/special/collections/quaker-specialtopics.html

Western Pennsylvania Genealogical Society
http://www.wpgs.org/

4400 Forbes Avenue
Pittsburgh, PA 15213-4080

Online Library Catalog
http://wpgs.library.net/

RHODE ISLAND

STATE HOME PAGE

Rhode Island Public Information Kiosk
http://www.state.ri.us/

Office of Vital Records
http://www.healthri.org/management/vital/home.htm

STATE LIBRARY

Rhode Island Department of Library Services
http://www.state.ri.us/library/web.htm

82 Smith Street   *Phone*   *(401) 222-2473*
State House Room 208   *Fax*   *(401) 222-3034*
Providence, RI 02903

Rhode Island Government Directory
http://www.state.ri.us/library/blue.htm

Rhode Island Governors
http://www.state.ri.us/library/governors.htm

STATE HISTORICAL SOCIETY

Rhode Island Historical Society
http://www.rihs.org/index.shtml

110 Benevolent Street   *Phone*   *(401) 331-8575*
Providence, RI 02906

Overview
http://www.rihs.org/rihsinfo.htm

SOUTH CAROLINA

STATE HOME PAGE

South Carolina Home Page
http://www.myscgov.com/SCSGPortal/static/home_tem1.html

Division of Vital Records
http://www.scdhec.net/vr/index.htm

STATE ARCHIVES

South Carolina Department of Archives and History
http://www.state.sc.us/scdah/homepage.htm

8301 Parklane Road	*Phone*	*(803) 896-6100*
Columbia, SC 29223	*Fax*	*(803) 896-6198*

Archives Guide
http://www.state.sc.us/scdah/guide/guide.htm

British Government Records, Collections Guide
http://www.state.sc.us/scdah/guide/britguide.htm

Confederate States of America, Collection Guide
http://www.state.sc.us/scdah/guide/confedguide.htm

Genealogy Resources
http://www.state.sc.us/scdah/genealre.htm

Local Government Records, Collection Guide
http://www.state.sc.us/scdah/guide/locguide.htm

Revolutionary War Letters, Diaries, Documents
http://www.schistory.org/displays/RevWar/archives-online/index.html

South Carolina Historical Marker Program
http://www.state.sc.us/scdah/historic.htm

Vital Records at the South Carolina State Archives
http://www.state.sc.us/scdah/vit.htm

STATE LIBRARY

South Carolina State Library
http://www.state.sc.us/scsl/

1500 Senate Street	*Phone*	*(803) 734-8666*
P.O. Box 11469	*Fax*	*(803) 734-8676*
Columbia, SC 29211		

Bibliographies
http://www.state.sc.us/scsl/readmore.html

County Histories
http://www.state.sc.us/scsl/cnties.html

DISCUS, South Carolina's Virtual Library
http://www.state.sc.us/scsl/discus/

Online Library Catalog
http://www.state.sc.us/scsl/lion.html

Public Library Links
http://www.state.sc.us/scsl/colibs1.html

STATE HISTORICAL SOCIETY

South Carolina Historical Society
http://www.schistory.org/

100 Meeting Street　　　　　*Phone*　*(803) 723-3225*
Charleston, SC 29401　　　　*Fax*　　*(803) 723-8584*
　　　　　　　　　　　　　　　E-mail　*info@schistory.org*

Bibliography
http://www.schistory.org/library/catalogs/bbrowse.html

County and Local Histories Surname Index
http://www.schistory.org/library/catalogs/locbrowse.html

Family Surname Guide
http://www.schistory.org/library/catalogs/gbrowse.html

Manuscript Collections
http://www.schistory.org/library/catalogs/mbrowse.html

Photographs in the South Carolina Historical Society
http://www.schistory.org/library/catalogs/pbrowse.html

Plat Maps
http://www.schistory.org/library/catalogs/mpbrowse.html

OTHER STATE SITES

University of South Carolina
http://www.sc.edu/

Columbia, SC 29208　　　　　*Phone*　*(803) 777-5183*
　　　　　　　　　　　　　　　Fax　　*(803) 777-5747*
　　　　　　　　　　　　　　　E-mail　*fulmerh@gwm.sc.edu*

Genealogical Collections
http://www.sc.edu/library/socar/mnscrpts/index.html#genies

Manuscript Collections
http://www.sc.edu/library/socar/mnscrpts/index.html

South Caroliniana Library
http://www.sc.edu/library/socar/index.html

SOUTH DAKOTA

STATE HOME PAGE

South Dakota Home Page
http://www.state.sd.us/

Ordering South Dakota Vital Records
http://www.state.sd.us/doh/VitalRec/Vital.htm

STATE ARCHIVES

South Dakota State Archives
http://www.sdhistory.org/archives.htm

900 Governors Drive   *Phone   (605) 773-3458*
Pierre, SD 57501-2217   *Fax   (605) 773-6041*
                               E-mail   Archref@state.sd.us

Genealogy Resources
http://www.sdhistory.org/archives.htm

Naturalization Records
http://www.sdhistory.org/arc_nat.htm

Newspaper Collections
http://www.sdhistory.org/arc_npap.htm

Railroad Records
http://www.sdhistory.org/arc_rroad.htm

STATE LIBRARY

South Dakota State Library
http://www.sdstatelibrary.com/

800 Governors Drive   *Phone   (605) 773-3131*
Pierre, SD 57501-2294   *(800) 423-6665*
                               Fax   (605) 773-4950
                               E-mail   refrequest@stlib.state.sd.us

South Dakota Libraries
http://webpals.sdln.net/cgi-bin/pals-cgi?palsAction=newSearchandsetWeb=SDSdir

STATE HISTORICAL SOCIETY

South Dakota State Historical Society

http://www.sdhistory.org/

900 Governors Drive   *Phone   (605) 773-3458*
Pierre, SD 57501-2217

Biographies of Dakotans

http://www.sdhistory.org/mus_dapr.htm

Museum

http://www.sdhistory.org/museum.htm

South Dakota History. (Serial). Semi-annual. Table of Contents. Vol. 30, No. 1 (Fall 2000)– .

http://www.sdhistory.org/rp_sdhst.htm

TENNESSEE

STATE HOME PAGE

Tennessee State Home Page

http://www.state.tn.us/

Office of Vital Records

http://www.state.tn.us/health/vr/

STATE LIBRARY AND ARCHIVES

OUTSTANDING SITE

Tennessee State Library and Archives

http://www.state.tn.us/sos/statelib/

403 7th Avenue North   *Phone   (615) 741-2764*
Nashville, TN 37243-0312   *Fax   (615) 741-6471*
                                E-mail   referenc@mail.state.tn.us

Acts of Tennessee, 1796–1830. Index

http://www.state.tn.us/sos/statelib/pubsvs/actindex.htm

Archives and Record Repositories in Tennessee, Directory

http://www.state.tn.us/sos/statelib/techsvs/ArchDirectory.pdf

Bibliography

http://www.state.tn.us/sos/statelib/pubsvs/intro.htm#tn_bibliographies

Census Indexes, 1820–1840
http://www.state.tn.us/sos/statelib/pubsvs/cen1820.htm

Census Indexes, 1850–1880
http://www.state.tn.us/sos/statelib/pubsvs/cen1850.htm

Census Records
http://www.state.tn.us/sos/statelib/pubsvs/intro.htm#census_records

Cherokee Research
http://www.state.tn.us/sos/statelib/pubsvs/cherokee.htm

City Directories
http://www.state.tn.us/sos/statelib/pubsvs/cdirect.htm

Civil War Records
http://www.state.tn.us/sos/statelib/pubsvs/civilwar.htm

Collections
http://www.state.tn.us/sos/statelib/techsvs/collections.htm

County Archives, Repositories
http://www.state.tn.us/sos/statelib/pubsvs/govtarch.htm

County Historians
http://www.state.tn.us/sos/statelib/pubsvs/historns.htm

County Records
http://www.state.tn.us/sos/statelib/pubsvs/intro.htm#county_records

Court Records
http://www.state.tn.us/sos/statelib/pubsvs/court.htm

Genealogical Guides, by County
http://www.state.tn.us/sos/statelib/pubsvs/countypg.htm

Libraries of Tennessee, Directory
http://www.state.tn.us/sos/statelib/publib/

Maps and Tennessee Place Names
http://www.state.tn.us/sos/statelib/pubsvs/intro.htm#place_names

Military Records
http://www.state.tn.us/sos/statelib/pubsvs/intro.htm#military_records

Newsapers and Obituary Indexes
http://www.state.tn.us/sos/statelib/pubsvs/intro.htm#tn_newspapers

Online Indexes
http://www.state.tn.us/sos/statelib/pubsvs/intro.htm#indexes

Online Library Catalog
http://www.auto-graphics.com/cgipac/mmx/tns

Post Card Collection
http://www.state.tn.us/sos/statelib/pubsvs/tpc.htm

Vital Records
http://www.state.tn.us/sos/statelib/pubsvs/intro.htm#vital_records

OTHER STATE SITES

Middle Tennessee State University
http://mtsu.edu/

Library
http://www.mtsu.edu/~library/

John E. Walker Library   *Phone*   *(615) 904-8524*
Box 013   *E-mail* *kmiddlet@frank.mtsu.edu*
Murfreesboro, TN 37132

Biographical Index to Tennessee Women
http://www.mtsu.edu/~library/wtn/bio/wtn-biog2.html

Special Collections Department
http://ulibnet.mtsu.edu/SpecialCollections/index.html

Women in Tennessee History
http://www.mtsu.edu/~library/wtn/wtn-home.html

Women's Studies Sources
http://frank.mtsu.edu/~kmiddlet/history/women.html

Women's Studies—Civil War Sources
http://frank.mtsu.edu/~kmiddlet/history/women/wh-cwar.html

Women's Studies—Resources, by State
http://frank.mtsu.edu/~kmiddlet/history/women/wh-digcoll.html

University of Tennessee, Knoxville
http://www.utk.edu/

Special Collections Department
http://www.lib.utk.edu/spcoll/

1401 Cumberland Avenue   *Phone*   *(865) 974-4480*
Knoxville, TN 37996-4000   *Fax*   *(865) 974-0560*
                             E-mail *special@aztec.lib.utk.edu*

Manuscripts Guide
http://www.lib.utk.edu/spcoll/scripts.html

World War II Collections
http://www.lib.utk.edu/spcoll/manuscripts/ww2index.html

TEXAS

STATE HOME PAGE

OUTSTANDING SITE

Texas State Home Page
http://www.state.tx.us/

Bureau of Vital Statistics
http://www.tdh.state.tx.us/bvs/

Texas General Land Office
http://www.glo.state.tx.us/

1700 N. Congress Avenue   *Phone*   *(512) 463-5288*
Austin, TX 78701-1495   *E-mail*   *archives@glo.state.tx.us*

Archives and Documents
http://www.glo.state.tx.us/archives.html

Archives, Finding Aids
http://www.glo.state.tx.us/archives/findaid.html

History of Texas Public Lands
http://www.glo.state.tx.us/history/

Map Collection
http://www.glo.state.tx.us/archives/mapscol.html

Spanish and Mexican Texas Land Records
http://www.glo.state.tx.us/archives/find_spanmex.html

Texas Historical Commission
http://www.thc.state.tx.us/

P.O. Box 12276   *Phone*   *(512) 463-6100*
Austin, TX 78711-2276   *Fax*   *(512) 475-4872*
                          E-mail *thc@thc.state.tx.us*

Historic Cemeteries in Texas
http://www.thc.state.tx.us/cemeteries/cemhtc.html

Historic Courthouse Preservation Project
http://www.thc.state.tx.us/courthouses/chdefault.html

Official Texas Historical Markers
http://www.thc.state.tx.us/markersdesigs/maddefault.html

Texas Department of Public Safety
http://www.txdps.state.tx.us/

P.O. Box 4087   *Phone* *(512) 424-2811*
Austin, TX 78773-0422

Fallen Officers Memorial
http://www.txdps.state.tx.us/memorial/

Missing Persons Clearinghouse
http://www.txdps.state.tx.us/mpch/

Texas State Cemetery
http://www.cemetery.state.tx.us/

909 Navasota Street   *Phone   (512) 463-0605*
Austin, TX 78702   *Fax   (512) 463-8811*
                              E-mail   state.cemetery@gsc.state.tx.us

History of the Confederate Section
http://www.cemetery.state.tx.us/html/historyconfed.htm

Master List of Burials
http://www.cemetery.state.tx.us/pub/database.htm

STATE LIBRARY AND ARCHIVES

Texas State Library
http://www.tsl.state.tx.us/

Lorenzo de Zavala Building   *Phone   (512) 463-5463   Genealogy Collection*
1201 Brazos   *E-mail   geninfo@tsl.state.tx.us   Genealogy*
Austin, TX 78701

Mailing Address:
P.O. Box 12927
Austin, TX 78711-2927

City Directories
http://www.tsl.state.tx.us/arc/citydirs.html

Confederate Indigent Families Database
http://www.tsl.state.tx.us/arc/cif/index.html

Confederate Pension Records Index (1863–1865)
http://www.tsl.state.tx.us/arc/pensions/index.html

County Records; Microfilm Loan Collection
http://www.tsl.state.tx.us/arc/local/index.html

Genealogy Resources
http://www.tsl.state.tx.us/arc/genfirst.html

Libraries in Texas, Directory
http://www.tsl.state.tx.us/ld/libraries/

Local Record. (Serial). Semi-annual. (Winter 1996)– .
http://www.tsl.state.tx.us/slrm/recordspubs/localrec/index.html

Map Collection
http://www.tsl.state.tx.us/arc/maps/index.html

Military Records, Texas Adjutant General Service Records, 1836–1935
http://www.tsl.state.tx.us/arc/service/index.html

Newspapers
http://www.tsl.state.tx.us/ref/abouttx/news.html

Republic of Texas Claims Database
http://www.tsl.state.tx.us/arc/repclaims/index.html

State Record. (Serial). Semi-annual. (July 1998)– .
http://www.tsl.state.tx.us/slrm/recordspubs/staterec/index.html

Tax Records
http://www.tsl.state.tx.us/arc/taxrolls.html

Telephone Directories
http://www.tsl.state.tx.us/arc/phondirs.html

TRAIL: Texas Records and Information Locator
http://www.tsl.state.tx.us/trail/index.html

Vital Records
http://www.tsl.state.tx.us/arc/vitalfaq.html

Voter Registration Records, 1867
http://www.tsl.state.tx.us/arc/votersreg.html

OTHER STATE SITES

Austin Public Library
http://www.ci.austin.tx.us/library/

Austin History Center
http://www.ci.austin.tx.us/library/ahc/default.htm

9th and Guadalupe Streets	*Phone* *(512) 974-7480*
P.O. Box 2287	*E-mail ahc_reference@ci.austin.tx.us*
Austin, TX 78768-2287	

Austin Archives Newsletter. (Serial). Semi-annual. (May 1997)– .
http://www.ahca.net/archives.htm

Austin History Center Association
http://www.ahca.net/

Biographical Sources
http://www.ci.austin.tx.us/library/ahc/biography.htm

Census Records
http://www.ci.austin.tx.us/library/ahc/census.htm

Clipping Files
http://www.ci.austin.tx.us/library/ahc/vertical.htm

Manuscript Collections
http://www.ci.austin.tx.us/library/ahc/manuscript.htm

Photograph Collections
http://www.ci.austin.tx.us/library/ahc/photo.htm

Preserving Your History
http://www.ci.austin.tx.us/library/ahc/preserve.htm

Catholic Archives of Texas
http://www.onr.com/user/cat/

Diocese of Austin Chancery Building   *Phone*   *(512) 476-4888*
1600 North Congress Avenue   *Fax*   *(512) 476-3715*
Austin, TX 78701   *E-mail*   *cat@onr.com*

Mailing Address:
P.O. Box 13327, Capitol Station
Austin, TX 78711

Corporate Records
http://www.onr.com/user/cat/cathol95.html#corporate_records

Manuscripts
http://www.onr.com/user/cat/cathol95.html

Personal Papers
http://www.onr.com/user/cat/cathol95.html#personal_papers

Sacramental Records
http://www.onr.com/user/cat/sacraments.htm

OUTSTANDING SITE

Dallas Genealogical Society
http://www.dallasgenealogy.org/

P.O. Box 12446   *Phone*   *(214) 670-7932*
Dallas, TX 75225-0446   *Fax*   *(214) 670-7932*
    E-mail   *info@dallasgenealogy.org*

Daughters of the Republic of Texas Library
http://www.drtl.org/

P.O. Box 1401   *Phone*   *(210) 225-1071*
San Antonio, TX 78295-1401   *Fax*   *(210) 212-8514*
    E-mail   *drtl@drtl.org*

Alamo: An Illustrated Chronology
http://www.drtl.org/History/index.asp

OUTSTANDING SITE

Denton County History Page
http://mikecochran.net/history.html

E-mail   gm.cochran@home.com

African American History
http://mikecochran.net/Blackhistory.html

Biographical Sketches
http://mikecochran.net/biographies.html

Cemetery Records, Index
http://mikecochran.net/cemeterypage.html

Confederate Pension Abstracts
http://mikecochran.net/Confeder@pens.html

County Records on Microfilm
http://mikecochran.net/CountyRecords.html

German Colonies in Denton County
http://mikecochran.net/germans.html

Oral Histories
http://mikecochran.net/oralhist.html

Site Index
http://mikecochran.net/Index.html

Fort Worth Public Library
http://www.fortworthlibrary.org/
500 West 3rd Street   *Phone   (817) 871-7740*
Fort Worth, TX 76102-7305   *E-mail   genlhist@forthworthlibrary.org*

Archival Collections
http://www.fortworthlibrary.org/archive.htm

Genealogy and Local History Section
http://www.fortworthlibrary.org/genlhst.htm

OUTSTANDING SITE

Hood County Genealogical Society
http://www.granburydepot.org/

P.O. Box 1623   *Phone   (817) 573-2557*
Granbury, TX 76048-8623   *E-mail   ancestor@GranburyDepot.org*

Biographical Sketches
http://www.granburydepot.org/z/biog.htm

Index of Genealogical Databases for Hood County
http://www.granburydepot.org/MainIndex.htm

Military Veterans of Hood County
http://www.hcnews.com/depot/

OUTSTANDING SITE

Houston Public Library
http://www.hpl.lib.tx.us/hpl/index.html

Central Library   *Phone   (713) 236-1313*
500 McKinney
Houston, TX 77002

Clayton Library for Genealogical Research
http://www.hpl.lib.tx.us/clayton/

5300 Caroline   *Phone   (713) 284-1999*
Houston, TX 77004-6896

Census Records
http://www.hpl.lib.tx.us/clayton/cla_c1.html

Friends of the Clayton Library
http://www.hpl.lib.tx.us/clayton/clf.html

Genealogical Periodicals
http://www.hpl.lib.tx.us/clayton/cla_c6.html

Genealogical Resources, by State
http://www.hpl.lib.tx.us/clayton/clmca0.html

Genealogies in the Clayton Library
http://www.hpl.lib.tx.us/clayton/cla_c5.html

Genealogies on Microfilm
http://www.hpl.lib.tx.us/clayton/clmcd0.html

History of the Clayton Library
http://www.hpl.lib.tx.us/clayton/cla_a6.html

Houston Metropolitan Research Center
http://www.hpl.lib.tx.us/hpl/hmrc.html

Houston Public Library History
http://www.hpl.lib.tx.us/hpl/libhist.html

International Records
http://www.hpl.lib.tx.us/clayton/clmcc0.html

Maps
http://www.hpl.lib.tx.us/clayton/cla_c7.html

Military Records
http://www.hpl.lib.tx.us/clayton/cla_c2.html

Passenger Lists
http://www.hpl.lib.tx.us/clayton/cla_c3.html

Texas and Local History Department
http://www.hpl.lib.tx.us/hpl/txr.html

OUTSTANDING SITE

Lone Star Junction
http://www.lsjunction.com/

Biography
http://www.lsjunction.com/people/people.htm

Full-text Books Online
http://site17585.dellhost.com/lsj/olbooks/olb_home.htm

Historic Documents
http://www.lsjunction.com/docs/docs.htm

Historic Places
http://www.lsjunction.com/places/ismap2b.htm

Photographs
http://site17585.dellhost.com/lsj/images/images.htm

The Texians: Online Database of Early Texans
http://site17585.dellhost.com/lsj/texians/

San Antonio Public Library
http://www.sat.lib.tx.us/

600 Soledad Street   *Phone   (512) 299-7790*
San Antonio, TX 78205

African American Genealogy
http://www.sat.lib.tx.us/central/genafam.htm

Czech Genealogy
http://www.sat.lib.tx.us/central/genczech.htm

Preserving San Antonio's History
http://www.sat.lib.tx.us/central/preserve.htm

San Antonio Bibliography, 1820–1859
   http://www.sat.lib.tx.us/central/account.htm

San Antonio, A Chronology, 1691–1997
   http://www.sat.lib.tx.us/central/sanevents.htm

San Antonio City Officers, 1837–1983
   http://www.sat.lib.tx.us/central/cityofficers.htm

Texana—Genealogy Collection
   http://www.sat.lib.tx.us/central/texana.htm

Texas Catholic Historical Society
   http://www.onr.com/user/cat/TCHS.htm

   c/o Texas Catholic Conference   *E-mail   jd10@swt.edu*
   1625 Rutherford Lane, Bldg. D
   Austin, TX 78754-5105

Catholic Southwest, A Journal of History and Culture. (Serial). Annual. Vols. 1–4
(1990–1993). Table of Contents. Vol. 2 (1991); Vol. 5 (1994)– .
   http://www.history.swt.edu/Catholic_Southwest.htm

University of Arizona
Special Collections Department, Library
   P.O. Box 210055   *Phone   (520) 621-4345*
   Tucson, AZ 85721-0055   *E-mail   stuartg@u.arizona.edu*

Archival Guides
   http://www.library.arizona.edu/images/swja/findingaids/findingaids.htm

Arizona Jewish Pioneers
   http://www.library.arizona.edu/images/swja/arizona.htm

Bibliography
   http://www.library.arizona.edu/images/swja/suggreads.htm

Jewish Pioneers of the Southwest
   http://www.library.arizona.edu/images/swja/pioneers.htm

Leona G. and David Bloom Southwest Jewish Archives
   http://www.library.arizona.edu/images/swja/swjalist.html

Manuscript Collections
   http://dizzy.library.arizona.edu/branches/spc/homepage/alphlist/alphlist.htm

New Mexico Jewish Pioneers
   http://www.library.arizona.edu/images/swja/newmexico.htm

Southwest Jewish History. (Serial). 3/year. Vol. 1, No. 1 (Fall 1992–Winter 1995).
   http://www.library.arizona.edu/images/swja/newsletter.html

Synagogues of the Southwest
http://www.library.arizona.edu/images/swja/synagogues.htm

West Texas Jewish Pioneers
http://www.library.arizona.edu/images/swja/westtexas.htm

University of Texas at Arlington
http://www.uta.edu

Libraries
http://www.uta.edu/library/

Special Collections Department
http://libraries.uta.edu/SpecColl/

702 College Street	*Phone (817) 272-3393*
P.O. Box 19497	*E-mail scref@library.uta.edu*
Arlington, TX 76019-0497	

Compass Rose. (Serial). Semi-annual. Current Issue and Selected Articles.
http://libraries.uta.edu/SpecColl/comprose.html

Guide to Collections
http://libraries.uta.edu/SpecColl/findaids/guidelntr.htm

Spanish-Language Historical Manuscripts
http://libraries.uta.edu/SpecColl/findaids/index.html#Span%20Lang

Texas Labor Archives
http://libraries.uta.edu/SpecColl/findaids/index.html#TX%20Labor

Topographical Maps of Texas, 1890–1972
http://libraries.uta.edu/SpecColl/findaids/topomaps.htm

University of Texas at Austin
http://www.utexas.edu/

Benson Latin American Collection
http://www.lib.utexas.edu/benson/index.html

Sid Richardson Hall 1.108	*Phone (512) 495-4520*
University of Texas at Austin	*Fax (512) 495-4568*
Austin, TX 78713-8916	*E-mail blac@lib.utexas.edu*

Censuses of Population, Latin America and the Caribbean
http://www.lib.utexas.edu/benson/bibnot/bn-79-1.html

Dumble Geological Survey of Texas, 1887–1894
http://www.lib.utexas.edu/books/dumble/

Jews in Latin America
http://www.lib.utexas.edu/benson/bibnot/bn-61-1.html

Manuscripts, Little-Known Latin American Manuscripts at the University of Texas
http://www.lib.utexas.edu/benson/larr.html

Mexican Archives
http://www.lib.utexas.edu/benson/Mex_Archives/Collection_list.html

Newspapers in the Benson Latin American Collection
http://www.lib.utexas.edu/benson/bibnot/bn-77-1.html

UTAH

STATE HOME PAGE

Utah Home Page
http://www.utah.gov/

Office of Vital Records and Statistics
http://www.health.state.ut.us/bvr/html/forms.html

STATE ARCHIVES

Utah State Archives
http://utstdpwww.state.ut.us/~archives/

P.O. Box 141021   Phone   (801) 538-3012
State Capitol, Archives Building   Fax   (801) 538-3354
Salt Lake City, UT 84114-1021   E-mail   research@das.state.ut.us

Agency Histories
http://archives.utah.gov/agencyhistories.htm

Military Records
http://archives.utah.gov/referenc/militar2.htm

Vital Records, Birth Records
http://archives.utah.gov/referenc/birth.htm

Vital Records, Death Records
http://archives.utah.gov/referenc/death.htm

Vital Records, Divorce Records
http://archives.utah.gov/referenc/Divorce.htm

STATE LIBRARY

Utah State Library
http://www.state.lib.ut.us/

2150 South 300 West, Suite 15   Phone   (801) 715-6757
Salt Lake City, UT 84115

Libraries Directory
http://www.state.lib.ut.us/directories.html

STATE GENEALOGICAL SOCIETY

SINGLE MOST IMPORTANT GENEALOGICAL WEB SITE ONLINE

**Genealogical Society of Utah
Family History Library of The Church of Jesus Christ of Latter-day Saints**
www.FamilySearch.org

*35 North West Temple Street
Salt Lake City, UT 84150-3400*

*Phone   (800) 453-3860 Ext. 22331
E-mail   fhl@ldschurch.org*

Directory of Family History Centers (Branch Libraries)
http://www.familysearch.org/Eng/Library/FHC/frameset_fhc.asp

Genealogy Research Guides
http://www.familysearch.org/Eng/Search/RG/frameset_rg.asp

Letter Writing Guides
http://www.familysearch.org/Eng/Library/Education/frameset_education.asp?PAGE=education_publications.asp

Word Lists (Multilingual Genealogical Vocabulary Lists)
http://www.familysearch.org/Eng/Library/Education/frameset_education.asp?PAGE=education_publications.asp

Online Library Catalog
http://www.familysearch.org/Eng/Library/FHLC/frameset_fhlc.asp

STATE HISTORICAL SOCIETY

Utah Historical Society
http://www.dced.state.ut.us/history/index.html

*300 Rio Grande
Salt Lake City, UT 8410-1143*

*Phone   (801) 533-3500
Fax   (801) 533-3503
TDD   (801) 533-3502
E-mail cehistry.ushs@email.state.ut.us*

Beehive History. (Serial). Annual. Table of Contents. Vol. 1 (1975)– .
http://history.utah.gov/publications/beehivehistory.html

Cemeteries and Burials Database Online Index
http://history.utah.gov/library/burials.html

Currents, News of the Utah State Historical Society. (Serial). Bi-monthly. Full-text.
Vol. 51, No. 2 (April 2001)– .
http://history.utah.gov/news/currents.html

Family History Research
http://history.utah.gov/library/familyhist.html

Historic Markers Searchable Database
http://history.utah.gov/library/markers.html

How to Research Your House
http://history.utah.gov/library/markers.html

Manuscripts and Photograph Collections
http://history.utah.gov/library/registers.html

Mormon Pioneer Bibliography
http://history.utah.gov/library/pionbibli.htm

Newspaper Holdings
http://history.utah.gov/library/newspaper.html

Telephone Directories
http://history.utah.gov/library/phone.html

Utah Historical Quarterly. (Serial). Quarterly. Table of Contents. Vol. 1, No. 1 (January 1928)– .
http://history.utah.gov/library/uhq.html

Utah Historical Quarterly. (Serial). Quarterly. Index. Vols. 46–64 (1978–1996).
http://history.utah.gov/historyprograms/uhqindex3.html

Yearbook Collection
http://history.utah.gov/library/yearbook.html

VERMONT

STATE HOME PAGE

State of Vermont
http://vermont.gov/

Vermont Vital Records
http://www.state.vt.us/health/_hs/vitals/records/vitalrecords.htm

STATE ARCHIVES

Vermont State Archives
http://vermont-archives.org/

Office of the Secretary of State
Redstone Building
26 Terrace Street, Drawer 9
Montpelier, VT 05609-1101

Phone   *(802) 828-2363*
E-mail   *gsanford@sec.state.vt.us*

ArcCat, Searchable Online Catalog of Vermont Archives
http://www.state.vt.us/vhs/arccat/

Collections
http://vermont-archives.org/guide/aguide.htm

Photograph Collections
http://vermont-archives.org/photos/photohome.html

Public Records Access
http://www.sec.state.vt.us/access/records/pubrec.htm

STATE LIBRARY

Vermont Department of Libraries
http://dol.state.vt.us/

109 State Street   *Phone   (802) 828-3268*
Montpelier, VT 05609-0601

Vermont Library Directory
http://dol.state.vt.us/GOPHER_ROOT5/LIBRARIES/DIR/dir.html

STATE HISTORICAL SOCIETY

Vermont Historical Society
http://www.state.vt.us/vhs/

109 State Street   *Phone   (802) 828-2291*
Montpelier, VT 05609-0901

Civil War Manuscripts
http://www.state.vt.us/vhs/civilw.htm

Genealogical Research in Vermont
http://www.state.vt.us/vhs/generes.htm

Local Historical Societies
http://www.state.vt.us/vhs/lhs/lhsindex.htm

OTHER STATE SITES

University of Vermont
http://www.uvm.edu/

Special Collections Department
http://bailey.uvm.edu/specialcollections/

Bailey/Howe Library
http://library.uvm.edu/

Burlington, VT 05405-40036   *Phone   (802) 656-2138*
                                      Fax   (802) 656-4038
                                      E-mail   edow@zoo.uvm.edu

Guide to Collections
http://bailey.uvm.edu/specialcollections/scinfo.html

Manuscripts
http://bailey.uvm.edu/specialcollections/scinv.html

Wilbur Collection of Electronic Vermontiana
http://bailey.uvm.edu/specialcollections/scev.html

VIRGINIA

STATE HOME PAGE

Virginia Home Page
http://www.state.va.us/

Office of Vital Records
http://www.vdh.state.va.us/misc/f_08.htm

STATE LIBRARY

EXTRAORDINARY SITE
One of the Most Extraordinary Web Sites Online

Library of Virginia
http://www.lva.lib.va.us/

800 East Broad Street   *Phone   (804) 692-3599*
Richmond, VA 23219-8000

African American Newspapers
http://www.lva.lib.va.us/whatwehave/news/AA_newspaper_holdings.pdf

Archives and Manuscripts Department
http://eagle.vsla.edu/bible/virtua-basic.html

Biographical Resources
http://www.lva.lib.va.us/whatwehave/bio/rn16_biographical.htm

Census Records
http://www.lva.lib.va.us/whatwehave/census/index.htm

Civil War Records
http://www.lva.lib.va.us/pubserv/archives/Guides_Databases/RN14CivilWar.htm

Court Records, County and City
http://www.lva.lib.va.us/whatwehave/local/rn6_localrecs.htm

Dictionary of Virginia Biography
http://www.lva.lib.va.us/whatwedo/pubs/dvb/index.htm

Digital Library Program
http://www.lva.lib.va.us/dlp/index.htm

Historical Societies in Virginia, Directory
http://www.lva.lib.va.us/whoweare/directories/vhs/index.htm

Kentucky Records at the Library of Virginia
http://www.lva.lib.va.us/whatwehave/local/va18_kentuckyrecs.htm

Land Office Patents and Grants, Virginia Office. Online Searchable Databases
http://eagle.vsla.edu/lonn/

Land Records
http://www.lva.lib.va.us/whatwehave/land/index.htm

Library Directory, Virginia Libraries
http://www.lva.lib.va.us/whoweare/directories/valib/index.htm

Military History Resources
http://www.lva.lib.va.us/whatwehave/mil/index.htm

Naturalization Records, 1657–1756
http://www.lva.lib.va.us/whatwehave/notes/rn9_natural1657.pdf

Naturalizations Records, 1776–1900
http://www.lva.lib.va.us/whatwehave/notes/rn12_natural1776.pdf

Newspaper Indexes
http://www.lva.lib.va.us/whatwehave/news/index.htm

Researching Virginia Place Names
http://www.lva.lib.va.us/whatwehave/map/researching_place_names.pdf

Revolutionary War Records
http://www.lva.lib.va.us/whatwehave/mil/rn8_varev.htm

Special Collections Department
http://www.lva.lib.va.us/whatwedo/special/index.htm

Virginia Newspaper Project
http://www.lva.lib.va.us/whatwedo/vnp/index.htm

Vital Records, Death Records Indexing Project
http://eagle.vsla.edu/drip/

Vital Records, Marriage Records Index
http://lvaimage.lib.va.us/collections/MG.html

Vital Records, Obituary Indexes and Related Sources
http://eagle.vsla.edu/henley/virtua-basic.html

STATE HISTORICAL SOCIETY

Virginia Historical Society
http://www.vahistorical.org/

428 North Boulevard　　　　　　　*Phone   (804) 358-4901*
P.O. Box 7311
Richmond, VA 23220

Library and Manuscript Collections
http://www.vahistorical.org/Research.htm

Virginia Magazine of History and Biography. (Serial). Quarterly. Table of Contents. Vol. 104, No. 1 (1996)– .
http://www.vahistorical.org/publications/vmhb.htm

OTHER STATE SITES

College of William and Mary
Special Collections Department
http://swem.wm.edu/SpColl/index.html

College of William and Mary　　　*Phone   (757) 253-4841*
Earl Gregg Swem Library　　　　　*E-mail   spcoll@mail.wm.edu*
P.O. Box 8794
Williamsburg, VA 23187-8794

Alumni List
http://www.swem.wm.edu/SpColl/Archives/provlist/frame.htm

Civil War Research
http://www.swem.wm.edu/spcoll/CivilWar/webcw2.html

Guide to Special Collections
http://www.swem.wm.edu/spcoll/guidetoc.html

University of Virginia
Special Collections Department
http://www.lib.virginia.edu/speccol/

Alderman Library　　　　　　　　*Phone   (434) 924-3143*
P.O. Box 400110　　　　　　　　　　　　　*(434) 924-3025*
Charlottesville, VA 22903-2498　*E-mail   mssbks@virginia.edu*

Afro-American Resources in Virginia, a Guide to Manuscripts
http://www.upress.virginia.edu/plunkett/mfp.html

Collections
http://www.lib.virginia.edu/speccol/collections/

Newspapers
http://www.statelib.wa.gov/wa_newspapers.aspx

Virginia Heritage Project
http://www.lib.virginia.edu/vhp/index.html

WASHINGTON

STATE HOME PAGE

Washington Home Page
http://access.wa.gov/

Center for Health Statistics
http://www.doh.wa.gov/ehsphl/chs/cert.htm

STATE ARCHIVES

Washington State Archives
http://www.secstate.wa.gov/archives/

East Capitol   *Phone   (360) 920-4151*
P.O. Box 40220   *E-mail   mail@secstate.wa.gov*
Olympia, WA 98504-0220

Genealogy
http://www.secstate.wa.gov/archives/genealogy.aspx?m=undefined

Oral History Program
http://www.secstate.wa.gov/oralhistory/

State Archives Regional Centers
http://www.secstate.wa.gov/archives/archives.aspx?m=undefined

STATE LIBRARY

Washington State Library
http://www.statelib.wa.gov/

415 15th Ave., SW   *Phone   (360) 753-4024*
P.O. Box 42460   *Fax   (360) 586-2475*
Olympia, WA 98504-2460

Libraries in Washington, Online
http://wlo.statelib.wa.gov/

Newspapers
http://www.statelib.wa.gov/wa_newspapers.aspx

STATE HISTORICAL SOCIETY

Washington State Historical Society
http://www.wshs.org/index.htm

Heritage Resource Center   Phone   *(253) 272-3500*
1911 Pacific Avenue
Tacoma, WA 98403

Columbia, Magazine of Northwest History. (Serial). Table of Contents. Vol. 11, No. 1 (Spring 1997)– .
http://www.wshs.org/columbia/topic_index.htm

OTHER STATE SITES

Gonzaga University
http://www.gonzaga.edu/

Special Collections Department
http://www.gonzaga.edu/Academics/Libraries/Foley+Library/Departments/Special+Collections/default.htm

Foley Center Library   Phone   *(509) 323-3847*
Spokane, WA 99258   Fax   *(509) 323-5904*
                             E-mail   *spcoll@its.gonzaga.edu*

Bing Crosby Collection
http://www.gonzaga.edu/Academics/Libraries/Foley+Library/Departments/Special+Collections/Collections/Bing+Crosby+Collection/default.htm

Jesuit Oregon Province Archives
http://www.gonzaga.edu/Academics/Libraries/Foley+Library/Departments/Special+Collections/Collections/JOPA/default.htm

Manuscripts
http://www.gonzaga.edu/Academics/Libraries/Foley+Library/Departments/Special+Collections/Collections/default.htm

Seattle Municipal Archives
http://www.cityofseattle.net/cityarchives/

600 Fourth Avenue, Room 104   Phone   *(206) 233-7807*
Seattle, WA 98104   Fax   *(206) 386-9025*
                             E-mail   *archives@ci.seattle.wa.us*

Archives Guide, Online
http://www.cityofseattle.net/cityarchives/Tools/Guide/Titletoc1.htm

Indexes to Holdings
http://www.cityofseattle.net/cityarchives/Tools/refindexestest.html

Photograph Collections
http://clerk.ci.seattle.wa.us/~public/phot1.htm

Northwest Room
http://www.tpl.lib.wa.us/v2/NWRoom/nwroom.htm

1102 Tacoma Avenue, South	*Phone*	*(253) 591-5622*
Tacoma, WA 94802	*Fax*	*(253) 627-1693*

Genealogy
http://www.tpl.lib.wa.us/v2/nwroom/genea.htm

Obituary Online Database Index
http://search.tpl.lib.wa.us/obits/

Photograph Collection
http://www.tpl.lib.wa.us/v2/nwroom/photo.htm

Ships and Shipping Online Database
http://www.tpl.lib.wa.us/v2/nwroom/ships.htm

Tacoma Building Index
http://www.tpl.lib.wa.us/v2/nwroom/WaNames.htm

Washington Place Names Online Database
http://www.tpl.lib.wa.us/v2/nwroom/WaNames.htm

WEST VIRGINIA

STATE HOME PAGE

West Virginia Home Page
http://www.state.wv.us/

West Virginia Vital Records
http://www.wvdhhr.org/bph/oehp/hsc/vr/birtcert.htm

STATE ARCHIVES

West Virginia State Archives
http://www.wvculture.org/history/wvsamenu.html

Archives and History Library	*Phone*	*(304) 558-0230*
The Cultural Center		
1900 Kanawha Boulevard, East		
Charleston, WV 25305-0300		

Adoption Research
http://www.wvculture.org/history/adoption.html

African Americans in West Virginia
http://www.wvculture.org/history/blacks.html

Archives and History News. (Serial). Monthly. Full-text. (March 2000)– .
http://www.wvculture.org/history/news.html

Bibliography of West Virginia
http://www.wvculture.org/history/biblio.html

Civil War Genealogy Research
http://www.wvculture.org/history/civwaran.html

Civil War Medals
http://www.wvculture.org/history/medals.html

County Formation History
http://www.wvculture.org/history/wvcounties.html

Historical Societies Directory
http://www.wvculture.org/history/guide2.html

Historic Markers
http://www.wvculture.org/history/wvsafaq.html#marker

Manuscripts
http://www.wvculture.org/history/mancoll.html

Military, West Virginia Veteran's Memorial, Indexes
http://www.wvculture.org/history/wvvets.html

Naturalization Records
http://www.wvculture.org/history/mancoll.html

Newspapers
http://www.wvculture.org/history/newspapers/newsmic.html

Revolutionary War Genealogy Research
http://www.wvculture.org/history/civwaran.html

West Virginia Historical Society Quarterly. (Serial). Vol. 9, No. 4/Vol. 10, No. 1
(March 1986)– .
http://www.wvculture.org/history/wvhssoc.html

West Virginia History. (Serial). Author Index. (1939)– .
http://www.wvculture.org/history/journal_wvh/toc-aut.html

West Virginia History. (Serial). Subject Index. (1939)– .
http://www.wvculture.org/history/journal_wvh/subjects.html

West Virginia Memory Project
http://129.71.134.132/index.htm

West Virginia Research Collections, Outside of West Virginia
http://www.wvculture.org/history/reposits_not_wv/states.html

OTHER STATE SITES

OUTSTANDING SITE

Allegheny Regional Family History Society
http://www.swcp.com/~dhickman/arfhs.html

P.O. Box 1804   *E-mail   dhickman@swcp.com*
Elkins, WV 26241

Barbour County Cemetery Descriptions
http://www.swcp.com/~dhickman/bcodes.html

Census, 1850 Database
http://www.swcp.com/~dhickman/census/census.html

Journal of the Allegheny Regional Ancestors. (Serial). Table of Contents and Index.
Vol. 1, No. 1 (Spring 1992)– .
http://www.swcp.com/~dhickman/journal.html

Pocahontas County Cemetery Descriptions
http://www.swcp.com/~dhickman/pcodes.html

Randolph County Cemetery Descriptions
http://www.swcp.com/~dhickman/randcem.htm

Shay Family
http://www.swcp.com/~dhickman/shay.html

Vital Records
http://www.swcp.com/~dhickman/vital.html

Marshall University
http://www.marshall.edu/

Special Collections Department
http://www.marshall.edu/speccoll/index.html

James E. Morrow Library   *Phone   (304) 696-2343*
400 Hal Greer Blvd.   *Fax   (304) 696-2361*
Huntington, WV 25755

Guide to Local History and Genealogy Resources
http://www.marshall.edu/speccoll/TOC.html

West Virginia Historical Resources Bibliography
http://www.marshall.edu/speccoll/RG-title.html

WISCONSIN

STATE HOME PAGE

Wisconsin State Home Page
http://www.wisconsin.gov/state/home

Vital Records Office
http://www.dhfs.state.wi.us/VitalRecords/birth.htm

STATE ARCHIVES AND HISTORICAL SOCIETY

Wisconsin Historical Society
http://www.shsw.wisc.edu/index.html

Archives
http://www.shsw.wisc.edu/archives/index.html

Library
http://www.shsw.wisc.edu/library/index.html

816 State Street, 2nd Floor   *Phone*   *(608) 264-6535*
Madison, WI 53706   *Fax*   *(608) 264-6520*

African American Newspapers
http://www.shsw.wisc.edu/library/aanp/index.html

Digital Collection
http://www.shsw.wisc.edu/library/collections/digital.html

Genealogy
http://www.wisconsinhistory.org/genealogy/index.html

Newspapers
http://www.shsw.wisc.edu/library/collections/news.html

http://www.shsw.wisc.edu/wlhba/index.asp

Wisconsin Magazine of History. (Serial). Quarterly. Index. Vol. 84, No. 1 (Fall 2000)– .
http://www.shsw.wisc.edu/wmh/annual_indexes.html

OUTSTANDING SITE

University of Wisconsin, Milwaukee
http://www.uwm.edu/Library/

Golda Meir Library
http://www.uwm.edu/Library/

2311 East Hartford Avenue,
*   Room W250*
P.O. Box 604
Milwaukee, WI 53201-0604

Phone   *(414) 229-5402*
Fax   *(414) 229-3605*
E-mail   *archives@gml.lib.uwm.edu*

Division of Archives and Special Collections
http://www.uwm.edu/Dept/Library/arch/division/

African American Collections
http://www.uwm.edu:80/Library/arch/blacks.htm

American Geographical Society Collection
http://leardo.lib.uwm.edu/

Birth Records
http://www.uwm.edu:80/Library/arch/birth.htm

Cemetery, Church, and Synagogue Records
http://www.uwm.edu/Library/arch/church.htm

Census, Federal, State, Local
http://www.uwm.edu/Library/arch/census.htm

Change of Name Records
http://www.uwm.edu/Library/arch/names.htm

Civil War Collections
http://www.uwm.edu/Library/arch/civilwar.htm

Court Records
http://www.uwm.edu/Library/arch/court.htm

Genealogical Records
http://www.uwm.edu/Library/arch/genie.htm

German American Records
http://www.uwm.edu/Library/arch/death.htm

Jewish Collections
http://www.uwm.edu/Library/arch/jewsal.htm

Naturalization Records
http://www.uwm.edu/Library/arch/citizen.htm

Polish American Records
http://www.uwm.edu/Library/arch/jewsal.htm

Probate Records
http://www.uwm.edu/Library/arch/property.htm

Vital Records, Death Records
http://www.uwm.edu/Library/arch/death.htm

Vital Records, Marriage Records
http://www.uwm.edu/Library/arch/marriage.htm

WYOMING

STATE HOME PAGE

Wyoming State Home Page
http://www.state.wy.us/

Wyoming Vital Records
http://wdhfs.state.wy.us/vital_records/certificate.htm

STATE LIBRARY

Wyoming State Library
http://www-wsl.state.wy.us/

2301 Capitol Avenue   *Phone*   *(307) 777-7281*
Cheyenne, WY 82002-0060   *Fax*   *(307) 777-6289*

Directory of Wyoming Libraries
http://cowgirl.state.wy.us/directory/

OTHER STATE SITES

University of Wyoming
http://www.uwyo.edu

American Heritage Center
http://uwadmnweb.uwyo.edu/AHC/default.htm

P.O. Box 3924   *Phone*   *(307) 766-4114*
Laramie, WY 82071   *Fax*   *(307) 766-5511*

Collection Guides
http://uwadmnweb.uwyo.edu/AHC/inventories.htm

Digital Manuscript Collections
http://uwadmnweb.uwyo.edu/AHC/digital/mss.htm

INTERNATIONAL SOURCES

AFGHANISTAN
Dowlat-e Eslami-ye Afghanestan

Library of Congress

Afghanistan Law Library
http://www.loc.gov/law/guide/afghanistan.html

World Factbook: Afghanistan
http://www.odci.gov/cia/publications/factbook/geos/af.html

ALBANIA
Republika e Shqipërisë

Library of Congress

Albania Law Library
http://www.loc.gov/law/guide/albania.html

World Factbook: Albania
http://www.cia.gov/cia/publications/factbook/geos/al.html

ALGERIA
Jumhuriya al-Jazairiya ad-Dimuqratiya ash-Shabiya

Archives Nationales D'Algérie
National Archives of Algeria
http://www.archives-dgan.gov.dz/

BP 61
Alger Gare, Algerie

Phone   (011) + 213 2 54 21 60/61
Fax   (011) + 213 2 54 16 16
E-mail   dgan@ist.cerist.dz

Library of Congress

Algeria Law Library
http://www.loc.gov/law/guide/algeria.html

World Factbook: Algeria
http://www.odci.gov/cia/publications/factbook/geos/ag.html

ANDORA
Principat d'Andorra

Arxiu Històric Nacional
National Historical Archives
http://www.andorra.ad/arxius/

Ministeri de Cultura   Phone   (011) + 376 861 889
Edifici Prada Casadet   Fax   (011) + 376 868 645
c. Prada Casadet, 8-12   E-mail: ahncultura.gov@andorra.ad
Andorra la Vella
Principat d'Andorra

Collections
http://www.andorra.ad/arxius/angles/fons/fons.htm

La Biblioteca Nacional D'Andora
http://www.andorra.ad/bibnac/

Placeta Sant Esteve, s/n   Phone   (011) + 376 826 445
Principat d'Andorra   Fax   (011) + 376 829 445
                                    E-mail   bncultura.gov@andorra.ad

Catàlegs de publicacions del Govern d'Andorra. (Serial). Annual. (1981)– .
http://www.andorra.ad/bibnac/catala/publica.htm

Ex-Libris Casa Bauró. Bibliografia d'Andorra. (Serial). Annual. (1998)–.
http://www.andorra.ad/bibnac/catala/publica.htm

Embassy of Andora
http://www.andorra.be/en/index.htm

Communs, Parishes, Town Halls in Andora
http://www.andorra.ad/catala/parroquia.htm

Library of Congress
Andora Law Library
http://www.loc.gov/law/guide/andorra.html

World Factbook: Andora
http://www.odci.gov/cia/publications/factbook/geos/an.html

ANGOLA
República Popular de Angola

Embassy of Angola
http://www.angola.org/

The Embassy of the Republic   Phone   (202) 785-1156
    of Angola   Fax   (202) 785-1258
2100-2108 16th Street, NW   E-mail   angola@angola.org
Washington, DC 20009

Library of Congress

Angola Law Library
   http://www.loc.gov/law/guide/angola.html

World Factbook: Angola
   http://www.odci.gov/cia/publications/factbook/geos/ao.html

ANTIGUA AND BARBUDA

Library of Congress

Antigua and Barbuda Law Library
   http://www.loc.gov/law/guide/antigua.html

Handbook of Latin American Studies
   http://lcweb2.loc.gov/hlas/

World Factbook: Antigua and Barbuda
   http://www.odci.gov/cia/publications/factbook/geos/ac.html

ARGENTINA
República Argentina

Archivo General de la Nación
National Archives
   http://www.archivo.gov.ar/

   Av. Leandro N. Alem 246 (1003)   Phone   *(011) + 54 (11) 4331 5531/2/3/6642*
   Buenos Aires, Argentina   Fax   *(011) + 54 (11) 44334 0065*
                                         E-mail   *archive@mininterior.gov.ar*

Passenger Lists, 1821–1870, Immigración
   http://www.archivo.gov.ar/

Biblioteca Nacional de la República Argentina
National Library of Argentina
   http://iris.bibnal.edu.ar/english/home_page.htm
   Agüero 2502
   Cuidad Autónoma de Buenos Aires, Argentina 1425

EBooks, Digital Library
   http://iris.bibnal.edu.ar/salavirtual/index.html

Online Catalog
   http://www.bibnal.edu.ar/

Registro del Estado Civil y Capacidad de Personas
Civil Registration (Vital Records)
   http://www.registrocivil.gov.ar/

Fees
   http://www.registrocivil.gov.ar/tasas.htm

Laws and Regulations
   http://www.registrocivil.gov.ar/normativa.htm

Registros Civiles de la República Argentina, Local Offices
   http://www.registrocivil.gov.ar/registros.htm

Asociacíon de Genealogía Judía de Argentina
Jewish Genealogical Association of Argentina
   http://www.agja.org.ar/

                              E-mail   genarg@invo.ar

Library of Congress
Argentina Law Library
   http://www.loc.gov/law/guide/argentina.html

Handbook of Latin American Studies
   http://lcweb2.loc.gov/hlas/

World Factbook: Argentina
   http://www.odci.gov/cia/publications/factbook/geos/ar.html

ARMENIA
Hayastani Hanrapetut'yun

National Library of Armenia
   http://www.iatp.am/sites/nla/index.html
   72 Teryan Street   *Phone   (011) + (3742) 56 48 66*
   Yerevan, Republic of Armenia   *Fax   (011) + (3742) 52 97 11*
       375009   *E-mail   nla@arm.r.am*

Library of Congress
Armenia Law Library
   http://www.loc.gov/law/guide/armenia.html

World Factbook: Armenia
   http://www.odci.gov/cia/publications/factbook/geos/am.html

ASIA

Council on East Asian Libraries
   http://purl.oclc.org/net/ceal

Committee on Chinese Materials
http://www.lib.uchicago.edu/o/cealccm/

Committee on Japanese Materials
http://www.library.arizona.edu/users/hkamada/CJM/cjmhome.html

Committee on Korean Materials
http://www.usc.edu/isd/locations/ssh/korean/kmc/

Japan Databases
http://hcl.harvard.edu/harvard-yenching/japandatabase.html

AUSTRALIA

OUTSTANDING SITE

National Archives of Australia
http://www.naa.gov.au/

Queen Victoria Terrace   *Phone*   *(011) + 61 (02) 6212 3600*
Parkes ACT 2600, Australia   *E-mail   archives@naa.gov.au*

Mailing Address:
P.O. Box 7425
Canberra Mail Centre ACT 2610, Australia

Convict Records
http://www.naa.gov.au/the_collection/family_history/other_records.html#convictRecords

Family History Materials
http://www.naa.gov.au/the_collection/family_history.html

Genealogy Fact Sheets
http://www.naa.gov.au/publications/fact_sheets/default.html#genealogy

Immigration Records
http://www.naa.gov.au/the_collection/family_history/immigrants.html

Indigenous Australians
http://www.naa.gov.au/the_collection/indigenous_records.html

Military Records
http://www.naa.gov.au/the_collection/family_history/armed_services.html

Preservation, *Archives Advices*. Fact Sheets
http://www.naa.gov.au/recordkeeping/rkpubs/advices/index.html

Vital Records
http://www.naa.gov.au/publications/fact_sheets/fs89.html

National Library of Australia

http://www.nla.gov.au/

Parkes Place   *Phone   (011) + 61 (0) 2 6262 1266*
Canberra ACT 2600, Australia   *Fax   (011) + 61 (0) 2 6273 5081*
                                            E-mail   www@nla.gov.au

Mailing Address:
P.O. Box E333
Queen Victoria Terrace
Parkes ACT 2600, Australia

Australian Periodical Publications, 1840–1845

http://www.nla.gov.au/ferg/

Collection Guides

http://www.nla.gov.au/guides/

Indexes and Databases

http://www.nla.gov.au/pathways/jnls/newsite/

Libraries in Australia

http://www.nla.gov.au/libraries/

Manuscript Collections

http://www.nla.gov.au/ms/findaids/

Online Catalog

http://www.nla.gov.au/catalogue/

OUTSTANDING SITE

Australian War Memorial

http://www.awm.gov.au/index_flash.asp

GPO Box 345   *Phone   (011) + 61 2 6243 4211*
Canberra ACT 2601 Australia   *Fax   (011) + 61 2 6243 4325*

Boer War Nominal Roll Database

http://www.awm.gov.au/database/boer.asp

Commemorative Roll Database

http://www.awm.gov.au/database/croll.asp

Family History Resources

http://www.awm.gov.au/research/family.htm

Journal of the Australian War Memorial. (Serial). Irregular. No. 28 (April 1996)– .
http://www.awm.gov.au/journal/index.htm

Online Encyclopedia of the Australian War Memorial
http://www.awm.gov.au/encyclopedia/index.htm

Personal Service Records
http://www.awm.gov.au/encyclopedia/ww1service.htm

Photograph and Other Media Collections Database Indexes
http://www.awm.gov.au/database/collection.asp

Roll of Honor
http://www.awm.gov.au/database/roh.asp

Wartime. (Serial). Irregular. Table of Contents. No. 1 (November 1997)– .
http://www.awm.gov.au/wartime/index.htm

World War I Nominal Roll Database
http://www.awm.gov.au/database/133.asp

OUTSTANDING SITE

Passenger Ships Arriving in Australasian Ports
http://members.iinet.net.au/~perthdps/shipping/mig-sa1.htm

Convicts to Australia
http://members.iinet.net.au/~perthdps/convicts/con-wa.html

New South Wales, 1837–1899
http://members.iinet.net.au/~perthdps/shipping/mig-nsw.htm

New Zealand Shipping, 1839–1905
http://members.iinet.net.au/~perthdps/shipping/mig-nz1.htm

Queensland, 1840–1915
http://members.iinet.net.au/~perthdps/shipping/mig-qld1.htm

South Australia, 1836–1840
http://members.iinet.net.au/~perthdps/shipping/mig-sa1.htm

Victoria, 1837–1899
http://members.iinet.net.au/~perthdps/shipping/mig-vic.htm

Western Australia, 1829–1889
http://members.iinet.net.au/~perthdps/shipping/mig-vic.htm

OTHER STATE SITES

Archival Authority of New South Wales

http://www.records.nsw.gov.au/

Globe Street	*Phone*	*(011) + 61 (02) 8276 5600*
The Rocks, Sydney NSW 2000	*Fax*	*(011) + (02) 8276 5604*
Australia	*E-mail*	*srecords@records.nsw.gov.au*

Mailing Address:
P.O. Box R625
Royal Exchange NSW 1225
Australia

Archives Investigator, Onine Search System

http://investigator.records.nsw.gov.au/investigator.htm

Census, 1788–1901, Convict Muster and Census Records

http://www.records.nsw.gov.au/publications/shortguides/12/page4.htm

Census, 1901 Census—Collectors' Books

http://www.records.nsw.gov.au/publications/shortguides/07/sg7-1.htm

Concise Guide to the Archives, 3rd Edition

http://www.records.nsw.gov.au/cguide/httoc.htm

For the Record. Newsletter. (Serial). No. 9 (February 1996)– .

http://www.records.nsw.gov.au/publications/fortherecord/backissues.htm

Land Grants, 1788–1856

http://www.records.nsw.gov.au/publications/shortguides/08/sg8-4.htm

Links, Australian Sites

http://www.records.nsw.gov.au/links/links.htm

Naturalization and Denization Records, 1834–1903

http://www.records.nsw.gov.au/publications/shortguides/09/page2.htm

Vital Records

http://www.records.nsw.gov.au/publications/shortguides/02/sg2-2.htm

Vital Records—Attorney General and Justice—Registry of Births, Deaths, and Marriages

http://www.records.nsw.gov.au/publications/shortguides/04/sg4-1.htm

Archives Office of Tasmania

http://www.archives.tas.gov.au/

77 Murray Street	*Phone*	*(011) + 61 3 6233 7488*
Hobart, Tasmania 7000	*Fax*	*(011) + 61 3 6233 7471*
Australia	*E-mail*	*archives.tasmania@education.*
		tas.gov.au

Collection Guides
http://www.archives.tas.gov.au/guides-to-holdings/

Colonial Tasmanian Family Links Database
http://pioneers.archives.tas.gov.au/

Convict Records
http://www.archives.tas.gov.au/guides-to-holdings/guide13.htm

District Registers of Births and Deaths Available on Microfilm
http://www.archives.tas.gov.au/guides-to-holdings/guide9.htm

Guide to the Records of the Colonial Secretary's Office
http://www.archives.tas.gov.au/publications/guides.htm

Guide to the Records of the Convict Department
http://www.archives.tas.gov.au/publications/guides.htm

Guide to the Records of the Governor's Office
http://www.archives.tas.gov.au/publications/guides.htm

Historical Tasmanian Photograph Collection, Index
http://www.archphotos.archives.tas.gov.au/

Naturalization Records
http://www.archives.tas.gov.au/guides-to-holdings/guide10.htm

Naturalization Records—Applications Index, 1835–1905
http://www.archives.tas.gov.au/genealogies/idxnatapps.htm

Probate Records
http://www.archives.tas.gov.au/guides-to-holdings/guide12.htm

Probate Records—Index to Wills, 1824–1915
http://www.archives.tas.gov.au/genealogies/idxofwills.htm

Vital Records
http://www.archives.tas.gov.au/guides-to-holdings/guide15.htm

Library and Information Service of Western Australia
http://www.liswa.wa.gov.au/index.html

Genealogy Centre
http://web.liswa.wa.gov.au/geneocent.html

State Records Office
http://www.sro.wa.gov.au/

Alexander Library Building	*Phone* *(011) + 61 8 9427 3111*
Perth Cultural Centre	*Fax* *(011) + 61 8 9427 3256*
Perth, Western Australia 6000	*E-mail* *info@liswa.wa.gov.au*
Australia	

Northern Territory Archives Service

http://www.nt.gov.au/nta/

2nd Floor	*Phone* (011) + (08) 8924 7677*
25 Cavenagh Street	*Fax* (011) + (08) 8924 7660*
Darwin NT 0800	*E-mail nt.archives@nt.gov.au*
Australia	

Mailing Address:
GPO Box 874
Darwin NT 0801
Australia

Biographical Archives

http://www.nt.gov.au/nta/4_guides/4-3_person/4-3_personal.htm

Collection Guides

http://www.nt.gov.au/nta/4_guides/guides.htm

Guide to Northern Territory Government and Local Government Organizations (Includes Registrar General's Office)

http://www.nt.gov.au/nta/4_guides/4-9_centaus/localgov.htm

Guide to Records of Aboriginal People in the Northern Territory

http://www.nt.gov.au/nta/4_guides/4-10_aborig/4-10_ab.htm

Guide to Records of Chinese in the Northern Territory

http://www.nt.gov.au/nta/4_guides/4-13_chinese/4-13%20chinese.htm

Oral History Program

http://www.nt.gov.au/nta/5_oral/oral1.htm

Protocols for Aboriginal Access to Records

http://www.nt.gov.au/nta/2_research/2-6_protocol.htm

Records Territory. (Serial). Irregular. No. 12 (September 1996)– .

http://www.nt.gov.au/nta/6_news/newslet1.htm

Queensland State Archives

http://www.archives.qld.gov.au/

435 Compton Road	*Phone* (011) + 61 7 875 8755*
Runcorn, Queensland 4113	*Fax* (011) + 61 7 875 8764*
Australia	*E-mail qsa@iie.qld.gov.au*

Mailing Address:
P.O. Box 1397
Sunnybank Hills, Queensland 4109
Australia

Aboriginal Records

http://www.archives.qld.gov.au/resserv/atsip.html

Database Search

http://www.archivessearch.qld.gov.au/Production/QsaMain.Asp

Family History Resources

http://www.archives.qld.gov.au/aids/famhist1.html

Finding Aids

http://www.archives.qld.gov.au/aids/aidslist.html

Runcord Record. (Serial). Vol. 7, No. 1 (January 2001)– .

http://www.archives.qld.gov.au/index_publications.html

Vital Records

http://www.archives.qld.gov.au/resserv/bdm.html

State Archives of South Australia

http://www.archives.sa.gov.au/

P.O. Box 1056	*E-mail* *staterecords@saugov.sa.gov.au*
Blair Athol West 5084	
South Australia	
Australia	

Aboriginal Records

http://www.archives.sa.gov.au/aboriginal/index.html

Family History Records

http://www.archives.sa.gov.au/archives/family_index.htm

recordSAarchive. (Serial). Quarterly. (September 1999)– .

http://www.archives.sa.gov.au/new/newsletter.htm

State Library of New South Wales

http://www.slnsw.gov.au/

Macquarie Street	*Phone*	*(011) + 61 2 9273 1414*
Sydney, NSW Australia 2000	*Fax*	*(011) + 61 2 9273 1255*

Newspaper Indexes. *Sydney Morning Herald, Sun Herald, Eastern Herald, Northern Herald,* and *Good Weekend* 1988– .

http://www.slnsw.gov.au/find/

Online Catalog

http://www.slnsw.gov.au/eres/

State Library of South Australia

http://www.slsa.sa.gov.au/

North Terrace	*Phone*	*(011) + 61 8 82077200*
Adelaide 5000, South Australia	*Fax*	*(011) + 61 8 82077247*
Australia	*E-mail*	*research@slsa.sa.gov.au*

Archival Database

http://www.catalog.slsa.sa.gov.au:1083/screens/opacmenu.html

Family History Service

http://www.slsa.sa.gov.au/gateway/lib_guide/fh/famhist.htm

Immigration and Passenger Lists
http://www.slsa.sa.gov.au/gateway/lib_guide/fh/shipping.htm

Newspaper Indexes and Databases
http://www.slsa.sa.gov.au/gateway/lib_guide/subjects/sgw070.htm

Online Catalog
http://www.catalog.slsa.sa.gov.au/screens/opacmenu.html

South Australiana Database
http://www.catalog.slsa.sa.gov.au:1084/screens/opacmenu.html

Vital Records
http://www.slsa.sa.gov.au/gateway/lib_guide/fh/births_deaths.htm

State Library of Tasmania
http://www.statelibrary.tas.gov.au/

91 Murray Street	*Phone*	*(011) + 61 3 6233 7511*
Hobart Tasmania 7000	*Fax*	*(011) + 61 3 6131 0927*
Australia	*E-mail*	*state.library@education.tas.gov.au*

Almanacs and Directories
http://www.statelibrary.tas.gov.au/collections/Famhistory/almanacs.htm

Cemetery Records
http://www.statelibrary.tas.gov.au/collections/Famhistory/Cemetery.htm

Census and Convict Muster Records
http://www.statelibrary.tas.gov.au/collections/Famhistory/census.htm

Convict Records
http://www.statelibrary.tas.gov.au/collections/Famhistory/convict.htm

Family History Journals
http://www.statelibrary.tas.gov.au/collections/famhistory/newsletters.htm

Family History Resources
http://www.statelibrary.tas.gov.au/collections/Famhistory/

Military Records
http://www.statelibrary.tas.gov.au/collections/Famhistory/military.htm

Newspapers
http://www.statelibrary.tas.gov.au/collections/Famhistory/newspapers.htm

Online Catalog
http://www.talis.tas.gov.au:8000/

Our Digital Island (Collection of Preserved Tasmanian Web Sites)
http://www.statelibrary.tas.gov.au/odi/

Passenger Lists and Records
http://www.statelibrary.tas.gov.au/collections/Famhistory/shippingrecords.htm

Photograph and Related Collections
http://images.statelibrary.tas.gov.au/

Research Collections
http://www.statelibrary.tas.gov.au/collections/refcoll.htm

Tasmanian Index of Community Organizations (TICO)
http://tico.tased.edu.au/

Tasmania's eHeritage Collection
http://www.statelibrary.tas.gov.au/eheritage/

Victorian and Edwardian Collections
http://www.statelibrary.tas.gov.au/vande/

Vital Records
http://www.statelibrary.tas.gov.au/collections/Famhistory/BDMindexes.htm

State Library of Victoria
http://www.slv.vic.gov.au/

328 Swanston Street	*Phone (011) + (03) 8664 7008*
Melbourne, Victoria, 3000	*Fax (011) + (03) 9639 3673*
Australia	

Australiana Collections
http://www.statelibrary.vic.gov.au/slv/latrobe/

Australian and New Zealand Post Office Directories
http://www.statelibrary.vic.gov.au/slv/latrobe/postdir2.htm

Australian Manuscripts Collection
http://www.statelibrary.vic.gov.au/slv/manuscripts/

Genealogy Centre
http://www.statelibrary.vic.gov.au/slv/genealogy/

Manuscripts Catalog
http://catalogue.slv.vic.gov.au/webvoy.htm

Melbourne Street Directories
http://www.statelibrary.vic.gov.au/slv/latrobe/streetdi.htm

Newspaper Collection
http://www.statelibrary.vic.gov.au/slv/newspapers/

Online Catalog
http://catalogue.slv.vic.gov.au/webvoy.htm

OUTSTANDING SITE

Victoria, Public Records Office
http://www.prov.vic.gov.au/welcome.htm

Keeper of Public Records   *Phone*   *(011) + (03) 9348 5600*
P.O. Box 2100   *Fax*   *(011) + (03) 9285 7953*
North Melbourne Victoria 3051 *E-mail* *ask.prov@dpc.vic.gov.au*
Australia

AUSTRIA
Republik Österreich

Österreichischen Staatsarchiv
Austrian State Archives
   http://www.oesta.gv.at/index.htm

   Nottendorfergrasse 2   *Phone*   *(011) + 43 1 795 40 452*
   A-1030, Vienna, Austria   *Fax*   *(011) + 43 1 795 40 109*

Archives
   http://www.oesta.gv.at/engdiv/organiza.htm

Family Court and State Archives
   http://www.oesta.gv.at/ebestand/ehh/efr1hh.htm

Genealogy Research
   http://www.oesta.gv.at/engdiv/geneal.htm

Military Archives
   http://www.oesta.gv.at/ebestand/ekv/efr1_kv.htm

Österreichischen Nationalbibliothek
Austrian National Library
   http://www.onb.ac.at/

   Josefsplatz 1   *Phone*   *(011) + 43 1 534 10*
   Postfach 308   *Fax*   *(011) + 43 1 534 10 Ext. 280*
   A-1015, Vienna, Austria   *E-mail* *onb@email.onb.ac.at*

Austrian National Union Catalog
   http://www.onb.ac.at/ev/catalogues/index.htm

Manuscripts
   http://www.onb.ac.at/ev/collections/manuscripts/index.htm

Map Department
   http://www.onb.ac.at/ev/collections/maps/index.htm

Online Library Catalog
http://www.onb.ac.at/ev/catalogues/index.htm

Society of Friends of the Austrian National Library
http://www.onb.ac.at/ev/about/friends.htm

Library of Congress

Austria Law Library
http://www.loc.gov/law/guide/armenia.html

World Factbook: Austria
http://www.odci.gov/cia/publications/factbook/geos/au.html

AZERBAIJAN
Azarbaijchan Respublikasy

Library of Congress

Azerbaijan Law Library
http://www.loc.gov/law/guide/azerbaijan.html

World Factbook: Azerbaijan
http://www.odci.gov/cia/publications/factbook/geos/aj.html

BAHAMAS

Library of Congress

Bahamas Law Library
http://www.loc.gov/law/guide/bahamas.html

Handbook of Latin American Studies
http://lcweb2.loc.gov/hlas/

World Factbook: Bahamas
http://www.odci.gov/cia/publications/factbook/geos/bf.html

BAHRAIN
Dawlat al Bahrayn

Library of Congress

Bahrain Law Library
http://www.loc.gov/law/guide/bahrain.html

World Factbook: Bahrain
http://www.odci.gov/cia/publications/factbook/geos/ba.html

BANGLADESH
Gana Prajatantri Bangladesh

Family History in India
http://members.ozemail.com.au/%7Eclday/index.html

Church Records in Colonial India
http://members.ozemail.com.au/%7Eclday/churches.htm

European Cemeteries in India
http://members.ozemail.com.au/%7Eclday/cem.htm

European Surnames in India
http://members.ozemail.com.au/%7Eclday/misc.htm

Goa Church Records
http://users.rootsweb.com/~indwgw/FIBIS/LDSGoa.htm

Indian Genealogy
http://members.ozemail.com.au/~clday/indian.htm

Madras Female Asylum (Orphanage). 1839 Register
http://users.rootsweb.com/~indwgw/orphan2.htm

Military and Other Sources for India Genealogical Research
http://members.ozemail.com.au/%7Eclday/other.htm

Regimental Histories of British Army Units That Served in India
http://members.ozemail.com.au/%7Eclday/regiments.htm

Library of Congress

Bangladesh Law Library
http://www.loc.gov/law/guide/bangladesh.html

World Factbook: Bangladesh
http://www.odci.gov/cia/publications/factbook/geos/bg.html

BARBADOS

Library of Congress

Barbados Law Library
http://www.loc.gov/law/guide/barbados.html

Handbook of Latin American Studies
http://lcweb2.loc.gov/hlas/

World Factbook: Barbados
http://www.odci.gov/cia/publications/factbook/geos/bb.html

BELARUS
Respublika Belarus

Library of Congress

Belarus Law Library
http://www.loc.gov/law/guide/belarus.html

World Factbook: Belarus
http://www.odci.gov/cia/publications/factbook/geos/bo.html

RAGAS Russian-American Genealogical Archival Service
http://feefhs.org/ragas/frgragas.html

U.S. Address:
1929 18th Street N.W., Suite 112
Washington, DC 20009-1710

Russian Address:
c/o Genealogy and Family History   *Fax*   *(011) + 246 20 20 to M-200*
* Society*   *E-mail vladrag@glas.apc.org*
P.O. Box 459
Moscow 123749, Russia

Genealogical Sources
http://feefhs.org/ragas/rag-sour.html

Overview
http://feefhs.org/ragas/rag-ltr.html

BELGIUM
Koninkrijk België

Belgische Genealogische Verenigingen
Genealogy in Belgium
http://users.skynet.be/sky60754/genealbe/geneabelgver.htm

Belgische Federatie voor Genealogie en Heraldiek and the Belgian Federation of Geneology and Heraldry
http://users.skynet.be/sky60754/genealbe/geneabelgverdet.htm#Federatie

Service de Centralisation des Études Généalogiques et Démographiques de Belgique
http://users.skynet.be/sky60754/genealbe/geneabelgverdet.htm#Service

Vlaamse Vereniging voor Familiekunde
http://users.skynet.be/sky60754/genealbe/geneabelgverdet.htm#Service

Library of Congress

Belgium Law Library
http://www.loc.gov/law/guide/belgium.html

World Factbook: Belgium
http://www.odci.gov/cia/publications/factbook/geos/be.html

Office Généalogique et Héraldique de Belgique
Office of Geneology and Heraldry of Belgium
http://www.oghb.org/

Avenue Charles Thielemans, 93   Phone   *(011) + 02 772 50 27*
B -1150 Bruxelles

Belgian Genealogy
http://www.oghb.org/

BELIZE

Library of Congress

Belize Law Library
http://www.loc.gov/law/guide/belize.html

Handbook of Latin American Studies
http://lcweb2.loc.gov/hlas/

World Factbook: Belize
http://www.odci.gov/cia/publications/factbook/geos/bh.html

BENIN
République du Bénin

Archives Nationales du Bénin
National Archives of Benin
http://www.unesco.org/webworld/archives/benin/anb.htm

Boîte Postale 629   Phone   *(011) + (229) 21 30 79*
Porto-Novo, Benin   Fax   *(011) + (229) 21 30 79*

Archival Guides
http://www.unesco.org/webworld/archives/benin/guidep03.html

Library of Congress

Benin Law Library
http://www.loc.gov/law/guide/benin.html

World Factbook: Benin
http://www.odci.gov/cia/publications/factbook/geos/bn.html

BHUTAN
Druk-yul

Library of Congress

Bhutan Law Library
http://www.loc.gov/law/guide/bhutan.html

World Factbook: Bhutan
http://www.odci.gov/cia/publications/factbook/geos/bt.html

BOLIVIA
República de Bolivia

La Biblioteca Nacional de Bolivia y el Archivo Nacional de Bolivia
National Library and National Archives of Bolivia
http://www.bcb.gov.bo/8fundacion/1infgeneral/biblioteca.html

Dirección: Calle España N° 43   *Phone   (011) + 0591 64 52986*
Casilla de Correos: 793   *E-mail   director@abnb.nch.edu.bo*
Sucre–Bolivia

Library of Congress

Bolivia Law Library
http://www.loc.gov/law/guide/bolivia.html

Handbook of Latin American Studies
http://lcweb2.loc.gov/hlas/

World Factbook: Bolivia
http://www.odci.gov/cia/publications/factbook/geos/bl.html

BOSNIA AND HERZEGOVINA
Republika Bosna i Hercegovina

Bosnian Ingathering Manuscript Program
http://www.kakarigi.net/manu/ingather.htm

E-mail   riedlmay@fas.harvard.edu

Library of Congress

Bosnia and Herzegovina Law Library
http://www.loc.gov/law/guide/bosnia.html

World Factbook: Bosnia and Herzegovina
http://www.odci.gov/cia/publications/factbook/geos/bk.html

BOTSWANA

Library of Congress

Botswana Law Library
> http://www.loc.gov/law/guide/botswana.html

World Factbook: Botswana
> http://www.odci.gov/cia/publications/factbook/geos/bc.html

BRAZIL

República Federativa do Brasil

Arquivo Nacional do Brasil
National Archives of Brazil
> http://www.arquivonacional.gov.br/

R. Azeredo Coutinho, 77	*Phone* *(011) + 55 21 232 4564*
Centro	*Fax* *(011) + 55 21 232 8430*
CEP 20.230-170	
Rio de Janeiro, RJ, Brazil	

Collection Guides
> http://www.arquivonacional.gov.br/cgi/GF_Pesquisa.htm

Immigration and Naturalization Records
> http://www.arquivonacional.gov.br/serv_pub/con_est.htm

Virtual Publications
> http://www.arquivonacional.gov.br/pub/virtual/virtual.htm

Library of Congress

Brazil Law Library
> http://www.loc.gov/law/guide/brazil.html

Handbook of Latin American Studies
> http://lcweb2.loc.gov/hlas/

World Factbook: Brazil
> http://www.odci.gov/cia/publications/factbook/geos/br.html

BRUNEI

Negara Brunei Darussalam

Library of Congress

Brunei Law Library
> http://www.loc.gov/law/guide/brunei.html

World Factbook: Brunei
http://www.odci.gov/cia/publications/factbook/geos/bx.html

BULGARIA
Republika Bulgaria

Library of Congress

Bulgaria Law Library
http://www.loc.gov/law/guide/bulgaria.html

World Factbook: Bulgaria
http://www.odci.gov/cia/publications/factbook/geos/bu.html

BURKINA FASO
République Democratique Populaire de Burkina Faso

Library of Congress

Burkina Faso Law Library
http://www.loc.gov/law/guide/burkina.html

World Factbook: Burkina Faso
http://www.odci.gov/cia/publications/factbook/geos/uv.html

BURMA
Myanma Naingngandaw

Library of Congress

Burma Law Library
http://www.loc.gov/law/guide/burma.html

World Factbook: Burma
http://www.odci.gov/cia/publications/factbook/geos/bm.html

BURUNDI
Republika y'Uburundi

Library of Congress

Burundi Law Library
http://www.loc.gov/law/guide/burundi.html

World Factbook: Burundi
http://www.odci.gov/cia/publications/factbook/geos/by.html

CAMBODIA
Preah Réachéanachâkr Kâmpuchéa

National Archives of Cambodia

http://www.camnet.com.kh/archives.cambodia/English/welcome.htm

P.O. Box 1109   Phone   (011) + 855 23 430 582
Phnom Penh, Cambodia   E-mail   archives.cambodia@camnet.com.kh

Archives at Risk in Cambodia. A Report

http://www.camnet.com.kh/archives.cambodia/English/archrisk.htm

Collections

http://www.camnet.com.kh/archives.cambodia/English/naccoll.htm

Library of Congress

Cambodia Law Library

http://www.loc.gov/law/guide/cambodia.html

World Factbook: Cambodia

http://www.odci.gov/cia/publications/factbook/geos/cb.html

CAMEROON
République du Cameroun

Library of Congress

Cameroon Law Library

http://www.loc.gov/law/guide/cameroon.html

World Factbook: Cameroon

http://www.odci.gov/cia/publications/factbook/geos/cm.html

CANADA

OUTSTANDING SITE

National Archives of Canada

http://www.archives.ca/08/08_e.html

Genealogy Unit   Phone   (613) 996-7458
Researcher Services Division   Fax   (613) 995-6274
395 Wellington Street
Ottawa, Ontario, Canada K1A 0N3

Colonial Archives
http://www.archives.ca/02/0201/020128_e.html

Genealogy
http://www.archives.ca/02/0201/020130_e.html

Immigration Records
http://www.archives.ca/02/02020204_e.html

Military Records
http://www.archives.ca/02/020203_e.html

Probate Records
http://www.archives.ca/02/020202/02020208_e.html

Western Land Grants
http://www.archives.ca/02/020111_e.html

National Library of Canada
http://www.nlc-bnc.ca/

395 Wellington Street	*Phone* (613) 996-5278
Ottawa, Ontario, Canada K1A 0N4	*Fax* (613) 943-1112
	E-mail reference@nlc-bnc.ca

Canadiana, National Bibliography
http://www.nlc-bnc.ca/canadiana/index-e.html

Canadian Library Gateway
http://www.nlc-bnc.ca/gatepasse/index_e.htm

Cemetery Records
http://www.nlc-bnc.ca/6/5/s5-201-e.html

Directory of Special Collections of Research Value in Canadian Libraries
http://www.nlc-bnc.ca/collectionsp/intro_e.htm

eBooks
http://collection.nlc-bnc.ca/e-coll-e/index-e.htm

Family Histories
http://www.nlc-bnc.ca/6/5/s5-203-e.html

Genealogical and Historical Periodicals
http://www.nlc-bnc.ca/6/5/s5-209-e.html

Genealogy and Family History at the National Library of Canada
http://www.nlc-bnc.ca/6/5/

Local Histories
http://www.nlc-bnc.ca/6/5/s5-202-e.html

Newspapers, Indexes to Canadian Newspapers, a Checklist
http://www.nlc-bnc.ca/8/12/index-e.html

Online Library Catalog, AMICUS
http://www.nlc-bnc.ca/amicus/index-e.html

Parish Registers
http://www.nlc-bnc.ca/6/5/s5-206-e.html

Library of Congress

Canada Law Library
http://www.loc.gov/law/guide/canada.html

World Factbook: Canada
http://www.odci.gov/cia/publications/factbook/geos/ca.html

OTHER PROVINCIAL SITES

Archives nationales du Québec
Quebec National Archives
http://www.anq.gouv.qc.ca/

225, Grande Allée Est   Phone   (418) 380-2399
Bloc C, 1er étage   Fax   (418) 380-2320
Québec G1R 5G5, Canada

Collections
http://www.anq.gouv.qc.ca/ANQ-D.html

Directory, Regional Centers
http://www.anq.gouv.qc.ca/institution/centres.htm

Genealogical Services
http://www.anq.gouv.qc.ca/ANQ-E-02.html

OUTSTANDING SITE

Archives of Ontario
http://www.archives.gov.on.ca/

77 Grenville St., Unit 300   Phone   (416) 327-1582
Toronto, Ontario, Canada M5S 1B3   Fax   (416) 327-1999
                                    E-mail   sommerc@archives.gov.on.ca

Divorce Records
http://www.archives.gov.on.ca/english/virtualrr/infohandout.htm

Genealogy Research
http://www.archives.gov.on.ca/english/geneal/index.html

Guides
http://www.archives.gov.on.ca/english/virtualrr/infohandout.htm

Probate Records
http://www.archives.gov.on.ca/english/virtualrr/info15.htm

Vital Records
http://www.archives.gov.on.ca/english/virtualrr/info9.htm

British Columbia Archives
http://www.bcarchives.gov.bc.ca/index.htm

655 Belleville Street   *Phone* *(250) 387-1952*
Victoria, BC, Canada V8V 1X4   *Fax*   *(250) 387-2072*
                               E-mail *access@www.bcarchives.gov.bc.ca*

Mailing Address:
865 Yates Street
Victoria, BC, Canada V8V 1X4

Collections
http://www.bcarchives.gov.bc.ca/sn-45E88AE/textual/general/textual.htm

Genealogical Resources
http://www.bcarchives.gov.bc.ca/textual/general/genealog.htm

Map Collection
http://www.bcarchives.gov.bc.ca/sn-45E88AE/cartogr/general/maps.htm

Online Library Catalog
http://www.bcarchives.gov.bc.ca/sn-45E88AE/library/general/library.htm

Vital Records
http://www.bcarchives.gov.bc.ca/textual/governmt/vstats/v_events.htm

Vital Records, Birth Registration Index, 1872–1901
http://www.bcarchives.gov.bc.ca:9000/sn-400ACDA/gbsearch/Births

Vital Records, Death Registration Index, 1872–1981
http://www.bcarchives.gov.bc.ca:9000/sn-45E88AE/gbsearch/Deaths

Vital Records, Marriage Registration Index, 1872–1926
http://www.bcarchives.gov.bc.ca:9000/sn-3B675C0/gbsearch/Marriages

Prince Edward Island Public Archives and Records Office
http://www.edu.pe.ca/paro/

Hon. George Coles Building   *Phone* *(902) 368-4290*
Richmond Street
Charlottetown, PEI, Canada

Census Records
http://www.edu.pe.ca/paro/research/census.asp

Genealogical Research
http://www.edu.pe.ca/paro/research/research.asp

Land Records
http://www.edu.pe.ca/paro/research/land.asp

Tracing Your Family Tree on Prince Edward Island
http://www.edu.pe.ca/paro/familyhistory/default.asp

Vital Records
http://www.edu.pe.ca/paro/research/births.asp

CAPE VERDE

República de Cabo Verde

Library of Congress

Cape Verde Law Library
http://www.loc.gov/law/guide/capeverde.html

World Factbook: Cape Verde
http://www.odci.gov/cia/publications/factbook/geos/cv.html

CARIBBEAN

Généalogie et Histoire de la Caraïbe
Caribbean Genealogy and History
http://members.aol.com/GHCaraibe/index.html

Pavillon 23   E-mail   *GHCaraibe@aol.com*
12 Avenue Charles de Gaulle
78230 La Pecq, France

Généalogie et Histoire de la Caraïbe. (Serial). No. 1 (1989)– .
http://members.aol.com/GHCaraibe/bul/sombul.html

Guadeloupe
http://members.aol.com/GHCaraibe/geo/geoguad1.html

Guyane
http://members.aol.com/GHCaraibe/geo/geoguya1.html

Martinique
http://members.aol.com/GHCaraibe/geo/geomart1.html

Saint-Pierre et Miquelon
http://members.aol.com/GHCaraibe/geo/geospmi1.html

CENTRAL AFRICAN REPUBLIC
République Centrafricaine Ködrö ti Bê Afrika

Library of Congress

Central African Republic Law Library
http://www.loc.gov/law/guide/car.html

World Factbook: Central African Republic
http://www.odci.gov/cia/publications/factbook/geos/ct.html

CHAD
République du Tchad

Library of Congress

Chad Law Library
http://www.loc.gov/law/guide/chad.html

World Factbook: Chad
http://www.odci.gov/cia/publications/factbook/geos/cd.html

CHILE
República de Chile

Archivo Nacional de Chile
National Archives of Chile
http://www.dibam.cl/archivo_nacional/index_arch.html

Miraflores # 50   Phone   *(011) + 562 633 89 57 Ext. 258*
Santiago, Chile

Archivo Siglo XX   Phone   *(011) + 562 681 79 79*
Agustinas # 3250
Santiago, Chile

Collections
http://www.dibam.cl/archivo_nacional/fondoarch.html

Departments
http://www.dibam.cl/archivo_nacional/seccionesarch.html

Biblioteca Nacional de Chile
National Library of Chile
http://www.dibam.cl/biblioteca_nacional/index_bn.html

Av. Bernardo O'Higgins 651   Phone   *(011) + 562 633 89 57 x227*
Santiago, Chile   E-mail   *egonzale@oris.renib.cl*

Online Catalog
www.bncatalogo.cl

Virtual Library
http://www.dibam.cl/biblioteca_nacional/index_bn.html

Dirección de Bibliotecas, Archivos y Museos
National Office of Libraries, Archives, and Museums
http://www.dibam.cl/

Public Libraries of Chile
http://www.dibam.cl/bibliotecas_publicas/fset_bp.html

Library of Congress
Chile Law Library
http://www.loc.gov/law/guide/chile.html

Handbook of Latin American Studies
http://lcweb2.loc.gov/hlas/

World Factbook: Chile
http://www.odci.gov/cia/publications/factbook/geos/ci.html

Servicio de Registro Civil e Identificación
Civil Registration and Identity Card Service
http://www.registrocivil.cl/registro/

Cathedral 1772 Piso 3   *Phone   (011) + 562 782-2000*
Santiago, Chile

CHINA

Chinese Historical Society of America
http://www.chsa.org/
965 Clay Street   *Phone   (415) 391-1188*
San Francisco, CA 94108   *Fax   (415) 391-1150*
                               E-mail   info@chsa.org

Bulletin. (Serial). Monthly. Table of Contents. No. 1 (February 1999)– .
http://www.chsa.org/resources/bulletin.htm

Chinese America: History and Perspectives. (Serial). Annual. Table of Contents.
Vol. 1 (1987)– .
http://www.chsa.org/resources/index.htm#Publications

Chinese Americans in the Civil War
http://www.chsa.org/resources/civilwar.htm

Chinese Historical Society of Southern California
http://www.chssc.org/

P.O. Box 862647   E-mail   chssc@chssc.org
Los Angeles, CA 90086-2647

Chinese Americans in World War II
http://www.chssc.org/ww2photos/index.html

Memorial Shrine, 1888
http://www.chssc.org/shrinededication.html

Overview
http://www.chssc.org/

Timeline, Chinese Americans in California
http://www.chssc.org/timeline.html

Chinese in Guyana: Their Roots
http://www.rootsweb.com/~guycigtr/

3495 Cambie Street   E-mail   Canereapers@Lycos.com
P.O. Box 556
Vancouver, BC V5Z 4R3
Canada

A History of the Chinese Indentured Labourers
http://www.rootsweb.com/~guycigtr/History.htm

Passenger Lists
http://www.rootsweb.com/~guycigtr/Passengers.htm

ChineseRoots.com
http://www.chineseroots.com/english/main.jsp

Surname Dictionary
http://www.chineseroots.com/english/manual/surnames/search/searchDic.jsp

Council on East Asian Libraries
http://purl.oclc.org/net/ceal

Committee on Chinese Materials
http://www.lib.uchicago.edu/o/cealccm/

Committee on Japanese Materials
http://www.library.arizona.edu/users/hkamada/CJM/cjmhome.html

Committee on Korean Materials
http://www.usc.edu/isd/locations/ssh/korean/kmc/

Japan Databases
http://hcl.harvard.edu/harvard-yenching/japandatabase.html

Library of Congress

China Law Library
> http://www.loc.gov/law/guide/china.html

World Factbook: China
> http://www.odci.gov/cia/publications/factbook/geos/ch.html

Northern Territory Archives Service
> http://www.nt.gov.au/nta/

2nd Floor	*Phone* *(011) + 61 (08) 8924 7677*
25 Cavenagh Street	*Fax* *(011) + 61 (08) 8924 7660*
Darwin NT 0800	*E-mail* *nt.archives@nt.gov.au*
Australia	

Mailing Address:
GPO Box 874
Darwin NT 0801
Australia

Guide to Records of Chinese in the Northern Territory
> http://www.nt.gov.au/nta/4_guides/4-13_chinese/4-13%20chinese.htm

Promise of Gold Mountain: Tucson's Chinese Heritage
> http://dizzy.library.arizona.edu/promise/

Bibliography
> http://dizzy.library.arizona.edu/promise/sources_041801.html

Biographies of Prominent Chinese American Tucsonans
> http://dizzy.library.arizona.edu/promise/bios_041801.html

Farms and Small Businesses
> http://dizzy.library.arizona.edu/promise/farmb_041801.html

Hi Wo Family
> http://www.library.arizona.edu/soza/hiwo.htm

"Immigrants to a Developing Society: The Chinese in Northern Mexico, 1875–1932," by Evelyn Hu DeHart
> http://dizzy.library.arizona.edu/promise/hu_041801.html

"Sojourners and Settlers, the Chinese Experience in Arizona," by Lawrence Michael Fong
> http://dizzy.library.arizona.edu/promise/lmfong_041801.html

Southern Pacific Railroad Workers
> http://dizzy.library.arizona.edu/promise/railroad_041801.html

Tucson's Chinatowns
> http://dizzy.library.arizona.edu/promise/chinat_041801.html

Video Clips
> http://dizzy.library.arizona.edu/promise/video_041801.html

COLOMBIA
República de Colombia

Archivo General de la Nación
National Archives of Colombia
> http://www.archivogeneral.gov.co/noticias/wmview.php?ArtID=2

Carrera 6a. No. 6 91	*Phone (011) + 57 3373111*
Bogotá, Colombia	*Fax (011) + 57 3372019*

La Superintendencia de Notariado y Registro
Superintendent of Notaries and Civil Registration
> http://www.anticorrupcion.gov.co/supernot/paginas/tramites_super.htm

Cl. 26 No. 13-49	*Phone (011) + 57 286 6286 Ext. 207*
Bogotá, Colombia	*(011) + 57 284 9456 Ext. 248*
	(011) + 57 281 1877 Ext. 270
	Fax (011) + 57 286 7136
	E-mail deleregi@latinonet.co

Library of Congress

Colombia Law Library
> http://www.loc.gov/law/guide/colombia.html

Handbook of Latin American Studies
> http://lcweb2.loc.gov/hlas/

World Factbook: Colombia
> http://www.odci.gov/cia/publications/factbook/geos/co.html

COMOROS
République Fédérale Islamique des Comores

Library of Congress

Comoros Law Library
> http://www.loc.gov/law/guide/comoros.html

World Factbook: Comoros
> http://www.odci.gov/cia/publications/factbook/geos/cn.html

CONGO, DEMOCRATIC REPUBLIC OF THE
République Democratique du Congo

Library of Congress

Congo Law Library
> http://www.loc.gov/law/guide/congodr.html

World Factbook: Congo
http://www.odci.gov/cia/publications/factbook/geos/cg.html

CONGO, REPUBLIC OF THE
République du Congo

Library of Congress

Congo Law Library
http://www.loc.gov/law/guide/congo.html

World Factbook: Congo
http://www.odci.gov/cia/publications/factbook/geos/cf.html

COSTA RICA
República de Costa Rica

Library of Congress

Costa Rica Law Library
http://www.loc.gov/law/guide/costarica.html

Handbook of Latin American Studies
http://lcweb2.loc.gov/hlas/

World Factbook: Costa Rica
http://www.odci.gov/cia/publications/factbook/geos/cs.html

CROATIA
Republika Hrvatska

Otvorena Vlada Pojmovno Kazalo Arhivi
Croatian State Archives
http://nippur.irb.hr/eng/crolibs.html

Collections
http://www.arhiv.hr/hr/fondovi/index.html

Otvorena Vlada Pojmovno Kazalo Knjiznice
Croatian Libraries
http://www.otvorena.vlada.hr/knjiz.htm

Library of Congress

Croatia Law Library
http://www.loc.gov/law/guide/croatia.html

World Factbook: Croatia
http://www.odci.gov/cia/publications/factbook/geos/hr.html

CUBA
República de Cuba

Library of Congress

Cuba Law Library
   http://www.loc.gov/law/guide/cuba.html

Handbook of Latin American Studies
   http://lcweb2.loc.gov/hlas/

World Factbook: Cuba
   http://www.odci.gov/cia/publications/factbook/geos/cu.html

Schomburg Center for Research in Black Culture
   http://www.nypl.org/research/sc/sc.html

   515 Malcolm X Boulevard   *Phone   (212) 491-2200*
   New York, NY 10037-1801

Fernando Ortiz Collection: A Bibliography of Afro-Cuban Material
   http://digital.nypl.org/schomburg/ortiz/ortizfront.htm

CYPRUS
Kypriaki Dimokratia

Library of Congress

Cyprus Law Library
   http://www.loc.gov/law/guide/cyprus.html

World Factbook: Cyprus
   http://www.odci.gov/cia/publications/factbook/geos/cy.html

CZECH REPUBLIC
Ceska Republika

Archivní správa Ministerstva vnitra České republiky
National Archives
   http://www.mvcr.cz/odbor/arch2.htm

   M.Horákové 133   *Phone   (011) + 420 2 3332 0274*
   166 21 Praha 6, Czech Republic   *Fax   (011) + 420 2 3334 1049*
                         E-mail   arch@mvcr.cz

Guide to Czech Archives
   http://www.cesarch.cz/adresar.aspx

OUTSTANDING SITE

Národní knihovna Ceské republiky
Czech National Library
http://www.nkp.cz/

Klementinum 190	*Phone* (011) + 420 2 2222 0348
CZ 110 01 Prague 1	*Fax* (011) + 420 2 2222 0367
Czech Republic	*E-mail* *hanus.hemola@nkp.cz*

Collections
   http://www.nkp.cz/fondy/English/altnk.htm

Online Catalog
   http://sigma.nkp.cz:4505/ALEPH/option?CON_LNG=eng

Online Catalogs—Other Czech Libraries
   http://www.nkp.cz/sluzby/English/othercat.htm

Library of Congress

Czech Law Library
   http://www.loc.gov/law/guide/czech.html

World Factbook: Czech Republic
   http://www.odci.gov/cia/publications/factbook/geos/ez.html

DENMARK
Kongeriget Danmark

Statens Arkiver Rigsarkivet
Danish State Archives
   http://www.sa.dk/default.htm

Rigsarkivet
Danish National Archives
   http://www.sa.dk/ra/

Rigsdagsgarden 9	*Phone* (011) + 45 33 12 33 10
DK-1218	*Fax* (011) + 45 33 15 33 39
Copenhagen K., Denmark	*E-mail* *mailbox@sa.dk*

Landsarkivet for Nørrejylland
Provincial Archives for Northern Jutland
   http://www.sa.dk/lav/aabtid/uk-intro.htm

Lille Sct. Hansgade 5	*Fax* (011) + 45 86 60 10 06
DK-8800 Viborg	
Denmark	

Landsarkivet for Sjælland, Lolland-Falster, and Bornholm
Provincial Archives of Zealand, Lolland-Falster, and Bornholm
   http://www.sa.dk/lak/engdefault.htm

   Jagtvej 10   *Fax*   *(011) + 45 35 39 05 35*
   DK-2200 Copenhagen N.
   Denmark

Landsarkivet for Sønderjylland
Provincial Archives for Southern Jutland
   http://www.sa.dk/laa/aabtid/UK-intro.htm

   Haderslevvej 45   *Fax*   *(011) + 45 74 62 32 88*
   DK-6200 Aabenraa
   Denmark

Genealogical Research in Denmark
   http://www.genealogi.dk/factwors.htm

Roots in Denmark
   http://www.sa.dk/ra/engelsk/Roots.htm

Det Kongelige Bibliotek
National Library of Denmark
   http://www.kb.dk/

   P.O. Box 2149   *Phone*   *(011) + 45 33 47 47 47*
   1016 Copenhagen K.   *Fax*   *(011) + 45 33 93 22 18*
   Denmark   *E-mail* *kb@kb.dk*

Aerial Photograph Collection
   http://www.kb.dk/kb/dept/nbo/kob/luft/index-en.htm

Danish Department Collections
   http://www.kb.dk/kb/dept/nbo/da/index-en.htm

Denmark's Electronic Research Library
   http://www.deff.dk/?lang=eng

Department of Maps, Prints, and Photographs
   http://www.kb.dk/kb/dept/nbo/kob/index-en.htm

OUTSTANDING SITE

Dansk Data Arkiv
Danish Data Archives
http://ddd.sa.dk/

Islandsgade 10   *Phone*   *(011) + 45 66 11 30 10*
DK-5000 Odense C.   *Fax*   *(011) + 45 66 11 30 60*
Denmark   *E-mail* *mailbox@dda.dk*

Census Indexes
http://ddd.sa.dk/kiplink_en.htm

Probate Index (Thisted, Viborg, Aalborg, and Randers Counties)
http://ddd.dda.dk/dprob/

OUTSTANDING SITE

Det Danske Udvandrerarkiv
Danish Emigration Archives
http://www.emiarch.dk/search.php3?l=en

Arkivstræde 1
P.O. BOX 1731
9100 Aalborg
Denmark

Phone   *(011) + 45 99 31 42 20*
Fax   *(011) + 45 98 10 22 48*
E-mail   *emiarch@emiarch.dk*

Library of Congress

Denmark Law Library
http://www.loc.gov/law/guide/denmark.html

World Factbook: Denmark
http://www.odci.gov/cia/publications/factbook/geos/da.html

Nordic Libraries Information Servers
http://www.lub.lu.se/resbyloc/Nordic_lib.html

Denmark
http://www.lub.lu.se/resbyloc/Nordic_lib.html#den

Estonia
http://www.lub.lu.se/resbyloc/Nordic_lib.html#est

Faroe Islands
http://www.lub.lu.se/resbyloc/Nordic_lib.html#far

Finland
http://www.lub.lu.se/resbyloc/Nordic_lib.html#fin

Iceland
http://www.lub.lu.se/resbyloc/Nordic_lib.html#ice

Latvia
http://www.lub.lu.se/resbyloc/Nordic_lib.html#lat

Lithuania
http://www.lub.lu.se/resbyloc/Nordic_lib.html#lit

Norway
   http://www.lub.lu.se/resbyloc/Nordic_lib.html#norw

Sweden
   http://www.lub.lu.se/resbyloc/Nordic_lib.html#swe

Samfundet for dansk genealogi og Personalhistorie
Society for Danish Genealogy and Biography
   http://www.genealogi.dk/

   Grysgårdsvej 2
   DK-2400 Copenhagen NV
   Denmark

DJIBOUTI
Jumhouriyya Djibouti

Library of Congress

Djibouti Law Library
   http://www.loc.gov/law/guide/djibouti.html

World Factbook: Djibouti
   http://www.odci.gov/cia/publications/factbook/geos/dj.html

DOMINICA

Library of Congress

Dominica Law Library
   http://www.loc.gov/law/guide/dominica.html

Handbook of Latin American Studies
   http://lcweb2.loc.gov/hlas/

World Factbook: Dominica
   http://www.odci.gov/cia/publications/factbook/geos/do.html

DOMINICAN REPUBLIC
República Dominicana

Library of Congress

Dominican Republic Law Library
   http://www.loc.gov/law/guide/dominican.html

Handbook of Latin American Studies
   http://lcweb2.loc.gov/hlas/

World Factbook: Dominican Republic
http://www.odci.gov/cia/publications/factbook/geos/dr.html

EAST TIMOR
Repúblika Demokrátika Timór-Leste

Library of Congress

East Timor Law Library
http://www.loc.gov/law/guide/easttimor.html

ECUADOR
República del Ecuador

Library of Congress

Ecuador Law Library
http://www.loc.gov/law/guide/ecuador.html

Handbook of Latin American Studies
http://lcweb2.loc.gov/hlas/

World Factbook: Ecuador
http://www.odci.gov/cia/publications/factbook/geos/ec.html

EGYPT
Jumhuriyat Misr al-Arabiya

National Library and Archives of Egypt
http://www.darelkotob.org/

Corniche El-Nil   *Phone   (011) + (202) 5750886*
Ramlet Boulac   *Fax   (011) + (202) 5765634*
Cairo, Egypt

Mailing Address:
8-Sabttiya
Cairo, Egypt 11638

National Archives
http://www.darelkotob.org/ENGLISH/HTML/NATIONAL%20_ARCHIVE.HTM

National Archives Collections
http://www.darelkotob.org/ENGLISH/HTML/ARCHIVE/DOCUM_COLL.HTM

Library of Congress

Egypt Law Library
http://www.loc.gov/law/guide/egypt.html

World Factbook: Egypt
http://www.odci.gov/cia/publications/factbook/geos/eg.html

EL SALVADOR
República de El Salvador

Library of Congress

El Salvador Law Library
http://www.loc.gov/law/guide/elsalvador.html

Handbook of Latin American Studies
http://lcweb2.loc.gov/hlas/

World Factbook: El Salvador
http://www.odci.gov/cia/publications/factbook/geos/es.html

ENGLAND

OUTSTANDING SITE

GENUKI, Genealogy, United Kingdom, and Ireland
http://www.genuki.org.uk/

Channel Islands
http://www.genuki.org.uk/big/irl/

Civil Registration
http://www.genuki.org.uk/big/#CivilRegistration

England
http://www.genuki.org.uk/big/eng/

Ireland
http://www.genuki.org.uk/big/irl/

Isle of Man
http://www.genuki.org.uk/big/iom/

Military Records
http://www.genuki.org.uk/big/MilitaryRecords.html

Scotland
http://www.genuki.org.uk/big/sct/

Wales
> http://www.genuki.org.uk/big/wal/

Library of Congress

England Law Library
> http://www.loc.gov/law/guide/england.html

World Factbook: England
> http://www.odci.gov/cia/publications/factbook/geos/uk.html

Office for National Statistics
> http://www.statistics.gov.uk/

General Register Office	*Phone (011) + 44 151 471 4801*
Overseas Registration Section	
Trafalgar Road	
Southport PR8 2HH UK	

Civil Registration
> http://www.statistics.gov.uk/registration/default.asp

Family Records Centre
> http://www.statistics.gov.uk/registration/family_records.asp

General Register Office (GRO)
> http://www.statistics.gov.uk/registration/general_register.asp

Vital Records, Overseas Requests
> http://www.statistics.gov.uk/nsbase/registration/CertificatesOverseas.asp

Public Record Office
> http://www.pro.gov.uk/

England, Wales, and the	*Phone (011) + 44 (0) 181 392 5200*
United Kingdom	*Fax (011) + 44 (0) 181 878 8905*
Ruskin Avenue	*E-mail enquiry.pro.rsd.kew@gtnet.gov.uk*
Kew, Surrey, England	
TW9 4DU UK	
Family Records Centre, FRC	*Phone (011) + 44 (0) 181 392 5300*
Office for National Statistics	*Fax (011) + 44 (0) 181 392 5307*
(Formerly Housed at St	*E-mail enquiry.pro.rsd.kew@gtnet.gov.uk*
Catherine's House)	
1 Myddelton Street	
London, England EC1R 1UW UK	

Divorce Records, After 1858
> http://catalogue.pro.gov.uk/ExternalRequest.asp?RequestReference=ri2289

Divorce Records, Before 1858
> http://catalogue.pro.gov.uk/ExternalRequest.asp?RequestReference=ri2288

Emigrants to America after 1776
http://catalogue.pro.gov.uk/ExternalRequest.asp?RequestReference=ri2107

Hearth Tax
http://catalogue.pro.gov.uk/ExternalRequest.asp?RequestReference=ri2139

Jacobite Risings
http://catalogue.pro.gov.uk/ExternalRequest.asp?RequestReference=ri2128

Online Collections
http://www.pro.gov.uk/online/default.htm

Research Leaflets
http://www.pro.gov.uk/leaflets/riindex.asp

Vital Records, at Sea
http://catalogue.pro.gov.uk/ExternalRequest.asp?RequestReference=ri2168

OUTSTANDING SITE

Royal Commission on Historical Manuscripts
http://www.hmc.gov.uk/

Quality House
Quality Court
Chancery Lane
London WC2A 1HP UK

Phone   (011) + 44 (0) 171 242 1198
Fax   (011) + 44 (0) 171 831 3550
E-mail   nra@hmc.gov.uk

Archives Directory
http://www.hmc.gov.uk/archon/archondirectory.htm

Genealogical Research
http://www.hmc.gov.uk/focus/text/famhisttxt.htm

Local History Research
http://www.hmc.gov.uk/focus/text/localintrotxt.htm

Manorial Documents Register
http://www.hmc.gov.uk/mdr/indexes.htm

Military Records Sources
http://www.hmc.gov.uk/sheets/8_armed.htm

National Registry of Archives
http://www.hmc.gov.uk/nra/search_nra.htm

EQUATORIAL GUINEA
República de Guinea Ecuatorial

Library of Congress

Equatorial Guinea Law Library
http://www.loc.gov/law/guide/equatorialguinea.html

World Factbook: Equatorial Guinea
http://www.odci.gov/cia/publications/factbook/geos/ek.html

ERITREA

Library of Congress

Eritrea Law Library
http://www.loc.gov/law/guide/eritrea.html

World Factbook: Eritrea
http://www.odci.gov/cia/publications/factbook/geos/er.html

ESTONIA
Eesti Vabariik

Rahvusarhiiv tagab Eesti
National Archives of Estonia
http://www.eha.ee/

J. Liivi 4	*Phone (011) + 372 7 387 500*
Tartu 50409	*Fax (011) + 372 7 387 510*
Estonia	*E-mail rahvusarhiiv@ra.ee*

Collections
http://www.eha.ee/english/english.htm

Eesti Rahvusraamatukogu
National Library of Estonia
http://www.nlib.ee/inglise/indexi.html

Tõnismägi 2, 15189	*Phone (011) + 372 630 7611*
Tallinn, Estonia	*E-mail nlib@nlib.ee*

Collections
http://www.nlib.ee/inglise/teen/servic.html

Online Catalog
http://helios.nlib.ee/search/

Virtual Library
http://www.nlib.ee/digi/digi.html

Library of Congress

Estonia Law Library
http://www.loc.gov/law/guide/estonia.html

World Factbook: Estonia
http://www.odci.gov/cia/publications/factbook/geos/en.html

Nordic Libraries Information Servers
http://www.lub.lu.se/resbyloc/Nordic_lib.html

Denmark
http://www.lub.lu.se/resbyloc/Nordic_lib.html#den

Estonia
http://www.lub.lu.se/resbyloc/Nordic_lib.html#est

Faroe Islands
http://www.lub.lu.se/resbyloc/Nordic_lib.html#far

Finland
http://www.lub.lu.se/resbyloc/Nordic_lib.html#fin

Iceland
http://www.lub.lu.se/resbyloc/Nordic_lib.html#ice

Latvia
http://www.lub.lu.se/resbyloc/Nordic_lib.html#lat

Lithuania
http://www.lub.lu.se/resbyloc/Nordic_lib.html#lit

Norway
http://www.lub.lu.se/resbyloc/Nordic_lib.html#norw

Sweden
http://www.lub.lu.se/resbyloc/Nordic_lib.html#swe

ETHIOPIA
Ityopia

Library of Congress

Ethiopia Law Library
http://www.loc.gov/law/guide/ethiopia.html

World Factbook: Ethiopia
http://www.odci.gov/cia/publications/factbook/geos/et.html

EUROPE

Ethnic, Religious, and National Index
http://feefhs.org/ethnic.html

Map Room
http://feefhs.org/maps/indexmap.html

FIJI

Library of Congress

Fiji Law Library
http://www.loc.gov/law/guide/fiji.html

World Factbook: Fiji
http://www.odci.gov/cia/publications/factbook/geos/fj.html

FINLAND
Suomen Tasavalta

Helsingin yliopiston kirjasto
National Library of Finland
http://www.lib.helsinki.fi/

P.O. Box 15 (Unioninkatu 36)   *Phone*   *(011) + 358 9 191 23196*
00014 Helsingin Yliopisto   *Fax*   *(011) + 358 9 191 22719*
Finland   *E-mail   HYK_palvelu@Helsinki.fi*

Library of Congress

Finland Law Library
http://www.loc.gov/law/guide/finland.html

World Factbook: Finland
http://www.odci.gov/cia/publications/factbook/geos/fi.html

Nordic Libraries Information Servers
    http://www.lub.lu.se/resbyloc/Nordic_lib.html

Denmark
    http://www.lub.lu.se/resbyloc/Nordic_lib.html#den

Estonia
    http://www.lub.lu.se/resbyloc/Nordic_lib.html#est

Faroe Islands
    http://www.lub.lu.se/resbyloc/Nordic_lib.html#far

Finland
    http://www.lub.lu.se/resbyloc/Nordic_lib.html#fin

Iceland
    http://www.lub.lu.se/resbyloc/Nordic_lib.html#ice

Latvia
    http://www.lub.lu.se/resbyloc/Nordic_lib.html#lat

Lithuania
    http://www.lub.lu.se/resbyloc/Nordic_lib.html#lit

Norway
    http://www.lub.lu.se/resbyloc/Nordic_lib.html#norw

Sweden
    http://www.lub.lu.se/resbyloc/Nordic_lib.html#swe

FRANCE

République Française

Le Centre d'accueil et de recherche des Archives nationales (CARAN)
French National Archives
    http://www.archivesnationales.culture.gouv.fr/chan/

60, rue des Francs-Bourgeois	*Phone*	*(011) + 33 (0)1 40 27 64 19*
75141 Paris Cedex 03, France	*Fax*	*(011) + 33 (0)1 40 27 66 28*

Archives in France
    http://www.archivesdefrance.culture.gouv.fr/

Bulletin des Archives de France. (Serial). Quarterly. No. 1 (June 2000)– .
    http://www.archivesdefrance.culture.gouv.fr/fr/archivistique/index.html

Collections
    http://www.archivesdefrance.culture.gouv.fr/fr/archivistique/index.html

Electronic Documents
    http://www.archivesdefrance.culture.gouv.fr/fr/archivistique/index.html

Faire une recherche au CHAN (Centre historique des Archives nationales)
Research at the CHAN (National Archives History Center)
> http://www.archivesnationales.culture.gouv.fr/chan/chan/rech.htm

Publications
> http://www.archivesdefrance.culture.gouv.fr/fr/publications/index.html

Bibliothèque nationale de France
National Library of France
> http://www.bnf.fr

Site François Mitterrand/Tolbiac   *Phone*   *(011) + 33 (0)1 53 79 59 59*
Quai François-Mauriac
75706 Paris Cedex 13
France

Collections
> http://www.bnf.fr/site_bnf_eng/collectionsgb/indexgb.htm

Digital Library
> http://www.bnf.fr/site_bnf_eng/bibnumgb/index.htm

Online Catalog
> http://www.bnf.fr/site_bnf_eng/cataloggb/indexgb.htm

Special Collections Department
> http://www.bnf.fr/site_bnf_eng/praticgb/indexgb.htm

Library of Congress

France Law Library
> http://www.loc.gov/law/guide/france.html

World Factbook: France
> http://www.odci.gov/cia/publications/factbook/geos/fr.html

GABON
République Gabonaise

Library of Congress

Gabon Law Library
> http://www.loc.gov/law/guide/gabon.html

World Factbook: Gabon
> http://www.odci.gov/cia/publications/factbook/geos/gb.html

GAMBIA

Library of Congress

Gambia Law Library
> http://www.loc.gov/law/guide/gambia.html

World Factbook: Gambia
http://www.odci.gov/cia/publications/factbook/geos/ga.html

GEORGIA
Sakartvelos Respublica

Library of Congress

Georgia Law Library
http://www.loc.gov/law/guide/georgia.html

World Factbook: Georgia
http://www.odci.gov/cia/publications/factbook/geos/gg.html

GERMANY
Bundesrepublik Deutschland

Die Deutsche Bibliothek
Library of Germany
http://www.ddb.de

Adickesallee 1   *Phone   (011) + 49 69 1525 2500*
60322 Frankfurt am Main *Fax   (011) + 49 69 1525 1010*
Germany   *E-mail   bossmeyer@dbf.ddb.de*

Digital Periodicals Online
http://deposit.ddb.de/online/exil/exil.htm

Gesellschaft für das Buch e. V.
Friends of Die Deutsche Bibliothek
http://www.ddb.de/wir/ges_buch_e.htm

Online Library Catalog
http://z3950gw.dbf.ddb.de/

Union Catalog of Serials
http://pacifix.ddb.de:7000/?SRT=YOPandIMPLAND=Y

OUTSTANDING SITE

German Genealogy Home Page
http://www.genealogienetz.de/genealogy.html

Translation Service   *E-mail   trans@genealogienetz.de*

Computergenealogie das Magazin für Familienforschung. (Serial). (January 2001)– .
http://www.genealogienetz.de/cg/

Computergenealogie. (Serial). Table of Contents. (1985–1998).
http://www.genealogienetz.de/cg/archiv/index.html

Emigration of Germans to America
http://www.genealogienetz.de/misc/emig/index.html

Familienforschung-Online. (Serial). Table of Contents. (July 1, 1999–October 24, 2000).
http://www.genealogienetz.de/cg/archiv/index.html

Geographic Index
http://www.genealogienetz.de/reg/rindex.htm

German-English, English-German Translation Service
http://www.genealogienetz.de/misc/translation.html

Hamburg Passenger Lists
http://www.genealogienetz.de/misc/emig/ham_pass.html

Listserv
http://list.genealogy.net/mailman/listinfo-e/News-L

Ortsfamilienbücher, Online Heritage Books
http://db.genealogy.net/ofb/

Regional History (Boundaries Over the Past Two Centuries)
http://www.genealogienetz.de/reg/gerhist.htm

U.S. Passport Applications
http://www.genealogienetz.de/misc/emig/pass1.html

Library of Congress

Germany Law Library
http://www.loc.gov/law/guide/germany.html

World Factbook: Germany
http://www.odci.gov/cia/publications/factbook/geos/gm.html

GHANA

Public Records and Archives Administration Department
http://www.praadgh-gov.org/

P.O. Box 3056	*Phone*	*(011) + 233 21 22 12 34*
Accra, Ghana	*Fax*	*(011) + 233 21 22 00 14*

Slave Trade Archives
http://www.internetghana.com/praad/stp.htm

Library of Congress

Ghana Law Library
  http://www.loc.gov/law/guide/ghana.html

World Factbook: Ghana
  http://www.odci.gov/cia/publications/factbook/geos/gh.html

GREECE
Elliniki Dimokratia

Elliniki Dimokratia

Εθνική Βιβλιοθήκη
National Library of Greece
  http://www.nlg.org

  Πανεπιστημίου 32
  32 Panepistimiou Avenue   *Phone   (011) +30 1 3382 600*
  1 06 79 Αθήνα   *Fax   (011) +30 1 3608 495*
  106 79 Athens, Greece

Site is written in Greek.

Library of Congress

Greece Law Library
  http://www.loc.gov/law/guide/greece.html

World Factbook: Greece
  http://www.odci.gov/cia/publications/factbook/geos/gr.html

GRENADA

Library of Congress

Grenada Law Library
  http://www.loc.gov/law/guide/grenada.html

World Factbook: Grenada
  http://www.odci.gov/cia/publications/factbook/geos/gj.html

GUATEMALA
República de Guatemala

Library of Congress

Guatemala Law Library
  http://www.loc.gov/law/guide/guatemala.html

Handbook of Latin American Studies
http://lcweb2.loc.gov/hlas/

World Factbook: Guatemala
http://www.odci.gov/cia/publications/factbook/geos/gt.html

GUINEA
République de Guinée

Library of Congress

Guinea Law Library
http://www.loc.gov/law/guide/guinea.html

World Factbook: Guinea
http://www.odci.gov/cia/publications/factbook/geos/gv.html

GUINEA-BISSAU
Republica da Guiné-Bissau

Library of Congress

Guinea-Bissau Law Library
http://www.loc.gov/law/guide/guineabissau.html

World Factbook: Guinea-Bissau
http://www.odci.gov/cia/publications/factbook/geos/pu.html

GUYANA

Chinese in Guyana: Their Roots
http://www.rootsweb.com/~guycigtr/

3495 Cambie Street   E-mail   *Canereapers@Lycos.com*
P.O. Box 556
Vancouver, BC V5Z 4R3
Canada

A History of the Chinese Indentured Labourers
http://www.rootsweb.com/~guycigtr/History.htm

Passenger Lists
http://www.rootsweb.com/~guycigtr/Passengers.htm

Library of Congress

Guyana Law Library
http://www.loc.gov/law/guide/guyana.html

Handbook of Latin American Studies
http://lcweb2.loc.gov/hlas/

World Factbook: Guyana
http://www.odci.gov/cia/publications/factbook/geos/gy.html

HAITI
République d' Haiti

Bibliothèque nationale d'Haïti
National Library Haiti
http://www.acctbief.org/structures/Haiti/Index.htm

193 rue du Centre   *Phone*   *(011) + (509) 222 02 36*
Port-au-Prince, Haïti   *Fax*   *(011) + (509) 221 20 86*

l'Association de Généalogie d'Haïti
Genealogical Association of Haiti
http://www.agh.qc.ca/

Library of Congress

Haiti Law Library
http://www.loc.gov/law/guide/haiti.html

Handbook of Latin American Studies
http://lcweb2.loc.gov/hlas/

World Factbook: Haiti
http://www.odci.gov/cia/publications/factbook/geos/ha.html

HONDURAS
República de Honduras

Library of Congress

Handbook of Latin American Studies
http://lcweb2.loc.gov/hlas/

Honduras Law Library
http://www.loc.gov/law/guide/honduras.html

World Factbook: Honduras
http://www.odci.gov/cia/publications/factbook/geos/ho.html

HUNGARY
Magyar Köztársaság

Magyar Országos Levéltár
National Archives of Hungary
http://www.natarch.hu/mol_e.htm

1014 Budapest, Hungary	*Phone*	*(011) + 36 1 356 5811*
Bécsi kapu tér 2-4.	*Fax*	*(011) + 36 1 212 1619*
	E-mail	*mail@natarch.hu*

Mailing Address:
1250 Budapest, Hungary
P.O. Box 3

Archives Guide
http://www.natarch.hu/fondx/fondxen.html

Collections Guide
http://www.natarch.hu/english/menu_31.htm

Family History
http://www.natarch.hu/english/menu_24a.htm

Parish Register Inventory
http://www.natarch.hu/fondx/akeren.html

Országos Széchényi Könyvtár (OSZK)
National Széchényi Library
http://www.oszk.hu/eng/index.html

Budavári Palota F épület	*Phone*	*(011) + 36 1 155 6169*
(Buda Royal Palace Wing F)		*(011) + 36 1 224 3845*
H-1827, Budapest, Hungary	*Fax*	*(011) + 36 1 202 0804*
	E-mail	*konkoz@oszk.hu*

Collections
http://www.oszk.hu/eng/collect/index.html

Hungarian Electronic Library
http://www.mek.iif.hu/

Hungarian National Bibliography. (Serial). Vol. 5, No. 21– .
http://www.oszk.hu/mnbkb/index-en.html

Hungarika Névkataszter. Hungarian Biographical Index.
http://www.iif.hu/db/hung/index.html

Írás tegnap és holnap. Writing Yesterday and Tomorrow. (Serial). Hungarian,
English, French. Vol. 1, No. 1. (August 1997)– .
http://www.oszk.hu/kiadvany/iras/index14e.html

Manuscript Collections
http://www.oszk.hu/eng/collect/kezirate.html

Microfilm Collections
http://www.oszk.hu/eng/services/mikroflm/mikroflm.html

Online Library Catalog
http://nektar.oszk.hu/

Budapest Föváros Levéltára
Budapest City Archives
http://www.bparchiv.hu/

H-1052 Budapest	*Phone*	*(011) + 36 1 317 2033*
Városház u. 9-11, Hungary	*Fax*	*(011) + 36 1 318 3319*
	E-mail	*bfl@bparchiv.hu*

Collections
http://www.bparchiv.hu/english/doc/iratok_e.htm

Library of Congress

Hungary Law Library
http://www.loc.gov/law/guide/hungary.html

World Factbook: Hungary
http://www.odci.gov/cia/publications/factbook/geos/hu.html

ICELAND
Lydveldid Ísland

Landsbókasafn Íslands
The National and University Library of Iceland
http://www.bok.hi.is/english/third.htm

Arngrimsgata 3	*Phone*	*(011) + 354 563 5600*
IS 107 Reykjavik, Iceland	*Fax*	*(011) + 354 563 5615*
	E-mail	*lbs@bok.hi.is*
		upplys@bok.hi.is Reference

Online Library Catalog
http://www.bok.hi.is/english/gegnir.htm

Library of Congress

Iceland Law Library
http://www.loc.gov/law/guide/iceland.html

World Factbook: Iceland
http://www.odci.gov/cia/publications/factbook/geos/ic.html

Nordic Libraries Information Servers
http://www.lub.lu.se/resbyloc/Nordic_lib.html

Denmark
http://www.lub.lu.se/resbyloc/Nordic_lib.html#den

Estonia
http://www.lub.lu.se/resbyloc/Nordic_lib.html#est

Faroe Islands
http://www.lub.lu.se/resbyloc/Nordic_lib.html#far

Finland
http://www.lub.lu.se/resbyloc/Nordic_lib.html#fin

Iceland
http://www.lub.lu.se/resbyloc/Nordic_lib.html#ice

Latvia
http://www.lub.lu.se/resbyloc/Nordic_lib.html#lat

Lithuania
http://www.lub.lu.se/resbyloc/Nordic_lib.html#lit

Norway
http://www.lub.lu.se/resbyloc/Nordic_lib.html#norw

Sweden
http://www.lub.lu.se/resbyloc/Nordic_lib.html#swe

INDIA

National Archives of India
http://nationalarchives.nic.in/

Janpath	*Phone*	*(011) + 91 338 3436*
New Delhi 110001, India	*Fax*	*(011) + 91 338 4127*

Andhra Pradesh State Archives
Taranaka
Hyderabad 500007
Andhra Pradesh, India

Karnataka State Archives		
Room 11, Ground Floor Vidhana	*Phone*	*(011) + 91 80 2254465*
Soudha	*Fax*	*(011) + 91 80 2254465*
Bangalore 560 001	*E-mail*	*Archives@Ren02.Nic.In*
Karnataka, India		

Kerala State Archives,
Directorate of Archives
Nalanda-Trivandrum 3
Kerala, India

Rajasthan State Archives
Bikaner
Rajasthan, India

State Archives of West Bengal
6 Bhowani Dutta Lane
Calcutta 700073, West Bengal
India

Collections
http://nationalarchives.nic.in/

Family History in India
http://members.ozemail.com.au/%7Eclday/index.html

Church Records in Colonial India
http://members.ozemail.com.au/%7Eclday/churches.htm

European Cemeteries in India
http://members.ozemail.com.au/%7Eclday/cem.htm

European Surnames in India
http://members.ozemail.com.au/%7Eclday/misc.htm

Goa Church Records
http://users.rootsweb.com/~indwgw/FIBIS/LDSGoa.htm

Indian Genealogy
http://members.ozemail.com.au/~clday/indian.htm

Madras Female Asylum (Orphanage). 1839 Register
http://users.rootsweb.com/~indwgw/orphan2.htm

Military and Other Sources for India Genealogical Research
http://members.ozemail.com.au/%7Eclday/other.htm

Regimental Histories of British Army Units That Served in India
http://members.ozemail.com.au/%7Eclday/regiments.htm

Library of Congress
India Law Library
http://www.loc.gov/law/guide/india.html

World Factbook: India
http://www.odci.gov/cia/publications/factbook/geos/in.html

Office of the Registrar General, India
http://www.censusindia.net/

2A, Mansingh Road   E-mail   *rgindia@censusindia.net*
New Delhi 110 011, India

INDONESIA
Republik Indonesia

Library of Congress

Indonesia Law Library
http://www.loc.gov/law/guide/indonesia.html

World Factbook: Indonesia
http://www.odci.gov/cia/publications/factbook/geos/id.html

IRAN
Jomhori-e-Islami-e-Iran

Library of Congress

Iran Law Library
http://www.loc.gov/law/guide/iran.html

World Factbook: Iran
http://www.odci.gov/cia/publications/factbook/geos/ir.html

IRAQ
Jumhouriya al 'Iraqia

Library of Congress

Iraq Law Library
http://www.loc.gov/law/guide/iraq.html

World Factbook: Iraq
http://www.odci.gov/cia/publications/factbook/geos/iz.html

IRELAND AND NORTHERN IRELAND

OUTSTANDING SITE

**An Chartlann Náisiúnta
National Archives of Ireland**
http://www.nationalarchives.ie/

*Bishop Street
Dublin 8, Ireland*

*Phone   (011) + 353 (1) 407 2300
Fax   (011) + 353 (1) 407 2333
E-mail   mail@nationalarchives.ie*

Genealogy Sources
http://www.nationalarchives.ie/genealogy.html

Great Famine, 1845–1850
http://www.nationalarchives.ie/famine.html

Ireland-Australia Transportation Database, 1791–1868
http://www.nationalarchives.ie/search01.html

Online Databases
http://www.nationalarchives.ie/onlinesearch.html

Ordnance Survey, Archives
http://www.nationalarchives.ie/osintro.html

Leabharlann Náisiúnta na hEireann
National Library of Ireland
http://www.nli.ie/

Kildare Street	*Phone* (011) + 353 1 603 02 00
Dublin, Ireland 2	*Fax* (011) + 353 1 676 66 90
	E-mail info@nli.ie

Collections
http://www.nli.ie/fr_coll.htm

Family History Resources
http://www.nli.ie/fr_servfamily.htm

Library Online Catalog
http://www.nli.ie/fr_cata.htm

Parish Registers in the National Library
http://www.nli.ie/pdfs/famil2.pdf

Public Record Office of Northern Ireland
http://proni.nics.gov.uk/index.htm

66 Balmoral Avenue	*Phone* (011) + 44 028 90 255905
Belfast, Northern Ireland	*Fax* (011) + 44 028 90 255999
	E-mail proni@dcalni.gov.uk

Church of Ireland Index
http://proni.nics.gov.uk/records/private/cofiindx.htm

Geographical Index
http://proni.nics.gov.uk/geogindx/geogindx.htm

Presbyterian Church Records
http://proni.nics.gov.uk/records/private/presindx.htm

Cavan Local
> http://cavan.local.ie/

Genealogy
> http://www.local.ie/genealogy/

Killeshandra
> http://cavan.local.ie/killeshandra/

Surnames
> http://www.local.ie/general/genealogy/family_names/

Irish Family History Foundation
> http://www.irishroots.net/

County Armagh Genealogy—Armagh Ancestry
> http://www.mayo-ireland.ie/Geneal/Armagh.htm

42 English Street	*Phone*	*(011) + 44 1861 521802*
Armagh, Co. Armagh BT61 7BA	*Fax*	*(011) + 44 1861 510033*
Northern Ireland		

Carlow Research Centre
> http://www.irishroots.net/Carlow.htm

Carlow Genealogy Project	*Phone*	*(011) + 353 (503) 30850*
Old School	*Fax*	*(011) + 353 (503) 30850*
College Street	*E-mail*	*carlowgenealogy@iolfree.ie*
Co. Carlow, Ireland		

Cavan Research Centre
> http://www.irishroots.net/Cavan.htm

Cana House	*Phone*	*(011) + 353 (0) 49 61094*
Farnham Street	*Fax*	*(011) + 353 (0) 49 4331494*
Cavan, Co. Cavan, Ireland	*E-mail*	*canahous@iol.ie*

Clare Heritage and Genealogical Centre
> http://clare.irish-roots.net/

Church Street	*Phone*	*(011) + 353 (0) 65 37955*
Corofin, Co. Clare, Ireland	*Fax*	*(011) + 353 (0) 65 6837540*
	E-mail	*clareheritage@eircom.net*

Emigration
> http://clare.irish-roots.net/emigration.htm

Mallow Heritage Centre
> http://www.irishroots.net/Cork.htm

County Cork, Ireland	*Phone*	*(011) + 353 (0) 22 21778*
27/28 Bank Place		
Mallow, Co. Cork, Ireland		
Cork City Ancestral Project	*Phone*	*(011) + 353 (0) 21 54699*
c/o County Library		
Farranlea Road		
Cork City, Ireland		

County Derry or Londonderry Genealogy Centre

http://www.irishroots.net/Derry.htm

4-22 Butcher Street	*Phone*	*(011) + 44 1504 373177*
Londonderry BT48 6HL	*Fax*	*(011) + 44 1504 374818*
Northern Ireland		

Donegal Ancestry in County Donegal

http://www.irishroots.net/Donegal.htm

Old Meeting House	*Phone*	*(011) + 353 74 51266*
Back Lane	*Fax*	*(011) + 353 74 51266*
Ramelton, Co. Donegal, Ireland		

East Galway Family History Society

http://www.irishroots.net/EtGalway.htm

Woodford	*Phone*	*(011) + 353 509 49309*
Loughrea, Co. Galway, Ireland	*Fax*	*(011) + 353 509 49309*

West Galway Family History Society

http://www.irishroots.net/WtGalway.htm

Research Unit	*Phone*	*(011) + 353 91 756737*
Venture Centre		
Liosbaun Estate		
Tuam Road		
Galway, Co. Galway, Ireland		

Kildare Heritage and Genealogy Company

http://www.irishroots.net/Kildare.htm

c/o Kildare County Library	*Phone*	*(011) + 353 45 431486*
Newbridge, Co. Kildare, Ireland		

Killarney Genealogical Centre

http://www.irishroots.net/Kilknny.htm

Cathedral Walk	*Phone*	*(011) + 353 64 35946*
Killarney, Co. Kerry, Ireland		

Laois and Offaly Family History Research Centre

http://www.irishroots.net/LaoisOff.htm

Bury Quay	*Phone*	*(011) + 353 506 21421*
Tullamore, Co. Offaly, Ireland	*Fax*	*(011) + 353 506 21421*
	E-mail	*ohas@iol.ie*

Leitrim Genealogy Centre

http://www.irishroots.net/Leitrim.htm

County Library	*Phone*	*(011) + 353 78 44012*
Ballinamore, Co. Leitrim, Ireland	*Fax*	*(011) + 353 78 44425*

Limerick Regional Archives

http://www.irishroots.net/limerick/index.htm

The Granary	*Phone*	*(011) + 353 61 410777*
Michael Street		
Limerick City, Ireland		

Longford Research Centre

http://www.irishroots.net/Longford.htm

Longford Roots   *Phone*   *(011) + 353 (0) 4341235*
1 Church Street
Longford, Co. Longford, Ireland

Mayo Family Research Centres

http://mayo.irishroots.net/mayo.htm

Enniscoe   *Phone*   *(011) + 353 96 31809*
Castlehill   *Fax*   *(011) + 353 96 31885*
Ballina, Co. Mayo, Ireland

Main Street   *Phone*   *(011) + 353 92 41214*
Ballinrobe, Co. Mayo, Ireland   *Fax*   *(011) + 353 92 41214*
                                          E-mail   *soumayo@iol.ie*

Meath Family Research Centre

http://www.irishroots.net/Louth.htm

Mill Street   *Phone*   *(011) + 353 46 36633*
Trim, Co. Meath, Ireland   *Fax*   *(011) + 353 46 37502*

Monaghan Research Centre

http://www.irishroots.net/Monaghan.htm

Monaghan Ancestry   *Phone*   *(011) + 353 (0) 47 82304*
Clogher Historical Society
6, Tully Street
Monaghan, Co. Monaghan, Ireland

County Roscommon Heritage and Genealogy Society

http://www.irishroots.net/Roscmmn.htm

Church Street   *Phone*   *(011) + 353 78 33380*
Strokestown, Co. Roscommon, Ireland

County Sligo Heritage and Genealogy Centre

http://www.irishroots.net/Sligo.htm

Aras Reddan   *Phone*   *(011) + 353 71 43728*
Temple Street
Sligo City, Co. Sligo, Ireland

Bru Boru Heritage Centre, Tipperary

http://www.irishroots.net/STipp.htm

Rock of Cashel   *Phone*   *(011) + 353 62 61122*
Co. Tipperary, Ireland   *Fax*   *(011) + 353 62 62700*

Tipperary North Family Research Centre

http://www.irishroots.net/NTipp.htm

The Gatehouse   *Phone*   *(011) + 353 67 33850*
Kickham Street   *Fax*   *(011) + 353 67 33586*
Nenagh, Co. Tipperary, Ireland

Waterford Research Centre
http://www.irishroots.net/Waterfrd.htm

St Patrick's Church	*Phone*	*(011) + 353 (0) 51 76123*
Jenkin's Lane	*Fax*	*(011) + 353 (0) 51 50645*
Waterford City, Co. Waterford,	*E-mail*	*mnoc@iol.ie*
Ireland		

Dun na Si Heritage Centre, Westmeath
http://www.irishroots.net/Wstmeath.htm

County Westmeath	*Phone*	*(011) + 353 902 81183*
Knockdanney	*Fax*	*(011) + 353 902 81661*
Co. Westmeath, Ireland		

Wexford Genealogy Centre
http://www.irishroots.net/Wexford.htm

| *Yola Farmstead* | *Phone* | *(011) + 353 53 31177* |
| *Tagoat, Co. Wexford, Ireland* | *Fax* | *(011) + 353 53 31177* |

Library of Congress

Ireland Law Library
http://www.loc.gov/law/guide/ireland.html

World Factbook: Ireland
http://www.odci.gov/cia/publications/factbook/geos/ei.html

Ulster Historical Foundation
http://www.uhf.org.uk/

12 College Square East	*Phone*	*(011) + 44 1232 332288*
Belfast BT1 6DD Northern Ireland	*Fax*	*(011) + 44 1232 239885*
	E-mail	*enquiry@uhf.org.uk*

Databases
http://www.uhf.org.uk/searchable.htm

ISRAEL
Medinat Israel

Yad Vashem
The Holocaust Martyrs' and Heroes' Remembrance Authority
http://www.yad-vashem.org.il

P.O. Box 3477	*Phone*	*(011) + 972 2 6751 611*
Jerusalem 91034, Israel	*Fax*	*(011) + 972 2 433511*
	E-mail	*holocaust.resources@yadvashem.org.il*
		library@yadvashem.org.il

Collections
http://www.yad-vashem.org.il/exhibitions/index_exhibitions.html

Hall of Names
http://www.yad-vashem.org.il/remembrance/index_remembrance.html

Yad Vashem Online Magazine. (Serial). Online. Vol. 1– .
http://www.yad-vashem.org.il/about_yad/index_about_yad.html

Yad Vashem Studies. (Serial). Annual. Vol. 26– .
http://www.yad-vashem.org.il/about_holocaust/temp_about_the_holocaust/temp_index_home_
studies.html

Library of Congress

Israel Law Library
http://www.loc.gov/law/guide/israel.html

World Factbook: Israel
http://www.odci.gov/cia/publications/factbook/geos/is.html

ITALY
Republica Italiana

OUTSTANDING SITE

Italian Genealogy Home Page
http://www.italiangenealogy.com/

Edmondo Tardio
Sinnigvelderstraat 395
1382 GB Weesp Netherlands

Adoption Records
http://www.italiangenealogy.com/

Citizenship Records
http://www.italiangenealogy.com/

Genealogy Tips
http://www.italiangenealogy.com/

Heraldry
http://www.italiangenealogy.com/

Medieval Research
http://www.italiangenealogy.com/

Names, Given Names
http://www.italiangenealogy.com/

Surnames Database

> http://www.italiangenealogy.com/

Vital Records

> http://www.italiangenealogy.com/

Library of Congress

Italy Law Library

> http://www.loc.gov/law/guide/italy.html

World Factbook: Italy

> http://www.odci.gov/cia/publications/factbook/geos/it.html

JAMAICA

Library of Congress

Handbook of Latin American Studies

> http://lcweb2.loc.gov/hlas/

Jamaica Law Library

> http://www.loc.gov/law/guide/jamaica.html

World Factbook: Jamaica

> http://www.odci.gov/cia/publications/factbook/geos/jm.html

JAPAN
Nihon-koku

Kokuritsu Kokkai Toshokan
National Diet Library

> http://www.ndl.go.jp/en/index.html

> *1-10-1 Nagata-cho*   *Phone*   *(011) + 81 3 3581 2331*
> *Chiyodaku, Tokyo 100-8924*   *Fax*   *(011) + 81 3 3508 2934*
> *Japan*

Electronic Library

> http://www.ndl.go.jp/en/data/endl.html

NDL Newsletter. (Serial). Quarterly. No. 103 (1997)– .

> http://www.ndl.go.jp/en/publication/ndl_newsletter/index.html

Online Library Catalog

> http://www.ndl.go.jp/en/data/opac.html

California Digital Library

> http://www.cdlib.org/

Council on East Asian Libraries
http://purl.oclc.org/net/ceal

Committee on Chinese Materials
http://www.lib.uchicago.edu/o/cealccm/

Committee on Japanese Materials
http://www.library.arizona.edu/users/hkamada/CJM/cjmhome.html

Committee on Korean Materials
http://www.usc.edu/isd/locations/ssh/korean/kmc/

Japan Databases
http://hcl.harvard.edu/harvard-yenching/japandatabase.html

Japanese American Digital Relocation Archives
http://jarda.cdlib.org/

Collection Guides
http://jarda.cdlib.org/guides.html

Oral Histories
http://jarda.cdlib.org/oral.html

Library of Congress

Japan Law Library
http://www.loc.gov/law/guide/japan.html

World Factbook: Japan
http://www.odci.gov/cia/publications/factbook/geos/ja.html

National Japanese American Historical Society
http://www.nikkeiheritage.org/

1684 Post Street   *Phone*   *(415) 921-5007*
San Francisco, CA 94115   *Fax*   *(415) 921-5087*
                              E-mail *njahs@njahs.org*

Nikkei Heritage. (Serial). Quarterly. Table of Contents. Vol. 3, No. 1 (Winter 1991)–.
http://www.nikkeiheritage.org/nh/index.htm

Tracing the Roots: Using a Regional Office of the National Archives
http://www.nikkeiheritage.org/nh/fvxin3.html

JORDAN
Al-Mamlakah al-'Urdunniyah al-Hashimiyah

Library of Congress

Jordan Law Library
http://www.loc.gov/law/guide/jordan.html

World Factbook: Jordan
http://www.odci.gov/cia/publications/factbook/geos/jo.html

KAZAKHSTAN
Kazak Respublikasy

Library of Congress

Kazakhstan Law Library
http://www.loc.gov/law/guide/kazakhstan.html

World Factbook: Kazakhstan
http://www.odci.gov/cia/publications/factbook/geos/kz.html

KENYA
Jamhuri ya Kenya

Kenya National Archives
http://www.kenyarchives.go.ke/

Moi Avenue
P.O. Box 49210
00100, Nairobi, Kenya

Phone   *(011) 254 02 228959*
E-mail   *knarchives@kenyaweb.com*

Collections
http://www.kenyarchives.go.ke/collection.htm

Library of Congress

Kenya Law Library
http://www.loc.gov/law/guide/kenya.html

World Factbook: Kenya
http://www.odci.gov/cia/publications/factbook/geos/ke.html

KIRIBATI

Library of Congress

Kiribati Law Library
http://www.loc.gov/law/guide/kiribati.html

World Factbook: Kiribati
http://www.odci.gov/cia/publications/factbook/geos/kr.html

KOREA
Taehan-min'guk

Council on East Asian Libraries
http://purl.oclc.org/net/ceal

Committee on Chinese Materials
http://www.lib.uchicago.edu/o/cealccm/

Committee on Japanese Materials
http://www.library.arizona.edu/users/hkamada/CJM/cjmhome.html

Committee on Korean Materials
http://www.usc.edu/isd/locations/ssh/korean/kmc/

Japan Databases
http://hcl.harvard.edu/harvard-yenching/japandatabase.html

Library of Congress
Korea Law Library
http://www.loc.gov/law/guide/southkorea.html

World Factbook: Korea
http://www.odci.gov/cia/publications/factbook/geos/ks.html

KUWAIT
Dowlat al Kuwait

Library of Congress
Kuwait Law Library
http://www.loc.gov/law/guide/kuwait.html

World Factbook: Kuwait
http://www.odci.gov/cia/publications/factbook/geos/ku.html

KYRGYZSTAN
Kyrgyz Respublikasy

Library of Congress
Kyrgyzstan Law Library
http://www.loc.gov/law/guide/kyrgyzstan.html

World Factbook: Kyrgyzstan
http://www.odci.gov/cia/publications/factbook/geos/kg.html

LAOS
Sathalanalat Paxathipatai Paxaxôn Lao

Library of Congress

Laos Law Library
http://www.loc.gov/law/guide/laos.html

World Factbook: Laos
http://www.odci.gov/cia/publications/factbook/geos/la.html

LATVIA
Latvijas Republika

Library of Congress

Latvia Law Library
http://www.loc.gov/law/guide/latvia.html

World Factbook: Latvia
http://www.odci.gov/cia/publications/factbook/geos/lg.html

Nordic Libraries Information Servers
http://www.lub.lu.se/resbyloc/Nordic_lib.html

Denmark
http://www.lub.lu.se/resbyloc/Nordic_lib.html#den

Estonia
http://www.lub.lu.se/resbyloc/Nordic_lib.html#est

Faroe Islands
http://www.lub.lu.se/resbyloc/Nordic_lib.html#far

Finland
http://www.lub.lu.se/resbyloc/Nordic_lib.html#fin

Iceland
http://www.lub.lu.se/resbyloc/Nordic_lib.html#ice

Latvia
http://www.lub.lu.se/resbyloc/Nordic_lib.html#lat

Lithuania
http://www.lub.lu.se/resbyloc/Nordic_lib.html#lit

Norway
http://www.lub.lu.se/resbyloc/Nordic_lib.html#norw

Sweden
http://www.lub.lu.se/resbyloc/Nordic_lib.html#swe

LEBANON
Jumhouriya al-Lubnaniya

National Archives of Lebanon
http://www.can.gov.lb/index.html

Rue Hamra – Imm. Picadelly – 6eme étage　　　*Phone*　　*(011) + 961 1 365783*
P.O. Box 113/6378
Beirut, Lebanon

Collections
http://www.can.gov.lb/french/collection/collection.htm

Library of Congress
Lebanon Law Library
http://www.loc.gov/law/guide/lebanon.html

World Factbook: Lebanon
http://www.odci.gov/cia/publications/factbook/geos/le.html

LESOTHO
Muso oa Lesotho

Library of Congress
Lesotho Law Library
http://www.loc.gov/law/guide/lesotho.html

World Factbook: Lesotho
http://www.odci.gov/cia/publications/factbook/geos/lt.html

LIBERIA

Library of Congress
Liberia Law Library
http://www.loc.gov/law/guide/liberia.html

World Factbook: Liberia
http://www.odci.gov/cia/publications/factbook/geos/li.html

LIBYA
Jamahiriya al-Arabiya al-Libiya al-Shabiya al-Ishtirakiya al-Uzma

Library of Congress
Libya Law Library
http://www.loc.gov/law/guide/libya.html

World Factbook: Libya
   http://www.odci.gov/cia/publications/factbook/geos/ly.html

LIECHTENSTEIN
Fürstentum Liechtenstein

Liechtensteinische Landesbibliothek
Liechtenstein National Library
   http://www.lbfl.li/

Gerberweg 5   *Phone*   *(011) + 423 41 75 236 63 62*
Postfact 385   *Fax*   *(011) + 412 41 75 233 14 19*
FL-9490 Vaduz, Liechtenstein

Online Library Catalog
   http://svllb1.lbfl.li/ALEPH

Library of Congress

Liechtenstein Law Library
   http://www.loc.gov/law/guide/liechtenstein.html

World Factbook: Liechtenstein
   http://www.odci.gov/cia/publications/factbook/geos/ls.html

LITHUANIA
Lietuvos Respublika

Lietuvos nacionaline Martyno Mazvydo biblioteka (LNB)
Martynas Mazvydas National Library of Lithuania
   http://www.lnb.lt/

Gedimino pr. 51   *Phone*   *(011) + 370 2 629 023*
2635 Vilnius, Lithuania   *Fax*   *(011) + 307 2 627 129*
                                      E-mail *biblio@lnb.lrs.lt*
                                                jolita@lnb.lrs.lt Manuscripts

Collections
   http://www.lnb.lt/coll_e.html

Online Library Catalog and Databases
   http://www.lnb.lt/catalogs_e.html

Library of Congress

Lithuania Law Library
   http://www.loc.gov/law/guide/lithuania.html

World Factbook: Lithuania
   http://www.odci.gov/cia/publications/factbook/geos/lh.html

Nordic Libraries Information Servers
> http://www.lub.lu.se/resbyloc/Nordic_lib.html

Denmark
> http://www.lub.lu.se/resbyloc/Nordic_lib.html#den

Estonia
> http://www.lub.lu.se/resbyloc/Nordic_lib.html#est

Faroe Islands
> http://www.lub.lu.se/resbyloc/Nordic_lib.html#far

Finland
> http://www.lub.lu.se/resbyloc/Nordic_lib.html#fin

Iceland
> http://www.lub.lu.se/resbyloc/Nordic_lib.html#ice

Latvia
> http://www.lub.lu.se/resbyloc/Nordic_lib.html#lat

Lithuania
> http://www.lub.lu.se/resbyloc/Nordic_lib.html#lit

Norway
> http://www.lub.lu.se/resbyloc/Nordic_lib.html#norw

Sweden
> http://www.lub.lu.se/resbyloc/Nordic_lib.html#swe

LUXEMBOURG
Grand-Duché de Luxembourg

Bibliothèque nationale Luxembourg
National Library of Luxembourg
> http://www.etat.lu/BNL/

37, boulevard F.-D. Roosevelt	*Phone* (011) + 352 22 97 55 1
L-2450 Luxembourg	*Fax* (011) + 352 47 56 72
	E-mail bib.nat@bi.etat.lu

Bibliographie d'histoire luxembourgeoise
Luxembourg Bibliography of History
> http://www.etat.lu/BNL/biblio/index.htm

Online Library Catalog
> http://aleph.etat.lu:4505/ALEPH/

Special Collections
> http://www.etat.lu/BNL/collspec/index.htm

Library of Congress

Luxembourg Law Library
http://www.loc.gov/law/guide/luxembourg.html

World Factbook: Luxembourg
http://www.odci.gov/cia/publications/factbook/geos/lu.html

MACEDONIA
Republika Makedonija

Library of Congress

Macedonia Law Library
http://www.loc.gov/law/guide/macedonia.html

World Factbook: Macedonia
http://www.odci.gov/cia/publications/factbook/geos/mk.html

MADAGASCAR
Repoblika Demokratika Malagasy

Library of Congress

Madagascar Law Library
http://www.loc.gov/law/guide/madagascar.html

World Factbook: Madagascar
http://www.odci.gov/cia/publications/factbook/geos/ma.html

MALAWI

Library of Congress

Malawi Law Library
http://www.loc.gov/law/guide/malawi.html

World Factbook: Malawi
http://www.odci.gov/cia/publications/factbook/geos/mi.html

MALAYSIA

Perpustakaan Negara Malaysia
National Library of Malaysia
http://www.pnm.my/

232, Jalan Tun Razak   *Phone   (011) + 603 268 71700*
50572 Kuala Lumpur, Malaysia *Fax   (011) + 603 269 27082*
                                E-mail pnmweb@www1.pnm.my

Online Library Catalog
   http://www.pnm.my/new/melayu/opac_m.htm

Library of Congress

Malaysia Law Library
   http://www.loc.gov/law/guide/malaysia.html

World Factbook: Malaysia
   http://www.odci.gov/cia/publications/factbook/geos/my.html

MALDIVES
Dhivehi Raajjeyge Jumhooriyyaa

Library of Congress

Maldives Law Library
   http://www.loc.gov/law/guide/maldives.html

World Factbook: Maldives
   http://www.odci.gov/cia/publications/factbook/geos/mv.html

MALI
République du Mali

Library of Congress

Mali Law Library
   http://www.loc.gov/law/guide/mali.html

World Factbook: Mali
   http://www.odci.gov/cia/publications/factbook/geos/ml.html

MALTA
Repubblika ta' Malta

Library of Congress

Malta Law Library
   http://www.loc.gov/law/guide/malta.html

World Factbook: Malta
   http://www.odci.gov/cia/publications/factbook/geos/mt.html

MARSHALL ISLANDS

Library of Congress

Marshall Islands Law Library
http://www.loc.gov/law/guide/marshall.html

World Factbook: Marshall Islands
http://www.odci.gov/cia/publications/factbook/geos/rm.html

MAURITANIA
République Islamique de Mauritanie

Library of Congress

Mauritania Law Library
http://www.loc.gov/law/guide/mauritania.html

World Factbook: Mauritania
http://www.odci.gov/cia/publications/factbook/geos/mr.html

MAURITIUS

Library of Congress

Mauritius Law Library
http://www.loc.gov/law/guide/mauritius.html

World Factbook: Mauritius
http://www.odci.gov/cia/publications/factbook/geos/mp.html

MEXICO
Estados Unidos Mexicanos

El Archivo General de la Nación
National Archives of Mexico
http://www.agn.gob.mx/indice.html

Online Library Catalogs
http://www.agn.gob.mx/bd.html

Library of Congress

Handbook of Latin American Studies
http://lcweb2.loc.gov/hlas/

Mexico Law Library
http://www.loc.gov/law/guide/mexico.html

World Factbook: Mexico
http://www.odci.gov/cia/publications/factbook/geos/mx.html

New Mexico State University
http://www.nmsu.edu/

New Mexico State University Library
http://lib.nmsu.edu/index.html

Rio Grande Historical Collections
http://archives.nmsu.edu/

P.O. Box 30006   Phone   (505) 646-3839
Las Cruces, NM 88003-8006   Fax   (505) 646-7477
                                      E-mail   archives@lib.nmsu.edu

Archivos General de Notarias del Estado de Durango, Mexico
http://archives.nmsu.edu/rghc/find.html

Archivos Históricos del Arzobispado de Durango (AHAD), Preliminary Guide
http://archives.nmsu.edu/rghc/durango/abtguide.html

MICRONESIA, THE FEDERATED STATES OF

Library of Congress

Micronesia Law Library
http://www.loc.gov/law/guide/micronesia.html

World Factbook: Micronesia
http://www.odci.gov/cia/publications/factbook/geos/fm.html

MOLDOVA
Republica Moldoveneasca

Library of Congress

Moldova Law Library
http://www.loc.gov/law/guide/moldova.html

World Factbook: Moldova
http://www.odci.gov/cia/publications/factbook/geos/md.html

MONACO
Principauté de Monaco

Library of Congress

Monaco Law Library
http://www.loc.gov/law/guide/monaco.html

World Factbook: Monaco
http://www.odci.gov/cia/publications/factbook/geos/mn.html

MONGOLIA

Library of Congress

Mongolia Law Library
http://www.loc.gov/law/guide/mongolia.html

World Factbook: Mongolia
http://www.odci.gov/cia/publications/factbook/geos/mg.html

MOROCCO
Mamlaka al-Maghrebia

Library of Congress

Morocco Law Library
http://www.loc.gov/law/guide/morocco.html

World Factbook: Morocco
http://www.odci.gov/cia/publications/factbook/geos/mo.html

MOZAMBIQUE
República de Moçambique

Library of Congress

Mozambique Law Library
http://www.loc.gov/law/guide/mozambique.html

World Factbook: Mozambique
http://www.odci.gov/cia/publications/factbook/geos/mz.html

NAMIBIA

National Archives of Namibia
http://global.stanford.edu/global/namibia/www.natarch.mec.gov.na/index.html

Private Bag 13250	*Phone* *(011) + 264 61 2934308*
4 Lüderitz Street	*Fax* *(011) + 264 61 239042*
Windhoek, Namibia	*E-mail* *natarch@natarch.mec.gov.na*

Annual Report. (Serial). Annual. (1996–1997).
http://global.stanford.edu/global/namibia/www.natarch.mec.gov.na/annual96.html

Databases
http://global.stanford.edu/global/namibia/www.natarch.mec.gov.na/search.html

Diaspora of Namibian Children
http://global.stanford.edu/global/namibia/www.natarch.mec.gov.na/exilephotos/exhibition.html

Listservs
http://global.stanford.edu/global/namibia/www.natarch.mec.gov.na/listserv.html

Library of Congress

Namibia Law Library
http://www.loc.gov/law/guide/namibia.html

World Factbook: Namibia
http://www.odci.gov/cia/publications/factbook/geos/wa.html

NAURU

Library of Congress

Nauru Law Library
http://www.loc.gov/law/guide/nauru.html

World Factbook: Nauru
http://www.odci.gov/cia/publications/factbook/geos/nr.html

NEPAL
Nepal Adhirajya

Library of Congress

Nepal Law Library
http://www.loc.gov/law/guide/nepal.html

World Factbook: Nepal
http://www.odci.gov/cia/publications/factbook/geos/np.html

THE NETHERLANDS
Koninkrijk der Nederlanden

Koninklijke Bibliotheek
National Library of The Netherlands
http://www.kb.nl/index-en.html

Prins Willem-Alexanderhof 5
2595 BE
The Hague, The Netherlands

Phone   (011) + 31 070 3140911
Fax   (011) + 31 070 3140450
Telex   34402 KB NL
E-mail   info@konbib.nl

Mailing Address:
P.O. Box 90407
2509 LK
The Hague, The Netherlands

Collections

http://www.kb.nl/kb/resources/frameset_collecties-en.html

Digital Collections

http://www.kb.nl/kb/menu/col-dig-en.html

Online Library Catalogs

http://www.kb.nl/kb/menu/cat-ove-en.html

The Holland Page

http://ourworld.compuserve.com/homepages/paulvanv/homepage.htm

Library of Congress

Netherlands Law Library

http://www.loc.gov/law/guide/netherlands.html

World Factbook: Netherlands

http://www.odci.gov/cia/publications/factbook/geos/nl.html

NEW ZEALAND

Te Whare Tohu Tuhituhinga o Aotearoa
National Archives of New Zealand

http://www.archives.govt.nz/index.html

10 Mulgrave Street	*Phone*	*(011) + 64 4 499 5595*
Thorndon, Wellington	*Fax*	*(011) + 64 4 495 6210*
	E-mail	*wellington@dia.govt.nz*

Mailing Address:
P.O. Box 12-050
Wellington, New Zealand

Auckland Regional Office	*Phone*	*(011) + 64 9 270 1100*
525 Mt. Wellington Highway	*Fax*	*(011) + 64 9 276 4472*
Auckland, New Zealand	*E-mail*	*auckland@archives.govt.nz*

Christchurch Regional Office	*Phone*	*(011) + 64 3 377 0760*
90 Peterborough Street	*Fax*	*(011) + 64 3 365 2662*
Christchurch, New Zealand	*E-mail*	*christchurch@archives.govt.nz*

Dunedin Regional Office	*Phone*	*(011) + 64-3 477 0404*
556 George Street	*Fax*	*(011) + 64-3 477 0422*
Dunedin, New Zealand	*E-mail*	*dunedin@archives.govt.nz*

Mailing Address:
P.O. Box 6183 Dunedin North
Dunedin, New Zealand

Collections

http://www.archives.govt.nz/holdings/holdings_frame.html

Local Government Records

http://www.archives.govt.nz/statutory_regulatory/schedules/local_government/index_frame.html

Reach Out—Kia Whakakautoro. (Serial). Semi-annual. (Autumn 1999–.)
http://www.archives.govt.nz/business/outreach/kia_whakakautoro/archive_frame.html

New Zealand National Library
http://www.natlib.govt.nz

P.O. Box 1467   *Phone   (011) + 64 4 474 3000*
Wellington, New Zealalnd   *Fax   (011) + 64 4 474 3035*
                                     E-mail   atl@natlib.govt.nz

New Zealand National Bibliography
http://www.natlib.govt.nz/en/catalogue/index.html#bibliography

Online Library Catalog
http://www.natlib.govt.nz/en/catalogue/index.html

Library of Congress

New Zealand Law Library
http://www.loc.gov/law/guide/newzealand.html

World Factbook: New Zealand
http://www.odci.gov/cia/publications/factbook/geos/nz.html

NICARAGUA
República de Nicaragua

Library of Congress

Handbook of Latin American Studies
http://lcweb2.loc.gov/hlas/

Nicaragua Law Library
http://www.loc.gov/law/guide/nicaragua.html

World Factbook: Nicaragua
http://www.odci.gov/cia/publications/factbook/geos/nu.html

NIGER
République du Niger

Library of Congress

Niger Law Library
http://www.loc.gov/law/guide/niger.html

World Factbook: Niger
http://www.odci.gov/cia/publications/factbook/geos/ng.html

NIGERIA

Library of Congress

Nigeria Law Library
http://www.loc.gov/law/guide/nigeria.html

World Factbook: Nigeria
http://www.odci.gov/cia/publications/factbook/geos/ni.html

NIUE

Library of Congress

Niue Law Library
http://www.loc.gov/law/guide/niue.html

World Factbook: Niue
http://www.odci.gov/cia/publications/factbook/geos/ne.html

NORTHERN MARIANA ISLANDS

Library of Congress

Northern Mariana Islands Law Library
http://www.loc.gov/law/guide/us-mp.html

World Factbook: Northern Mariana Islands
http://www.odci.gov/cia/publications/factbook/geos/cq.html

NORWAY

Kongeriket Norge

Arkivverket
State Archives of Norway
http://www.riksarkivet.no/english/about.html

Folke Bernadottes vei 21	*Phone*	*(011) + 47 22 02 26 00*
Postboks 4013 Ulleval Hageby	*Fax*	*(011) + 47 22 23 74 89*
N-0806 Oslo, Norway	*E-mail*	*riksarkivet@riksarkivaren.dep.no*

Digitalarkivet (Digital Archives)
http://digitalarkivet.uib.no/cgi-win/WebFront.exe?slag=visandtekst=meldingarandspraak=e

Directory of Archives, Norway
http://www.riksarkivet.no/english/about/contact.html

Electronic Recordkeeping
http://www.riksarkivet.no/english/electronic.html

Håndbok for Riksarkivet på nett
Guide to the National Archives
> http://www.riksarkivet.no/arkivverket/publikasjoner/nett/handbok-ra.html

How to Trace Your Ancestors in Norway
> http://digitalarkivet.uib.no/sab/howto.html

Register over arkivmateriale på mikrokort (Microfilm Register)
> http://www.riksarkivet.no/arkivverket/kilder/medier/mikrofilm/mikrokort.html

Nasjonalbiblioteket
The National Library of Norway
> http://www.nb.no/

Postboks 2674 Solli	*Phone (011) + 47 22 55 33 70*
N-0203 Oslo, Norway	*Fax (011) + 47 22 55 38 95*
	E-mail nb@nbr.no

Collections
> http://www.nb.no/html/innhold.html

Databases
> http://www.nb.no/html/databaser.html

Online Exhibits
> http://www.nb.no/html/nyheter.html

Library of Congress

Norway Law Library
> http://www.loc.gov/law/guide/norway.html

World Factbook: Norway
> http://www.odci.gov/cia/publications/factbook/geos/no.html

Nordic Libraries Information Servers
> http://www.lub.lu.se/resbyloc/Nordic_lib.html

Denmark
> http://www.lub.lu.se/resbyloc/Nordic_lib.html#den

Estonia
> http://www.lub.lu.se/resbyloc/Nordic_lib.html#est

Faroe Islands
> http://www.lub.lu.se/resbyloc/Nordic_lib.html#far

Finland
> http://www.lub.lu.se/resbyloc/Nordic_lib.html#fin

Iceland
> http://www.lub.lu.se/resbyloc/Nordic_lib.html#ice

Latvia
http://www.lub.lu.se/resbyloc/Nordic_lib.html#lat

Lithuania
http://www.lub.lu.se/resbyloc/Nordic_lib.html#lit

Norway
http://www.lub.lu.se/resbyloc/Nordic_lib.html#norw

Sweden
http://www.lub.lu.se/resbyloc/Nordic_lib.html#swe

Norwegian Historical Data Centre
http://www.rhd.uit.no/indexeng.html

The Faculty of Social Sciences   *Phone   (011) + 47 77 64 41 77*
University of Tromsø
N-9037 Tromsø, Norway

Censuses of Norway
http://www.rhd.uit.no/census.html

How to Trace Your Ancestry in Norway
http://odin.dep.no/odinarkiv/norsk/dep/ud/1996/eng/032005-990804/index-dok000-b-f-a.html

Searching the 1865, 1875, and 1900 Censuses for Norway
http://www.rhd.uit.no/folketellinger_aeng.html

A Study of Migration in the Province of Troms, 1865–1900, Based on the Censuses,
by Gunnar Thorvaldsen
http://www.rhd.uit.no/nhdc/summary.html

OMAN
Saltanat 'Uman

Library of Congress
Oman Law Library
http://www.loc.gov/law/guide/oman.html

World Factbook: Oman
http://www.odci.gov/cia/publications/factbook/geos/mu.html

PAKISTAN
Islami Jamhuriya e Pakistan

Family History in India
http://members.ozemail.com.au/%7Eclday/index.html

Church Records in Colonial India
http://members.ozemail.com.au/%7Eclday/churches.htm

European Cemeteries in India
http://members.ozemail.com.au/%7Eclday/cem.htm

European Surnames in India
http://members.ozemail.com.au/%7Eclday/misc.htm

Goa Church Records
http://users.rootsweb.com/~indwgw/FIBIS/LDSGoa.htm

Indian Genealogy
http://members.ozemail.com.au/~clday/indian.htm

Madras Female Asylum (Orphanage). 1839 Register
http://users.rootsweb.com/~indwgw/orphan2.htm

Military and Other Sources for India Genealogical Research
http://members.ozemail.com.au/%7Eclday/other.htm

Regimental Histories of British Army Units That Served in India
http://members.ozemail.com.au/%7Eclday/regiments.htm

Library of Congress

Pakistan Law Library
http://www.loc.gov/law/guide/pakistan.html

World Factbook: Pakistan
http://www.odci.gov/cia/publications/factbook/geos/pk.html

PALAU

Library of Congress

Palau Law Library
http://www.loc.gov/law/guide/palau.html

World Factbook: Palau
http://www.odci.gov/cia/publications/factbook/geos/ps.html

PANAMA
República de Panamá

Library of Congress

Handbook of Latin American Studies
http://lcweb2.loc.gov/hlas/

Panama Law Library
http://www.loc.gov/law/guide/panama.html

World Factbook: Panama
http://www.odci.gov/cia/publications/factbook/geos/pm.html

PAPUA NEW GUINEA

Library of Congress

Papua New Guinea Law Library
http://www.loc.gov/law/guide/papua.html

World Factbook: Papua New Guinea
http://www.odci.gov/cia/publications/factbook/geos/pp.html

PARAGUAY
República del Paraguay

Library of Congress

Handbook of Latin American Studies
http://lcweb2.loc.gov/hlas/

Paraguay Law Library
http://www.loc.gov/law/guide/paraguay.html

World Factbook: Paraguay
http://www.odci.gov/cia/publications/factbook/geos/pa.html

PERU
República del Perú

Library of Congress

Handbook of Latin American Studies
http://lcweb2.loc.gov/hlas/

Peru Law Library
http://www.loc.gov/law/guide/peru.html

World Factbook: Peru
http://www.odci.gov/cia/publications/factbook/geos/pe.html

PHILIPPINES
Republika ng Pilipinas

Library of Congress

Philippines Law Library
http://www.loc.gov/law/guide/philippines.html

World Factbook: Philippines
http://www.odci.gov/cia/publications/factbook/geos/rp.html

POLAND
Rzeczpospolita Polska

Biblioteka Narodowa
National Library of Poland
> http://www.bn.org.pl/

> *Al. Niepodleglosci 213*　　　　*Phone*　*(011) + 48 22 608 2999*
> *P.O. Box 36*　　　　　　　　　*Fax*　　*(011) + 48 22 825 5251*
> *00973 Warszawa 22, Poland*　　*E-mail*　*biblnar@bn.org.pl*

Collections
> http://www.bn.org.pl/COLLEC.htm

Databases
> http://193.59.172.222/wykaz.htm

eBooks
> http://www.bn.org.pl/elec.htm

National Bibliography
> http://www.bn.org.pl/AGENCY.htm

Online Resources
> http://www.bn.org.pl/zaspl_eng.htm

Reference Services
> http://www.bn.org.pl/refser.htm

Library of Congress

Poland Law Library
> http://www.loc.gov/law/guide/poland.html

World Factbook: Poland
> http://www.odci.gov/cia/publications/factbook/geos/pl.html

PORTUGAL
República Portuguesa

Biblioteca Nacional
National Library of Portugal
> http://www.bn.pt/

> *Campo Grande 83 – 1749 – 081*　　*Phone*　*(011) + 351 (1) 7950130*
> *Lisboa, Codex, Portugal*　　　　　*Fax*　　*(011) + 351 (1) 7933607*
> 　　　　　　　　　　　　　　　　　*E-mail*　*spires@ibl.pt*

Archives
> http://www.bn.pt/coleccoes/arquivos.html

Digital Collections
http://bnd.bn.pt/

Online Library Catalog
http://sirius.bn.pt/sirius/sirius.exe

Library of Congress

Portugal Law Library
http://www.loc.gov/law/guide/portugal.html

World Factbook: Portugal
http://www.odci.gov/cia/publications/factbook/geos/po.html

PUERTO RICO

Library of Congress

Handbook of Latin American Studies
http://lcweb2.loc.gov/hlas/

Puerto Rico Law Library
http://www.loc.gov/law/guide/us-pr.html

World Factbook: Puerto Rico
http://www.odci.gov/cia/publications/factbook/geos/rq.html

QATAR
Dawlat Qatar

Library of Congress

Qatar Law Library
http://www.loc.gov/law/guide/qatar.html

World Factbook: Qatar
http://www.odci.gov/cia/publications/factbook/geos/qa.html

ROMANIA

Biblioteca Nationala României
National Library of Romania
http://www.bibnat.ro/

Strada Ion Ghica 4, sector 3,
   cod 79708
Bucurest, Romania

Phone   (011) + 40 1 614 24 34
Fax   (011) + 40 1 312 33 81
E-mail go@bibnat.ro

Overview
http://www.bibnat.ro/english_version.html

Library of Congress

Romania Law Library
http://www.loc.gov/law/guide/romania.html

World Factbook: Romania
http://www.odci.gov/cia/publications/factbook/geos/ro.html

RUSSIA

Rossiiskaya Federatsiya

Library of Congress

Russia Law Library
http://www.loc.gov/law/guide/russia.html

World Factbook: Russia
http://www.odci.gov/cia/publications/factbook/geos/rs.html

RAGAS Russian-American Genealogical Archival Service

http://feefhs.org/ragas/frgragas.html

U.S. Address:
1929 18th Street N.W., Suite 112
Washington, DC 20009-1710

Russian Address:
c/o Genealogy and Family History   *Fax   (011) + 246 20 20 to M-200*
*   Society*   *E-mail   vladrag@glas.apc.org*
P.O. Box 459
Moscow 123749, Russia

Genealogical Sources
http://feefhs.org/ragas/rag-sour.html

Overview
http://feefhs.org/ragas/rag-ltr.html

RWANDA

Republika y'u Rwanda

Library of Congress

Rwanda Law Library
http://www.loc.gov/law/guide/rwanda.html

World Factbook: Rwanda
http://www.odci.gov/cia/publications/factbook/geos/rw.html

SAINT KITTS AND NEVIS

Library of Congress

Handbook of Latin American Studies
http://lcweb2.loc.gov/hlas/

Saint Kitts and Nevis Law Library
http://www.loc.gov/law/guide/stkitts.html

World Factbook: Saint Kitts and Nevis
http://www.odci.gov/cia/publications/factbook/geos/sc.html

SAINT LUCIA

Library of Congress

Handbook of Latin American Studies
http://lcweb2.loc.gov/hlas/

Saint Lucia Law Library
http://www.loc.gov/law/guide/stlucia.html

World Factbook: Saint Lucia
http://www.odci.gov/cia/publications/factbook/geos/st.html

SAINT VINCENT AND THE GRENADINES

Library of Congress

Handbook of Latin American Studies
http://lcweb2.loc.gov/hlas/

Saint Vincent and the Grenadines Law Library
http://www.loc.gov/law/guide/stvincent.html

World Factbook: Saint Vincent and the Grenadines
http://www.odci.gov/cia/publications/factbook/geos/vc.html

SAMOA
Samoa i Sisifo

Library of Congress

Samoa Law Library
http://www.loc.gov/law/guide/samoa.html

World Factbook: Samoa
http://www.odci.gov/cia/publications/factbook/geos/ws.html

SAN MARINO
Repubblica di San Marino

Library of Congress

San Marino Law Library
http://www.loc.gov/law/guide/sanmarino.html

World Factbook: San Marino
http://www.odci.gov/cia/publications/factbook/geos/sm.html

SÃO TOMÉ AND PRÍNCIPE
República Democrática de São Tomé e Príncipe

Library of Congress

São Tomé and Príncipe Law Library
http://www.loc.gov/law/guide/saotome.html

World Factbook: São Tomé and Príncipe
http://www.odci.gov/cia/publications/factbook/geos/tp.html

SAUDI ARABIA
Mamlaka al-'Arabiya as-Sa'udiya

Library of Congress

Saudi Arabia Law Library
http://www.loc.gov/law/guide/saudiarabia.html

World Factbook: Saudi Arabia
http://www.odci.gov/cia/publications/factbook/geos/sa.html

SCANDINAVIA

Nordic Libraries Information Servers
http://www.lub.lu.se/resbyloc/Nordic_lib.html

Denmark
http://www.lub.lu.se/resbyloc/Nordic_lib.html#den

Estonia
http://www.lub.lu.se/resbyloc/Nordic_lib.html#est

Faroe Islands
http://www.lub.lu.se/resbyloc/Nordic_lib.html#far

Finland
http://www.lub.lu.se/resbyloc/Nordic_lib.html#fin

Iceland
http://www.lub.lu.se/resbyloc/Nordic_lib.html#ice

Latvia
http://www.lub.lu.se/resbyloc/Nordic_lib.html#lat

Lithuania
http://www.lub.lu.se/resbyloc/Nordic_lib.html#lit

Norway
http://www.lub.lu.se/resbyloc/Nordic_lib.html#norw

Sweden
http://www.lub.lu.se/resbyloc/Nordic_lib.html#swe

SCOTLAND

National Library of Scotland
http://www.nls.uk/

George IV Bridge
Edinburgh, EH1 1EW, Scotland

Phone   (011) + 44 (0) 131 226 4531
Fax   (011) + 44 (0) 131 459 4532
E-mail   webmaster@nls.uk
enquiries@nls.uk   Special Collections

Manuscripts
http://www.nls.uk/collections/manuscripts/index.html

Online Library Catalogs
http://www.nls.uk/catalogues/index.html

OUTSTANDING SITE

General Register Office for Scotland
http://www.gro-scotland.gov.uk/

New Register House
Edinburgh, Scotland, EH1 3YT

Phone   (011) + 44 (0) 131 314 0380
Fax   (011) + 44 (0) 131 314 4400
E-mail   gros@gtnet.gov.uk

Civil Registration
http://www.gro-scotland.gov.uk/grosweb/grosweb.nsf/pages/bdm

Genealogy Records
http://www.gro-scotland.gov.uk/grosweb/grosweb.nsf/pages/famrec

Marriages at Gretna, 1975–2000
http://www.gro-scotland.gov.uk/grosweb/grosweb.nsf/pages/occpgg

Names, Popular Forenames in Scotland, 1900–2000
http://www.gro-scotland.gov.uk/grosweb/grosweb.nsf/pages/name00

1901 Census
http://www.gro-scotland.gov.uk/grosweb/grosweb.nsf/pages/leaflt11

Old Parish Registers
http://www.gro-scotland.gov.uk/grosweb/grosweb.nsf/pages/opr_cov

Scottish Registration Service
http://www.gro-scotland.gov.uk/grosweb/grosweb.nsf/pages/scotreg

Library of Congress

Scotland Law Library
http://www.loc.gov/law/guide/scotland.html

Registers of Scotland Executive Agency
http://www.ros.gov.uk/

Meadowbank House	*Phone*	*(011) + 44 (0) 131 659 6111 Ext. 3083*
153 London Road	*Fax*	*(011) + 44 (0) 131 479 3688*
Edinburgh, EH8 7AU, Scotland	*E-mail*	*alan.ramage@ros.gov.uk*

Property Registers
http://www.ros.gov.uk/r1.htm

Searching the Land and Sasine Registers
http://www.ros.gov.uk/sasreg.htm

Scottish Genealogy Society
http://www.sol.co.uk/s/scotgensoc/

15 Victoria Terrace	*Phone*	*(011) + 44 (0) 131 220 3677*
Edinburgh, EH1 2JL, Scotland	*E-mail*	*info@scotsgenealogy.com*

Family History Index
http://www.scotsgenealogy.com/fhi/fhi.htm

Land Registers and Valuation Rolls
http://www.scotsgenealogy.com/online/land_registers.htm

Scottish Jamaican Testaments
http://www.scotsgenealogy.com/online/scottish_jamaica_testaments.htm

SENEGAL
République du Sénégal

Library of Congress

Senegal Law Library
http://www.loc.gov/law/guide/senegal.html

World Factbook: Senegal
http://www.odci.gov/cia/publications/factbook/geos/sg.html

SEYCHELLES
République des Seychelles

Library of Congress

Seychelles Law Library
   http://www.loc.gov/law/guide/seychelles.html

World Factbook: Seychelles
   http://www.odci.gov/cia/publications/factbook/geos/se.html

SIERRA LEONE

Library of Congress

Sierra Leone Law Library
   http://www.loc.gov/law/guide/sierraleone.html

World Factbook: Sierra Leone
   http://www.odci.gov/cia/publications/factbook/geos/sl.html

SINGAPORE

National Archives of Singapore
   http://www.nhb.gov.sg/NAS/nas.shtml

140 Hill Street   *Phone*   *(011) + 65 375 2510*
Hill Street Building   *Fax*   *(011) + 65 339 3583*
Singapore 179369   *E-mail* *joeann_lee@nhb.gov.sg*

Cartographic and Architectural Records
   http://cards.nhb.gov.sg/index.htm

National Monuments
   http://www.heritagehub.com.sg/

Oral History Collection
   http://aavis.nhb.gov.sg/

Picture Archives
   http://nas.nhb.gov.sg/picas/

Posters Online Database
   http://www.postersonline.com.sg/index.html

Public Records
   http://www.a2o.com.sg:8080/nas/SilverStream/Objectstore/General/gindex.htm

Records of Private Organizations, Groups
   http://www.a2o.com.sg:8080/nas/SilverStream/Objectstore/General/pindex.htm

Library of Congress

Singapore Law Library
http://www.loc.gov/law/guide/singapore.html

World Factbook: Singapore
http://www.odci.gov/cia/publications/factbook/geos/sn.html

SLOVAKIA
Slovenska Republika

Slovenská národná kniznica v Matici slovenskej
The Slovak National Library in Matica slovenská
http://www.matica.sk/

Novomeského 32
036 52 Martin, Slovakia

Phone   (011) + 42 842 31371
Fax   (011) + 42 842 331 60
E-mail   snk@esix.matica.sk

Collections
http://www.matica.sk/uvod/pracovms.html

Library of Congress

Slovakia Law Library
http://www.loc.gov/law/guide/slovakia.html

World Factbook: Slovakia
http://www.odci.gov/cia/publications/factbook/geos/lo.html

SLOVENIA
Republika Slovenija

OUTSTANDING SITE

Slovenski Arhivi
Slovene Archives
http://www.sigov.si/ars/

Zvezdarska 1, p.p. 70
1000 Ljubljana, Slovenia

Phone   (011) + 386 61 125 12 22
Fax   (011) + 386 61 216 551
E-mail   ars@ars.sigov.mail.si

Collection Guide
http://www.sigov.si/ars/4a.htm

Databases
http://www.sigov.si/arhiv/index.html

Library of Congress

Slovenia Law Library
http://www.loc.gov/law/guide/slovenia.html

World Factbook: Slovenia
http://www.odci.gov/cia/publications/factbook/geos/si.html

SOUTH AFRICA

National Archives of South Africa
http://www.national.archives.gov.za/

24 Hamilton Street   *Phone*   *(011) 27 (012) 323 5300*
Private Bag X236   *Fax*   *(011) 27 (012) 323 5287*
Pretoria 0001, South Africa *E-mail* *arg02@dacst4.pwv.gov.za*

Genealogical Information
http://www.national.archives.gov.za/services_to_the_public.htm#research

National Automated Archival Information Retrieval System (NAAIRS)
http://www.national.archives.gov.za/naairs_content.htm

SPAIN
Reino de España

Biblioteca Nacional de Espana
National Library of Spain
http://www.bne.es/

Paseo de Recoletos 20-22   *Phone*   *(011) + 34 1 580 78 23*
28071, Madrid, Spain   *E-mail* *info@bne.es*

Inter-library Loan Service
http://www.bne.es/ingles/prest.htm

Library Online Union Catalog
http://www.mcu.es/ccpb/index.html

Online Exhibits
http://www.bne.es/ingles/exposicion-fra.htm

Library of Congress

Spain Law Library
http://www.loc.gov/law/guide/spain.html

World Factbook: Spain
http://www.odci.gov/cia/publications/factbook/geos/sp.html

SRI LANKA
Sri Lanka Prajatantrika Samajawadi Janarajaya Ilangai Jananayage Socialisak Kudiarasu

Library of Congress

Sri Lanka Law Library
http://www.loc.gov/law/guide/srilanka.html

World Factbook: Sri Lanka
http://www.odci.gov/cia/publications/factbook/geos/ce.html

SUDAN
Jamhuryat es-Sudan

Library of Congress

Sudan Law Library
http://www.loc.gov/law/guide/sudan.html

World Factbook: Sudan
http://www.odci.gov/cia/publications/factbook/geos/su.html

SURINAME
Republiek Suriname

Library of Congress

Suriname Law Library
http://www.loc.gov/law/guide/suriname.html

World Factbook: Suriname
http://www.odci.gov/cia/publications/factbook/geos/ns.html

SWAZILAND
Umbuso weSwatini

Library of Congress

Swaziland Law Library
http://www.loc.gov/law/guide/swaziland.html

World Factbook: Swaziland
http://www.odci.gov/cia/publications/factbook/geos/wz.html

SWEDEN
Konungariket Sverige

Riksarkivet
National Archives of Sweden
 http://www.ra.se/indexengelska.html

Box 12541	*Phone*	*(011) + 46 08 737 63 50*
102 29 Stockholm, Sweden	*Fax*	*(011) + 46 08 737 64 74*

Archives Database, ARKIS
 http://www.nad.ra.se/

Krigsarkivet, Military Archives
 http://www.ra.se/KRA/english.html

Regional Archives
 http://www.ra.se/la.html

SVAR (Svensk Arkivinformation) Research Center
 http://www.svar.ra.se/

Kungl. biblioteket, Sveriges nationalbibliotek
National Library of Sweden
 http://www.kb.se/ENG/kbstart.htm

Box 5039	*Phone*	*(011) + 46 08 463 40 00*
S-102 41 Stockholm, Sweden	*Fax*	*(011) + 46 08 463 40 04*
	E-mail	*kungl.biblioteket@kb.se*

Manuscript Collections
 http://www.kb.se/ENG/kbstart.htm

Newspaper Collections
 http://www.kb.se/ENG/kbstart.htm

Online Library Catalog
 http://regina.kb.se/ALEPH

Swedish Collection
 http://www.kb.se/ENG/kbstart.htm

Library of Congress

Sweden Law Library
 http://www.loc.gov/law/guide/sweden.html

World Factbook: Sweden
 http://www.odci.gov/cia/publications/factbook/geos/sw.html

Nordic Libraries Information Servers
 http://www.lub.lu.se/resbyloc/Nordic_lib.html

Denmark

    http://www.lub.lu.se/resbyloc/Nordic_lib.html#den

Estonia

    http://www.lub.lu.se/resbyloc/Nordic_lib.html#est

Faroe Islands

    http://www.lub.lu.se/resbyloc/Nordic_lib.html#far

Finland

    http://www.lub.lu.se/resbyloc/Nordic_lib.html#fin

Iceland

    http://www.lub.lu.se/resbyloc/Nordic_lib.html#ice

Latvia

    http://www.lub.lu.se/resbyloc/Nordic_lib.html#lat

Lithuania

    http://www.lub.lu.se/resbyloc/Nordic_lib.html#lit

Norway

    http://www.lub.lu.se/resbyloc/Nordic_lib.html#norw

Sweden

    http://www.lub.lu.se/resbyloc/Nordic_lib.html#swe

SWITZERLAND
Schweizerische Eidgenossenschaft

Schweizerisches Bundesarchiv
Swiss Federal Archives

    http://www.admin.ch/bar/

Schweizerisches Bundesarchiv	*Phone*	*(011) + 41 (0)31 322 89 89*
Archivstrasse 24	*Phone*	*(011) + 41 (0)31 322 78 23 Reference*
CH - 3003 Bern, Switzerland	*E-mail*	*Bundesarchiv@bar.admin.ch*

Collections

    http://www.bundesarchiv.ch/bar/engine/ShowPage?pageName=suchhilfen_bestaende.jsp

Guide to Swiss Archives

    http://www.staluzern.ch/vsa/archive/archive.html

Bibliothèque Nationale Suisse
Swiss National Library

    http://www.snl.ch/e/aktuell/index.htm

Hallwylstraße 15	*Phone*	*(011) + 41 31 322 89 11*
CH-3003 Bern, Switzerland	*Fax*	*(011) + 41 31 322 84 63*
	E-mail	*slb-bns@slb.admin.ch*

Collections
> http://www.snl.ch/e/aktuell/co_front.htm#collections

Library Online Catalog
> http://www.snl.ch/e/aktuell/co_front.htm#catalogues

Library of Congress

Switzerland Law Library
> http://www.loc.gov/law/guide/switzerland.html

World Factbook: Switzerland
> http://www.odci.gov/cia/publications/factbook/geos/sz.html

SYRIA
Jumhuriya al-Arabya as-Suriya

Library of Congress

Syria Law Library
> http://www.loc.gov/law/guide/syria.html

World Factbook: Syria
> http://www.odci.gov/cia/publications/factbook/geos/sy.html

TAJIKISTAN
Jumhurii Tojikiston

Library of Congress

Tajikistan Law Library
> http://www.loc.gov/law/guide/tajikistan.html

World Factbook: Tajikistan
> http://www.odci.gov/cia/publications/factbook/geos/ti.html

TANZANIA
Jamhuri ya Muungano wa Tanzania

Library of Congress

Tanzania Law Library
> http://www.loc.gov/law/guide/tanzania.html

World Factbook: Tanzania
> http://www.odci.gov/cia/publications/factbook/geos/tz.html

THAILAND
Prathes Thai or Muang-Thai

Library of Congress

Thailand Law Library
http://www.loc.gov/law/guide/thailand.html

World Factbook: Thailand
http://www.odci.gov/cia/publications/factbook/geos/th.html

TOGO
République Togolaise

Library of Congress

Togo Law Library
http://www.loc.gov/law/guide/togo.html

World Factbook: Togo
http://www.odci.gov/cia/publications/factbook/geos/to.html

TRINIDAD AND TOBAGO

National Library and Information System of Trinidad and Tobago
http://www.nalis.gov.tt/

Knox and Pembroke Streets   *Phone   (868) 623-6124 Heritage Library*
Port of Spain, Trinidad and Tobago   *(868) 624 1130 Public Library*

Online Library Catalog
http://catalog.nalis.gov.tt/pac.opac

Library of Congress

Trinidad and Tobago Law Library
http://www.loc.gov/law/guide/trinidad.html

World Factbook: Trinidad and Tobago
http://www.odci.gov/cia/publications/factbook/geos/td.html

TUNISIA
Jumhuriya at-Tunisiya

Library of Congress

Tunisia Law Library
http://www.loc.gov/law/guide/tunisia.html

World Factbook: Tunisia
http://www.odci.gov/cia/publications/factbook/geos/ts.html

TURKEY
Türkiye Çumhuriyeti

Millî Kütüphane
National Library of Turkey
http://www.mkutup.gov.tr/index-eng.html

Bahçelievler 06490   *Phone*   *(011) + 90 312 2126 200 / 339*
Ankara, Turkey   *E-mail*   *altinay@www.mkutup.gov.tr*
                                        davut@mkutup.gov.tr

Türk Kütüphaneciler Dernedi
Association of Turkish Librarians
http://www.kutuphaneci.org.tr/turk/

Necatibey Cad. Elgün Sok. 8/8   *Phone*   *(011) + 90 312 230 13 25*
06442 Kyzylay   *Fax*   *(011) + 90 312 232 04 53*
Ankara, Turkey

Library of Congress

Turkey Law Library
http://www.loc.gov/law/guide/turkey.html

World Factbook: Turkey
http://www.odci.gov/cia/publications/factbook/geos/tu.html

TURKMENISTAN
Turkmenostan Respublikasy

Library of Congress

Turkmenistan Law Library
http://www.loc.gov/law/guide/turkmenistan.html

World Factbook: Turkmenistan
http://www.odci.gov/cia/publications/factbook/geos/tx.html

TUVALU

Library of Congress

Tuvalu Law Library
http://www.loc.gov/law/guide/tuvalu.html

World Factbook: Tuvalu
http://www.odci.gov/cia/publications/factbook/geos/tv.html

UGANDA

Library of Congress

Uganda Law Library
http://www.loc.gov/law/guide/uganda.html

World Factbook: Uganda
http://www.odci.gov/cia/publications/factbook/geos/ug.html

UKRAINE
Ukraïna

Library of Congress

Ukraine Law Library
http://www.loc.gov/law/guide/ukraine.html

World Factbook: Ukraine
http://www.odci.gov/cia/publications/factbook/geos/up.html

RAGAS Russian-American Genealogical Archival Service

http://feefhs.org/ragas/frgragas.html

U.S. Address:
1929 18th Street N.W., Suite 112
Washington, DC 20009-1710

Russian Address:
c/o Genealogy and Family History   *Fax*   *(011) + 246 20 20 to M-200*
  Society   *E-mail* *vladrag@glas.apc.org*
P.O. Box 459
Moscow 123749, Russia

Genealogical Sources
http://feefhs.org/ragas/rag-sour.html

Overview
http://feefhs.org/ragas/rag-ltr.html

UNITED ARAB EMIRATES
Al Imarat al Arabiyah al Muttahidah

Library of Congress

United Arab Emirates Law Library
http://www.loc.gov/law/guide/uae.html

World Factbook: United Arab Emirates
http://www.odci.gov/cia/publications/factbook/geos/tc.html

URUGUAY
República Oriental del Uruguay

Library of Congress

Handbook of Latin American Studies
http://lcweb2.loc.gov/hlas/

Uruguay Law Library
http://www.loc.gov/law/guide/uruguay.html

World Factbook: Uruguay
http://www.odci.gov/cia/publications/factbook/geos/uy.html

UZBEKISTAN
Uzbekiston Respublikasi

Library of Congress

Uzbekistan Law Library
http://www.loc.gov/law/guide/uzbekistan.html

World Factbook: Uzbekistan
http://www.odci.gov/cia/publications/factbook/geos/uz.html

VANUATU
Library of Congress

Vanuatu Law Library
http://www.loc.gov/law/guide/vanuatu.html

World Factbook: Vanuatu
http://www.odci.gov/cia/publications/factbook/geos/nh.html

VENEZUELA
República de Venezuela

Biblioteca Nacional de Venezuela
National Library of Venezuela
http://www.bnv.bib.ve/

Edificio Nueva Sede Foro Libertador
Parroquia Altagracia *Phone* *(011) + (58 212) 505 91 25*
Final Avenida Panteón *Fax* *(011) + (58 212) 564 36 69*
Caracas, Venezuela

Public Libraries
http://www.bnv.bib.ve/frame5.htm

Rare Books and Manuscripts
http://www.bnv.bib.ve/frame33.htm

Reference Services
http://www.bnv.bib.ve/frame31.htm

Library of Congress

Handbook of Latin American Studies
http://lcweb2.loc.gov/hlas/

Venezuela Law Library
http://www.loc.gov/law/guide/venezuela.html

World Factbook: Venezuela
http://www.odci.gov/cia/publications/factbook/geos/ve.html

VIETNAM
Công Hòa Xã Hôi Chu Nghîa Viêt Nam

Library of Congress

Vietnam Law Library
http://www.loc.gov/law/guide/vietnam.html

World Factbook: Vietnam
http://www.odci.gov/cia/publications/factbook/geos/vm.html

YEMEN
Jamhuriya al Yamaniya

Library of Congress

Yemen Law Library
http://www.loc.gov/law/guide/yemen.html

World Factbook: Yemen
http://www.odci.gov/cia/publications/factbook/geos/ym.html

YUGOSLAVIA
Savezna Republika Jugoslavija

Library of Congress

Yugoslavia Law Library
http://www.loc.gov/law/guide/yugoslavia.html

World Factbook: Yugoslavia
http://www.odci.gov/cia/publications/factbook/geos/yi.html

ZAMBIA

Library of Congress

Zambia Law Library
> http://www.loc.gov/law/guide/zambia.html

World Factbook: Zambia
> http://www.odci.gov/cia/publications/factbook/geos/za.html

ZIMBABWE

Library of Congress

Zimbabwe Law Library
> http://www.loc.gov/law/guide/zimbabwe.html

World Factbook: Zimbabwe
> http://www.odci.gov/cia/publications/factbook/geos/zi.html

NOTES

NOTES

NOTES

NOTES

NOTES

NOTES

ABOUT THE CD

The CD version of *Virtual Roots 2.0,* **VR2.pdf,** can be viewed only with **Adobe Acrobat Reader,** whic
is provided on this CD.

OPENING VR2.PDF IF ACROBAT READER IS INSTALLED ON YOUR COMPUTER

Macintosh: VR2.pdf will open immediately upon placing the CD in your drive.

Windows: There are several ways to open a file on a CD:

1. From the desktop: double click on the hard-drive icon (My Computer), double click on the CD-driv
   icon, double click on the file named VR2.pdf. Acrobat Reader will launch and the file will open.
2. From the Menu Bar: Go to Start—Find and type in the file name VR2.pdf. Hit Enter when the file
   located on the CD drive.
3. From Acrobat Reader: Launch Acrobat Reader. Click on File in the menu bar and select Open. The
   locate the file VR2.pdf on the CD in the drive and hit Enter.

OPENING VR2.PDF IF ACROBAT READER IS NOT INSTALLED ON YOUR COMPUTER

Macintosh: double click on the Acrobat Reader Installer icon on the CD and follow the setup instruction

Windows: There are several ways to install a program from a CD:

1. From the desktop: double click on the hard-drive icon (My Computer), double click on the CD-driv
   icon, double click on the file named "ar505enu.exe"—this is the Acrobat Installer. The program wi
   launch, and then simply follow the setup instructions.
2. From the Menu Bar: Go to Start—Run—Browse and highlight the CD drive in the drop-down window
   The file named "ar505enu.exe" will appear. Double click on the file and proceed as in (1) above.

Acrobat Reader is provided free of charge by Adobe (http://www.adobe.com) and can also be down
loaded from their web site at: http://www.adobe.com/products/acrobat/readstep2.html or http://www
adobe.com/products/acrobat/alternate.html

README.PDF

Provided in text, rtf, and pdf formats, this document lists system requirements for using Acrobat Reade
describes the interactive features of VR2.pdf, and provides important information for users new to Acroba
Reader. The text and rtf versions can be viewed in WordPad or NotePad (Windows), in SimpleText (Mac), o
in your word-processing software. The pdf version can be viewed only in Acrobat Reader.
